Time Work

TIME WORK
STUDIES OF TEMPORAL AGENCY

Edited by
Michael G. Flaherty, Lotte Meinert,
and Anne Line Dalsgård

berghahn
NEW YORK · OXFORD
www.berghahnbooks.com

First published in 2020 by
Berghahn Books
www.berghahnbooks.com

© 2020, 2023 Michael G. Flaherty, Lotte Meinert, and Anne Line Dalsgård
First paperback edition published in 2023

Library of Congress Cataloging-in-Publication Data

A C.I.P. cataloging record is available from the Library of Congress

Library of Congress Cataloging in Publication Control Number: 2020937011

British Library Cataloguing in Publication Data

A catalogue record for this book is available from the British Library

ISBN 978-1-78920-704-0 hardback
ISBN 978-1-80073-929-1 paperback
ISBN 978-1-78920–705-7 ebook

https://doi.org/10.3167/9781789207040

Contents

Part I

Beginnings, Concepts, and Questions

Introduction

Michael G. Flaherty, Anne Line Dalsgård, and Lotte Meinert

Across the social sciences, the study of time has been preoccupied with causality. Despite the standardization of time, a particular interval can seem
to pass slowly or quickly from the standpoint of human perception. What
brings about variation in our temporal experience?

When social scientists address this question, they tend to employ an analytical framework borrowed from the natural sciences. Within that framework, it is assumed that the situation determines the perception of time.
One's objective circumstances are thought to be antecedent, external, and
coercive to one's subjective temporal experience. This is the causal logic of
determinism.

In recent years, an abundance of research has appeared in anthropology
and sociology that emphasizes other ways of understanding temporal experience. Michael Flaherty reviews some of this work in his chapter, and the
authors of other chapters acknowledge and discuss previous work specific
to their own ethnographic studies. With our introduction, then, we want to
identify the aims of this book, not review prior research.

If you ask people to describe situations during which they perceived
time to pass slowly, there will be stories that appear to fit the causal logic
of determinism. Let us consider, for example, the temporal experience of
a bystander during a terrorist incident at an airport (Magnuson 1986: 74).
A woman is working at a gift shop when, without warning, men pull out
guns and begin shooting people waiting for their flights. Security guards
arrive quickly and begin to shoot back at the terrorists. "It seemed to go on
forever," said the woman at the gift shop, but the incident lasted only five
minutes as measured by a clock. It is easy to attribute this temporal distortion to the effect of sudden violence. Yet this is only one way to alter time
and temporal experience.

If we examine temporal experience more carefully, we find countless cases that contradict the deterministic framework. These anomalous cases are so numerous that, once assembled, they provide the foundation for a very different line of inquiry. Time was imposed on the woman working in that gift shop, but, in the following excerpt from an interview (Flaherty 2011: 2), a young college student describes how she imposes herself on time:

> When I'm out with my boyfriend, especially when we take walks on the beach, I try to keep his mind, as well as my own, off the end of the school year when we have to separate for the summer. I talk about present problems with classes, past times, anything but the future. I try to keep him laughing to forget about leaving. I try to make the time we spend together seem longer.

We witness comparable distortion in temporal experience: time is perceived to pass slowly during the aforementioned terrorist incident as well as the last weeks that two college students spend together. But there is a crucial difference. This perception is inflicted upon the woman working in the gift shop, while it is desired and orchestrated by the college student. In the latter case, we see an individual change temporal experience by exercising a measure of willfulness.

Recognizing the relevance of self-determination, Flaherty (2002, 2003, 2011) has conceptualized time work or temporal agency. This concept sensitizes us to the intentional alteration of our own temporal experience, or that of others. Instead of assuming that time simply happens to us, the analysis of temporal agency reverses the direction of the causal arrow to show how we make time happen. This line of inquiry reveals how individuals and groups act as the architects of their own temporal experience (exemplified by the college student in the foregoing extract). In its original formulation, however, the concept of time work is more than fifteen years old, and the conceptualization emerged from data collected exclusively in the United States. The chapters in this edited collection show us how people in diverse societies modify various dimensions of temporal experience.

What is more, the original formulation sensitized us only to intended time work. The individuals in question chose to modify their own temporal experience. By and large, they were self-consciously aware of what they were doing and why they were doing it. With this book, we identify an exciting new direction for research: the study of less conscious or unintended forms of temporal agency. People in various social settings often follow local practices for reasons that have little or nothing to do with temporal agency. Nonetheless, it is evident to an outside observer that these practices influence their temporal experience. The chapters in our edited collection include examples such as praying, fasting or breaking a fast, making tea with other unemployed men, redefining the fraudulent past of one's family, and pursuing traditional activities in order to maintain ethnic identities. These studies greatly extend the analytical reach of time work as a frame of reference.

Is the theory of time work applicable to people across different societies and social situations? Intentionally or unintentionally, do people in diverse settings control, manipulate, or customize aspects of their own temporal experience? If so, what dimensions of temporal experience do they alter, and what local theories or practices do they employ? These questions are the impetus for ongoing collaboration between Flaherty and a team of anthropologists at Aarhus University in Denmark. One product of this collaboration is an edited collection of cross-cultural studies that focus on time as a problematic experience in the lives of young people (Dalsgård et al. 2014).

The publication of that book was followed by Flaherty's year-long stint (from October 2016 to September 2017) as senior fellow and visiting professor with the Aarhus Institute of Advanced Studies (AIAS). During this stay, Flaherty, Anne Line Dalsgård, and Lotte Meinert organized a symposium called Time Work: New Research on Temporal Agency. With funding from AIAS, this symposium brought together a distinguished group of interdisciplinary scholars to share their most recent work on temporal agency. These fascinating and rigorous studies are international in scope, including Argentina, Brazil, Canada, Denmark, Egypt, Georgia, Kyrgyzstan, Niger, Russia, Uganda, and the United States. With the assistance of our fine editor, Tom Bonnington, the essays were subjected to anonymous peer review. We thank the three anonymous reviewers for their very helpful comments. In this book, we present these essays as an edited collection that examines the current state of research on temporal agency.

OVERVIEW OF THE BOOK

In his chapter, "The Lathe of Time: Some Principles of Temporal Agency," Michael Flaherty establishes the conceptual framework for our book. A lathe is a machine for shaping material of some kind. With this metaphor, Flaherty introduces the reader to the notion of time work and provides a rationale for its conceptualization. In addition, he reviews existing research concerning time work and extracts some principles of temporal agency. Time work would not be possible were it not for the fact that human beings make constrained choices to intervene in, and thereby modify, the course of social interaction. We decide how to respond to our circumstances, but we are not at liberty to choose whatever temporal experience we might wish for. The realization of time work requires proper motivation, necessary skill, and other resources that may or may not be available. Hence, the outcome is uncertain: one's effort at time work may succeed or fail. Temporal agency may or may not be supported by one's relationships, organizational affiliations, and cultural heritage. In time work, people exhibit temporal dispositions, but these preferences are conditioned by one's socialization. Much of time work is directed toward solving existing or anticipated problems with temporal experience.

We have organized the balance of our edited collection into five thematic parts, each containing a pair of related chapters. In the first of these sections, "Temporal Afflictions," we present two chapters that investigate efforts to address the problematic experience of time as an unhealthy or disruptive factor in social interaction.

In their chapter, "Repetition Work: Healing Spirits and Trauma in the Churches of Northern Uganda," Lars Williams and Lotte Meinert argue that post-traumatic stress disorder (PTSD) or psychological trauma can be conceptualized as a form of time disturbance that collapses the past-present-future structure of time, causing flashbacks. Their findings suggest that repetition in the rhythms of prayer and other religious practices is an effective way to deal with these problems. The afflicted people regard praying as a religious practice, yet the authors suggest that this may also be a form of time work. The empirical material for this chapter is based on anthropological fieldwork in the Gulu area of northern Uganda between 2010 and 2017, where Williams and Meinert have examined how people attempt to heal the traumas and spiritual afflictions that remain after years of violent conflict in the area. Their data reveal the intrapersonal and interpersonal use of repetition in rituals, prayer, and the recitation of passages from the Bible and the Quran as techniques for handling trauma and spiritual troubles. By means of these strategies, the afflicted people stabilize and synchronize the flawed temporal experience at the heart of PTSD. Williams and Meinert explore these practices with the concept of time work and interpret the observed repetition as a form of temporal agency, which is used to alleviate the crippling legacies from a violent past.

What can we learn about attention deficit hyperactivity disorder (ADHD) if, in accord with Mikka Nielsen, we view it as a temporal disturbance? In her chapter, "ADHD and Temporal Experiences: Struggling for Synchronization," Nielsen describes how her Danish interlocutors modify temporal experience when struggling with the symptoms of ADHD. She observes that ADHD is not simply an individualistic phenomenon, because the symptoms arise in problematic relationships and clashing forms of interaction, and result in difficulty with interpersonal coordination in different social contexts.

Nielsen seeks to understand ADHD as a disruption in one's experience of time and a state of desynchronization or arrhythmia. Having interviewed adults diagnosed with ADHD in Denmark, she demonstrates how differences in their perception of time, their physical restlessness, and their experience of speedy thoughts are connected to temporal impairment, which is manifest in an embodied experience of being "out of sync" with others. Nielsen shows us how her interlocutors use ingenious strategies for resynchronizing with the temporal regimes of the surrounding world. This time work helps to integrate them with the collective rhythms of everyday life.

The next thematic section, "The Politics of Time," is devoted to the role of power in temporal agency. Here, we examine individual and collective efforts to impose or resist various forms of temporal experience. These studies concern how groups use temporal agency in response to state-sponsored time work.

Approximately thirty thousand people were abducted, tortured, and assassinated during the last civil-military dictatorship that ruled Argentina between 1976 and 1983. To date, 130 of their surviving offspring—the "living disappeared"—have been identified. As infants, they were abducted, and their identities were altered by people who had a hand in the suffering and disappearance of their parents. In many cases, they were subsequently raised as unwitting members of their abductors' families. In her chapter, "Hacking Time and Looping Temporalities in the Identification of the Adult 'Living Disappeared' in Argentina," Noa Vaisman explores the role of time work and temporality more broadly in the process of DNA identification of these individuals. The identification process can be viewed, she argues, as a form of time hacking—that is, an intervention and work on a person's sense of time through the decoding and uncovering of sensitive information. DNA identity tests transform an individual's understanding of chronological-biographical time. Vaisman conceptualizes this transformation as a looping of the past into the present, which brings about an individual's often uncertain or even reluctant manner of confronting the request to be identified and the information that emerges once relations with one's biological family are confirmed.

Prior to colonization, the Inuit people of northern Canada pursued a nomadic existence by living off the land. The government had forced them into small settlements by the early 1960s and had imposed a rational temporal regime through the domination of work, economics, and bureaucracy. Thus, the contemporary Inuit have a foot in each of two different ways of life—one indigenous and one colonial—with divergent temporal practices. In her chapter, "Temporal Front and Back Stages: Time Work as Resistance," Lisa-Jo van den Scott shows us how the Inuit strive to maintain their cultural boundaries by performing nonmembership in Western temporal practices. For example, they drop in rather than call first to arrange a meeting, and walk into someone's house instead of knocking and waiting at the door. Van den Scott lived in the village of Arviat, Nunavut territory, Canada, for more than five years. With meticulous ethnographic description, she immerses the reader in temporal resistance as a form of political time work. Erving Goffman famously demonstrated the analytical power of distinguishing between front stage and back stage settings. Van den Scott elaborates on this distinction by showing us that, during back stage intervals, the people of Arviat enact Inuit time in resistance to the encroaching temporal paradigms of Canadian society. Temporal practices demonstrate group membership; by the same token, violating these temporal norms is an effective way to perform nonmembership.

In the following thematic section, "Spirituality and Atheism as Temporal Agency," the juxtaposition of two chapters is both ironic and revealing. One of them describes how the inhabitants of a village in rural Brazil use Catholic beliefs and practices as time work. The other explores the performance of atheism as time work among young people in Kyrgyzstan mocking and resisting the resurgence of Islam in a formerly communist nation.

What would the concept of time work be like if, rather than emphasizing its subversive dimension, we shift our gaze to examine the ways in which it produces normal temporal experience? How is the concept of time work changed if we focus on practices that maintain or rectify temporal experiences considered acceptable or even prescribed by the people in a particular community? These questions have been largely overlooked in previous research. In her chapter, "*Se Deus Quiser*: Catholicism as Time Work among the Xukuru of Pernambuco," Clarissa Martins Lima considers these questions from the standpoint of the residents of Vila de Cimbres, an indigenous village of the Xukuru do Ororuba ethnic group located in northeast Brazil. Her findings show that even though time assumes a number of different forms among the Xukuru, God is considered to be responsible for determining the directions that they take. Thus, one's adherence to Catholicism is a way of confirming divine intentions concerning temporal experience. She also observes, however, that it is precisely in rectifying what is predicted by God through Catholicism that the Xukuru attempt to control their future and even interfere with divine will. In this sense, the Xukuru's Catholicism can be thought of as a form of time work that is simultaneously normative and subversive.

In Kyrgyzstan, atheism has gone from being state-imposed and conspicuously present in public space during Soviet times to being privatized, whereas religion—in particular Islam—has become more prominent in community life. Atheists, and young atheists in particular, perceive that their lack of faith is viewed as highly controversial by the larger community, and complete disengagement from religion is rarely an option for them. In her chapter, "'It is Just Doing the Motion': Atheist Time Work in Contemporary Kyrgyzstan," Maria Louw explores how young Kyrgyz atheists struggle to maintain their atheist sensibilities in social contexts that have become marked with religious practices. These practices include the five daily prayers and fasting in the Ramadan as well as more local rituals, such as the commemoration of ancestor spirits and subtler aspects of daily interaction. Together, these observances make for an Islamic rhythm to social life, thereby placing human lives in a larger temporal framework where ancestor spirits interfere with the lives of the living, and life here and now is merely a prelude to the afterlife. Young Kyrgyz atheists rarely contest this narrative openly and directly, but they do not succumb to it, either. Instead, they strive to create alternative temporal experiences through, for example, subtle ironizing, joking, and playfulness in everyday life, as well as on social media, and through efforts to empty religious acts and phrases of their eschatological meaning.

The two chapters in the next thematic section—"Reinventing the Past, Present, and Future"—both concern people confronting problematic circumstances. Facing very different dilemmas, they deal with their respective issues by inventing new versions of time comfortably at odds with the facts of life.

In their chapter, "Inventing New Time: Time Work in the Grief Practices of Bereaved Parents," Dorthe Christensen and Kjetil Sandvik conceptualize a novel category of temporal agency inspired by Martin Heidegger's (1962: 469) statement that "saying now . . . is the discursive articulation of a making-present." Extending their previous research on grief, they use ethnographic methods to study how bereaved parents engage in ritualized time work at the Danish website Mindet.dk, how they perform parenthood on their children's graves, and how they continue trying to be parents by including the dead child in the family's everyday life. Bereaved parents profoundly renegotiate basic social boundaries by creating innovative ways of keeping the child present in routine activities. Instead of trying to reinstall the temporal normality that existed prior to the death of their child, or conform to society's views concerning how to mourn, let go, and move on, they strive to invent delicate ways of making the dead child present in their lives and live on *with* rather than *without* the deceased. Christensen and Sandvik conclude that these mourning practices transgress the aim of returning to social normality. In fact, these practices can be seen as the parents installing not only a new temporality but a new social world. Through their time work, these parents eventually transform the temporal collapse instigated by the child's death into an unprecedented cosmological and temporal order.

In his chapter, "Now Is Not: Future Anteriority and a Georgian in Russia," Martin Demant Frederiksen revisits his 2009 conversations with Gosha, one of Frederksen's interlocutors during fieldwork in Batumi, Georgia. At that time, Gosha was a young unemployed musician desperate to migrate to Russia. He had been reluctant to talk about his life from the perspective of the troublesome present. Rather than admitting he was stuck, Gosha would narrate his present from a future-anterior perspective, pretending to be looking back from a new life in Moscow during 2019. Lightheartedly, he imagined a future when he would be a famous lead singer in Russia's most popular rock band and Frederiksen, who was equally assigned a fictional role, would be a reporter interviewing him for an article in the *Rolling Stone Magazine.* Frederiksen was skeptical, but, in retrospect, he had to revise his disbelief. As in the 1989 film, *Back to the Future Part II,* which presents a vision of the future with hoverboards, flying cars, and self-drying jackets, the future envisioned by Gosha did not really come about. Yet, in its own magical way, it did. In his tracing of Gosha's imagined and actual biography, from 2009 to 2019, Frederiksen describes the porous relationship between present and future in Gosha's life and accounts for a form of time work wherein the temporal experience of the present is actively suppressed and surpassed.

In our last thematic section, "Time and Deprivation," we have two studies that focus on time work occasioned by doing without the necessities of life. Via temporal agency, young men in Niger create a new social institution to fill the hours left empty by their unemployment. And, in Egypt, people fasting during Ramadan have recourse to time work while dealing with hunger and thirst as expressions of piety.

For young men in Niger who cannot secure stable employment, waiting has become something of an endemic condition. They have created spaces specifically for waiting, known as *fadas* (tea circles), and they repair to these spaces frequently to drink tea, socialize with friends, play cards, and listen to music. The *fadas* exemplify how young men carve out spaces of relevance in a landscape of unevenly distributed access to work and wealth. Some scholars have referred to the period of stagnation, helplessness, and vulnerability experienced by young unemployed college graduates in the Middle East and Africa as "waithood." Because it homogenizes the period of suspension that young men endure, waithood cannot account for the various forms of anticipatory temporality that emerge among youth in urban Niger. Waiting may be a suspension of time, but it is not necessarily a suspension of activity. In her chapter, "The Work of Waiting: Boredom, Teatime, and Future-Making in Niger," Adeline Masquelier considers how the *fada* constitutes a workspace-in-waiting and how waiting at the *fada* has become a form of temporal agency. In particular, her study reveals how waiting enables the emergence of a new sociality, epitomized by what she calls teatime. Time work, Flaherty (2003: 19) argues, "integrates agency with temporality." Inasmuch as idleness can be said to contain space for action, at the *fada*, it leads young men to intervene with the structuring of time to produce particular outcomes. In accord with this perspective, Masquelier suggests that far from being simple tactics for passing time, teatime—that is, the making and drinking of tea—creates agentive, purposeful forms of waiting. By creating ideal conditions for actualizing aspirations, these modes of waiting effectively constitute attempts to realize a collectively imagined future.

Ramadan is a special period set aside annually in the Muslim calendar to fast, pray, and study the Quran. In their chapter, "Balancing Blood Sugar: Fasting, Feeling, and Time Work during the Egyptian Ramadan," Mille Kjærgaard Thorsen and Anne Line Dalsgård argue that the Ramadan is not only a period of abstention and piety, but also a period of substantial time work. On the collective level, Ramadan structures time and its content; on the level of individuality, it operates through a disciplining of one's body, evoking certain emotions and concomitant microtemporalities throughout the day and month. As Thorsen and Dalsgård demonstrate, however, people who observe the Ramadan in Cairo are not just passive subjects to this disciplining; they are also experiencing and creative subjects who may try to change their circumstances. Drawing on Flaherty's notion of time work, Thorsen and Dalsgård show how, during the obligatory fast from dawn to dusk, certain perceptions of time are evoked and altered by means of temporal agency. Their approach to time work derives from an understanding of human agency as driven by cognitive reflections as well as physiological and emotional processes. Thus, their conceptual orientation is one of embodied sociality as they focus on the emotional substratum of temporal experience and the intertwining of the somatic, the subjective, and the social in the experience of the yearly fasting. They suggest that the biochemistry of the human body may provoke certain temporal experiences and drive us to a desire for change, but also constrain our attempts at making these changes come about. The ethnographic data stem from fieldwork conducted in Cairo during 2015 and 2017, including participant observation among families with members diagnosed with diabetes.

In these eleven chapters, we examine how people in very different social and cultural situations modify and customize their own temporal experience. All of the authors make use of observations from field notes or excerpts from in-depth interviews. We hope that the analytical contrasts and resonances make for new insights and inspire further research. The five thematic sections of the book are followed by an afterword written by Carmen Leccardi. We will let her have the final word and here simply express our gratitude for her interest in the work we have assembled.

Michael G. Flaherty
Professor, Department of Sociology
Eckerd College and University of South Florida, USA

Anne Line Dalsgård
Associate Professor, Department of Anthropology
Aarhus University, Denmark

Lotte Meinert
Professor, Department of Anthropology
Aarhus University, Denmark

REFERENCES

Dalsgård, Anne Line, Martin Demant Frederiksen, Susanne Højlund, and Lotte Meinert. 2014. *Ethnographies of Youth and Temporality: Time Objectified.* Philadelphia: Temple University Press.
Flaherty, Michael G. 2002. "Making Time: Agency and the Construction of Temporal Experience." *Symbolic Interaction* 25 (3): 379–88.
Flaherty, Michael G. 2003. "Time Work: Customizing Temporal Experience." *Social Psychology Quarterly* 66 (1): 17–33.
Flaherty, Michael G. 2011. *The Textures of Time: Agency and Temporal Experience.* Philadelphia: Temple University Press.
Magnuson, Ed. 1986. "Ten Minutes of Horror." *Time*, 6 January, 74.

Chapter 1

The Lathe of Time
Some Principles of Temporal Agency

Michael G. Flaherty

In its original formulation, "time work" is defined as personal or interpersonal enterprise directed toward provoking or preventing various kinds of temporal experience (Flaherty 2002, 2003, 2011). The study of time work reveals human effort to intervene in the trajectory of events. With this intervention, we attempt to control, manipulate, and customize our own temporal experience or that of others.

In effect, one asks oneself, "What type of temporal experience would I prefer?" Then, having answered this question, one employs local or personal theories and practices (which I call time work) to bring into being circumstances that elicit the desired form of temporal experience. As such, time work is temporal agency, and, from this perspective, choice is an essential attribute of social interaction as well as temporal experience.

The conceptual pedigree of time work can be traced back to the foundation of American pragmatism. "My experience is what I agree to attend to," argues William James (1890: 402). George Herbert Mead (1934: 25) adds that the self-conscious individual chooses how to respond to environmental stimuli (regardless of whether they are present in the setting or only imagined). It follows that, via the choices they make, human beings create or determine the environment to which they respond.

Time work has been the subject of considerable research since its conceptualization, but these studies are scattered across the academic landscape in various articles and books. This literature has not been assembled and assessed for what it tells us about temporal agency. What have we learned

from these studies? What has been overlooked? With this chapter, I hope
to illuminate the boundary between what we know and what we do not yet
know about time work. I review this line of inquiry with the aim of creating
a springboard for continued research.

CONSTRAINED CHOICES

Time work is rooted in human desire. One desires a certain form of temporal
experience, but it will not occur without one's intervention. The individual
must take steps to bring this temporal experience into being. Typically, this
process entails deliberation and planning, perhaps even a local or personal
theory that guides one's effort. The resulting temporal experience is a product of human endeavor. One chooses to experience time in a particular way.

This does *not* mean that we are free to choose whatever temporal experience we might wish for. The conceptualization of time work does not
contradict the epistemology of the social sciences. Human beings, always
and everywhere, make choices in the course of social interaction, but these
choices are constrained by one's circumstances (past, present, and future).
Put differently, temporal experience is a complicated mixture of determinism and self-determination.

Temporal norms are evident in any given society, but how do they come
about? Norms concerning punctuality provide a prototype. They may be
indigenous or imperialistic. Either way, we know that they are not hard-
wired into human physiology because they vary so much from place to place
and can be quickly changed by brutal regimes (Iutcovich, Babbitt, and Iutcovich 1979; Levine 1997; Mead [1951] 1966; Schulz, Knoki, and Knoki-
Wilson 1999; Thompson 1967). Within any particular society, however, there
is typically enormous uniformity: most people do most things at appropriate
times.

A young American girl, living with a family in Barcelona, learns that
dinner is served at an unfamiliar time. Wanting to be a polite visitor, she
chooses to conform with the local custom. Yet it is equally true that her
Spanish hosts choose to conform with the traditional norms of their native
country. From both sides of this encounter, punctuality is realized by means
of temporal agency. Choosing to conform with familiar or unfamiliar temporal norms is a variety of time work.

Yet it would be a mistake to view these respective choices as uncaused.
George Herbert Mead (1932: 15) observes that "even the emergent happens
under determining conditions." The decision to conform is, itself, a product
of enculturation because our desires are socialized. Everyone in the fore-

going scenario has been taught to want the temporal conformity he or she exhibits. In this sense, all cultural practices are enacted by means of human agency. As Giddens (1979: 56) would have it, both the visiting girl and her host family "could have acted otherwise." Agency figures in the outcome because constrained choices are crucial links in the causal chain of cultural reproduction. If two nations exhibit stable but divergent forms of punctuality, both of these patterns result from myriad, dispersed, and yet parallel decisions made by members of the respective populations.

Murray Melbin (1969: 650) found a distinct pattern when he examined the behavioral rhythms of patients at a mental hospital. There was a strong tendency for them to "behave crazily" during weekdays, but not weekends or evenings. They chose to exhibit their insanity at certain times: "The difference is accounted for by the weekday presence . . . of professional treatment personnel and clinical trainees who are receptive to the revelation of symptoms and react with interest and tolerance." During evenings and weekends, the available members of the staff are not likely to "react with interest and tolerance." These patients, though officially classified as insane, were not oblivious to the temporal rhythms of that hospital, and they made quite strategic, albeit constrained, choices concerning the timing of their behavior. With the assistance of this temporal agency, they brought about the semblance of temporal determinism.

Our temporal agency may enact what clients want from us (at some personal sacrifice), as when teachers are at pains to make time during class seem to pass quickly. Of course, teachers may not care whether students enjoy the experience, but this only highlights the fact that, one way or another, teachers must choose how to position their classroom performance vis-à-vis the known temporal desires of their audience. In short, among teachers who strive to make class interesting, time work does not spring from within themselves as an unbidden creature of whimsy. Kindred dynamics operate at a university where the administration demands that members of the faculty allocate a specific proportion of their time to research, teaching, and service. Again, members of the faculty can elect to respond in idiosyncratic fashion (perhaps incurring a penalty for temporal deviance), but most choose to conform with these expectations to one degree or another. Here, we should conceptualize two levels of time work. First, there is an effort by administrators to impose temporal parameters on members of the faculty. Second, there is the time work professors enact in their more or less uncertain response to these demands.

So, one's own temporal agency is often set in motion by the temporal desires or dictates of others. From a distance, this can look like determinism; up close, we discover that these processes are composed of countless deliberations, choices, and negotiations. Time work can be, and frequently is, individualistic. Yet it is also the case that religions, corporations, schools, hospitals, prisons, governments, and other organizations engage in time work. In one way or another, they attempt to control or manipulate the temporal experience of their own people or that of client populations. The use of power and coercion for the purposes of temporal agency is apparent in Javier Auyero's (2011: 5) ethnographic research among the applicants for social services in Buenos Aires. By means of interminable waiting, the needy and destitute of Argentina are persuaded "to be patient, thus conveying the implicit state request to be compliant" as citizens. They become "patients of the state."

All of which is to say that time work does not represent the triumph of "freedom" or self-determination. It is manifest as constrained choices in an effort to modify one's own temporal experience or that of others. According to Erving Goffman (1959: 114), "Individuals attempt to buffer themselves from . . . deterministic demands that surround them." Temporal agency can represent an attempt to buffer ourselves from deterministic demands or accede to them. What is more, time work can assume the guise of deterministic demands. Therefore, when we observe people enacting various forms of temporal agency, we should ask ourselves why they are making those choices and not others.

SUCCESS AND FAILURE

With time work, we attempt to realize our temporal desires, which can be selfish or altruistic. This concept invokes metaphorical labor because, regardless of motivation, some effort will be required. It follows that the effort in question may or may not succeed. To date, this point has received very little attention, but it is a worthy topic for our research.

There may be no effective way to modify a particular dimension of temporal experience. In the United States, couples who opt to homeschool their children almost always relegate this responsibility to the mother. Research by Jennifer Lois (2010: 421) reveals that these mothers face insurmountable challenges with temporal agency: "The intensive demands of homeschooling left them stressed and dissatisfied with the amount of time they had to pursue their own interests. Mothers tried to allocate their time differently to manage these feelings, yet their efforts were unsuccessful." There are only so many hours in the day, and they have filled them with too many aspirations. We must acknowledge, however, that they are encouraged to do so by an ideological perspective on motherhood.

By virtue of their social location, some people never learn how to engage in certain types of temporal agency. The requisite knowledge and motivation are not randomly distributed across the population. Consequently, one may not acquire the necessary cultural capital for particular kinds of time work (Bourdieu 1984). If the self-management of one's time is possible, but the requisite skill and motivation are lacking, then one is unlikely to be successful at the temporal agency in question or will not even attempt it in the first place. The techniques of time management that make for a middle-class lifestyle are not universal (Leshan 1952; Levine 1997: 95–96; O'Rand and Ellis 1974). This is not to say that only some people engage in time work. All human beings enact temporal agency, but, to some extent, the dimensions of time work emerge from and reflect one's social location.

By itself, however, one's desire for a particular type of temporal experience is insufficient. An individual may lack the resources for whole genres of time work. Temporal agency is conditioned by inequality. Affluent people pay others to wait in lines on their own behalf. They use money to buy time for themselves. This is not something everyone can afford to do. With diverse flowers blooming at distinct times of the year, people who inhabit the Andaman Islands have developed a "calendar of scents" (Radcliffe-Brown [1922] 1964: 311–12). People who live in Nigeria can agree to meet when the sun is at a certain point in the sky (Bohannan 1953: 252). These resources for the organization of temporal experience are simply unavailable to prison inmates who reside in windowless cells with solid steel doors twenty-four hours a day. Instead of flowers or the sun, they structure their own temporal experience in terms of the number of times they are counted each day and the contents of food trays shoved through a slot in the door.

Certain forms of time work will be encouraged by one's personal relationships, organizational affiliations, and cultural heritage. The opposite is equally true. Indeed, there may be contextual resistance to specific genres of temporal agency. Witness, for instance, the following excerpt from an interview with a twenty-nine-year-old insurance salesman:

> I work all week and I like to have the nights to myself to do my work and rest. My girlfriend would like to see me more often, but when she's around I can't concentrate. So I tell her she can only come over on the weekends, which she doesn't really like, but it has to be that way so I can get my work done. I'd like to see her more often, too, but it's more convenient this way.

He wants to be a good boyfriend, but he also wants to be a good employee. Striving for balance between these respective demands on his time, he engages in temporal agency by controlling the frequency with which he sees his girlfriend. Notice, however, that his success comes at the price of her failure to increase time with him. She cannot realize the temporal experience she desires. One person's temporal agency can become another person's temporal structure. Attention to success and failure sensitizes us to the fact that determinism and self-determination are abstractions—rhetorical devices that oversimplify the messy etiology of temporal experience. In everyday life, success (or failure) at time work is always contingent on the causal give and take of social interaction.

Finally, temporal agency can "succeed" but be dysfunctional or even self-destructive. By clinging to immutable remorse, for example, one chooses to live in a seemingly unalterable and grief-inducing past. This is a recipe for low self-esteem or even depression. Alternatively, one may generate chronic anxiety by imagining a future full of threats that do not exist. Various physical ailments and diverse mental or interpersonal disorders may be related to dysfunctional forms of time work. There is, as well, the self-abnegation of parents who sacrifice their own happiness in the present for the sake of their children's happiness in the future. These parents cannot recoup the past if their children reject a future to which they never really aspired. And there is the danger of nostalgia where one longs for a "lost" (or perhaps fictional) past. This is the reactionary time work of right-wing political parties and social movements.

TEMPORAL DISPOSITIONS

Much of time work appears to be dispositional. An individual or segment of the population seeks to satisfy temporal inclinations. The time work in question is not right or wrong in any absolute sense; it is, rather, more or less suited to one's temporal propensities. Of course, these tendencies emerge from prior social interaction, but, as previously noted, one must exercise some agency in order to actualize them.

Certain variations on this theme seem more voluntary than others. This observation suggests that we need to conceptualize and analyze gradations of temporal agency. In its most extreme forms, time work segues into something that resembles time play. One can, for example, elect to take LSD, peyote, mescaline, or psilocybin for the mind (and time) altering effects produced by these hallucinogenic drugs. Intense meditation can have a parallel impact on the perceived passage of time (Kramer, Weger, and Sharma 2013). Thus, time work may arise from one's predilection for an altered state of consciousness.

Temporal agency differs stylistically even among people who are, ostensibly, in similar circumstances. How do you spend time on your vacation? In

Karen Stein's (2012) study, she formulates two ideal types. There are those who strive to ignore time "and find release from schedules and routine" (2012: 335). They aspire to an expanse of empty time and seek "rest and relaxation" (2012: 341). It will be a mark of success if, at some point, they lose track of time and do not know what day of the week it is. In contrast, there are those who are engaged in "tourism," which "necessitates close attention to time" (2012: 341). They want to maximize the number of noteworthy activities, which makes for a tightly packed schedule of sights to see.

A very different body of research suggests that people use temporal agency in order to die at the right time. More than thirty years ago, David Phillips and Kenneth Feldman (1973: 678) found that "there are fewer deaths before three ceremonial occasions: one's birthday, Presidential elections, and the Jewish Day of Atonement." This is an enduring pattern, as demonstrated by Ellen Idler and S. V. Kasl (1992: 1052): "Religious group membership ... protected Christians and Jews against mortality in the month before their respective religious holidays during a six-year period." In a later study by Phillips, Barker, and Brewer (2010), there was a significant increase of deaths on Christmas and New Year's Day. Correspondingly, mortality dipped during the days preceding these holidays. Most recently, Murray Last (2013) discovered comparable tendencies in a Muslim area of Nigeria. It is worth noting that all of these studies concern so-called deaths from "natural" causes, not suicides. No one knows exactly how it happens, but it would appear that many people are timing their deaths in conjunction with meaningful dates.

Temporal dispositions are also manifest when people attempt to control or modify the experience of time while at work. Daphne Demetry (2013: 601) conducted "a natural ethnographic experiment" in her study of "a single restaurant under two chef regimes." The first chef created a temporal atmosphere of camaraderie in which employees "had no strict start time" (2013: 587). The second chef insisted on a temporal atmosphere of professionalism "by establishing a strict work schedule" (2013: 594). In turn, these respective temporal contexts shaped the way in which members of the staff perceived the passage of time. Van Eerde, Beeftink, and Rutte (2016) examine the pacing of one's own work among architects. A U-shaped pattern emerges from their data, with "most activity at the start of a project and right before a deadline" (2016: 676). This self-imposed pacing "allows for incubation" of ideas and creativity during the intermediate fallow period (2016: 677). Further stylistic contrast is evident in Clark Molstad's (1986) ethnographic research among people who choose and cope with boring work. Seeking to avoid the stress associated with more demanding jobs, they engage in temporal agency by self-selecting work that is known to be tedious. Doing so requires a subsequent stage of time work during which they attempt to manage the resulting boredom.

As with time work, it would be a mistake to conceive of temporal dispositions as simply individualistic tendencies. Instead, we should ask ourselves why certain people (and not others) exhibit such preferences. The widespread acceleration of activities in our society offers a case in point (Rosa 2003, 2013). Speed is intrinsic to efficiency and therefore advantageous in a competitive economic environment (Hassan 2009). Yet that which is merely functional in one sphere of society (such as commercial enterprise) can become something that is valorized in a diffuse and gratuitous way. Not surprisingly, a great deal of contemporary time work is devoted to accelerating various endeavors—including previously unhurried leisure activities, such as reading, dating, chess, baseball, and tennis (Fine 2012). Temporal dispositions are cultural phenomena, and they provide much of the motivation for our time work.

PROBLEMATIC CIRCUMSTANCES

With the aforementioned concept of temporal dispositions, we are sensitized to the fact that people have preferences concerning their experience of time. Nevertheless, existing or anticipated circumstances may be antagonistic to these preferences. Without intervention of some sort, one's temporal experience will be undesirable. Much of time work involves avoiding or modifying such circumstances. One's temporal experience will not be altered by wishing for it; something must be done. For this reason, time work is typically laborious. It entails deliberation, effort, and execution. With time work, one aims to revise problematic circumstances.

There are multiple variations on this theme. To begin with, there may be temporal obstacles to becoming the person one wishes to be. Harold Garfinkel's (1967: 178) famously intersexed subject, Agnes, wanted to be accepted as a "normal female." The manipulation of time was crucial to her efforts because she was acutely aware that she needed a particular past in order to achieve a desired future: "Time played a peculiar role in constituting for Agnes the significance of her present situation. With regard to the past, we have seen the prominence with which she historicised, making for herself and presenting us with a socially acceptable biography." Her version of the past ignored the inconvenient fact that she was raised as a boy until puberty.

In a related vein, homeless people confront the twin problems of self-esteem and respect from others. Emily Meanwell (2013) observes that these problems are most acute when they seek shelter from the state. To receive shelter, they must show that they need help (a stigmatized status) but also deserve help (a valorized status). The solution to this quandary entails temporal agency. Meanwell (2013: 439) finds that they "construct narratives that symbolically reconstruct the past from the standpoint of the present." In other words, they present "a temporally divided self." These stories profane their past selves in order to salvage their present selves. Paraphrasing the familiar hymn, they were lost, but now are found. Like Agnes, these homeless people create the past that is required for a particular future.

In contrast, research by Crystal Fleming (2017) reveals that Caribbean and black French activists are striving for the preservation of collective memory. Many of them are descendants of former slaves, but they have formed social movements opposed to French denial of past participation in slavery. The official political narrative is that France is color-blind, and racism is a problem that afflicts other nations. Yet black citizens of France suffer ubiquitous forms of racism, and they view their current conditions as the legacy of slavery in former French colonies. Their social movements profane the past as it is imagined by the French regime. France's effort to deny past participation in slavery is a genre of temporal agency; so are efforts to reject such denial. With Fleming's ethnography, we witness mnemonic conflict, and collective memory is the prize.

In the foregoing studies, people are modifying the way we define or understand the past. We must also be alert to temporal agency directed toward the realization of a particular future. Newborn children in Uganda are named for their ancestors or the circumstances of their birth. Meinert and Schneidermann (2014) argue that these traditional naming practices constitute a genre of temporal agency because they condense biographical time. When named for an ancestor, the child's identity is linked to the past; when named for the circumstances of his or her birth, the child's identity is linked to the present. Recently, however, Meinert and Schneidermann (2014: 163) have observed young men giving themselves new names more suitable for the world-renowned singers they aspire to become. Self-naming is an ambitious and mutinous form of time work. It rejects the present and past of one's people for the sake of one's own future.

Individuals have autobiographical stories, and societies have collective memories. These stories and memories are characterized by various themes and narrative structures. Strictly speaking, the informants in the studies by Garfinkel, Meanwell, Fleming, and Meinert and Schneidermann are not altering temporal experience, but they are attempting to change the way we see the past or the future. This exciting elaboration on the concept of time work does not supplant the analysis of narrative structures. Yet, with the conceptualization of temporal agency, we can examine the methods or procedures by which narratives are created, maintained, or changed. This new line of inquiry promises to reveal how narrative structures are accomplished via social interaction.

Different issues confront those who strive to maintain relationships with others despite the impediments of distance and death. In her study of Latvian couples in long-distance relationships (LDRs), Jurkane-Hobein (2015) finds extensive and multidimensional use of temporal agency. These couples co-construct the meaning of their time together and their time apart. By setting deadlines, long-distance partners "treat the situation between face-to-face meetings as temporary" (2015: 192). Jurkane-Hobein (2015: 195) notes that when opportunities arise, these couples engage in what I have called the savoring complex: "Time work during the present-together includes *creating an event* and *focusing on the here and now*." Jurkane-Hobein (2015: 198) adds that "a very important type of time work in LDRs is spending the present-apart together." For instance, they may eat dinner and watch a movie via Skype. It is also possible to maintain one's relationship with the dead, as Christensen and Sandvik (2013) demonstrate in their study of a Danish online memorial site. These online memorials are devoted to deceased children, most of whom lived only a brief period of time (in some cases, a single day). Yet the memorials are created and maintained indefinitely by parents who wish to prolong (dare we say "savor") the relationship.

Temporal agency can be found in behavior that, on the face of it, seems to have little or nothing to do with time, per se. Unemployment and poverty make for boredom and the perception that time is passing slowly (Levine 1997). Yet one's participation in gangs, crime, and violence can transform otherwise boring intervals into episodes of drama, excitement, and pageantry (Jensen 2014). In so doing, however, one strikes a bargain with the devil, because incarceration is typically the price one pays for altering temporal experience in this fashion. With incarceration, there is even greater monotony than one finds in disadvantaged neighborhoods (Bengtsson 2012). Moreover, many prisoners deal with this problem by means of continued participation in gangs, crime, and violence. There is, then, agentic complicity in the cyclical time of chronic recidivism.

Other prisoners, seeking to avoid the cycle of recidivism, have recourse to different types of temporal agency. Some of their strategies were chronicled by sociologist Rik Scarce (2002) when he was jailed for contempt of court. He describes several tactics by which inmates attempt to compress the perceived passage of time. For example, many prisoners spend as much of their sentence as possible sleeping (2002: 310). A related strategy entails manipulation of the calendar by counting only Saturdays: "Sunday through Friday was a blur of sleeping, card playing, and eating. Only Saturday counted.

The effect was to make seven weeks feel like seven days" (2002: 310). A more extreme version involves "deleting two months from the calendar" (2002: 311). In order to accomplish this feat, an inmate must discard the calendar and stop reading newspapers or watching the news on television, all of which remind one of the actual date. There is a price to pay for this tactic, however, in that the prisoner is less prepared for life outside of prison. Here, as is often the case, one's temporal agency has intended and unintended consequences.

Like incarceration, conversation transpires within a unique temporal framework. We are doing time work when we talk to each other. In most of our ordinary conversations, we strive to establish and maintain mutual understanding. Temporal agency is an essential part of this process. Much of it is taken for granted, and, once we have learned the rules, we hardly think about it. Yet, once again, we must continually choose to enact these temporal norms. Sequencing in conversational openings is a prime example because the turn-taking that produces this pattern is intrinsically temporal (Schegloff 1968). At a more intentional level, we choose how to refer to time during our conversations with others. The options from which we choose (e.g., "this afternoon" versus "at 3:30") enable us to pursue various agendas in our speech. As Raymond and White (2017: 112) put it, "if speakers select a particular way of referring to time because of its intended effect on subsequent interaction, then time reference should be conceptualized as a form of temporal agency or 'time work.'" At a still higher level of intentionality, there is the use of temporal agency to avoid or minimize conversational incompetence. One of Husting's (2015: 228) subjects, for instance, "waited to order food at the bar until only a few people were around."

Clearly, people strive to avoid or extricate themselves from problematic temporal experience. An interesting variation on this theme is the engineering of temporal experience in medical settings and processes. Notoriously, patients seeking medical care are forced to wait for it. The waiting is stressful and makes for the perception that time is passing slowly. Klingemann and his colleagues (2015: 1) note that traditional efforts to address this problem ignore the setting while "attempting to reduce objective waiting times." They report on a quasi-experiment that examined the impact of "holistic [i.e., multisensory] artistic waiting room transformations." A setting filled with opportunities for active involvement with artistic creations reduced waiting stress as well as perceived waiting time (2015: 11). In kindred fashion, Buetow (2004) asks how practices can accelerate the perceived passage of time in waiting rooms and slow the perceived passage of time during medical consultations. Carr, Teucher, and Casson (2014) examine perceived wait time for scheduled surgery. McCoy (2009) looks at how HIV-positive patients use time work in an effort to adhere to the prescribed schedule for antiretroviral drugs. Generous funding ensures the continued study of temporal agency in medical settings and processes.

DIRECTIONS FOR FUTURE RESEARCH

Time and temporal experience are aspects of every human endeavor. Likewise, agency is "a necessary feature of action" (Giddens 1979: 56). It follows that temporal agency is ubiquitous in social interaction. Often, however, time work is tacit, taken for granted, and hard to see. We are accustomed to thinking about time in terms of clocks and calendars, but temporal experience is multidimensional—it includes duration, frequency, sequence, timing, and allocation, as well as efforts to steal time from each other. Day in and day out, we try to modify or enact these dimensions of temporal experience. Further research is called for in order to identify other dimensions of time work. Relatedly, there is evidence suggesting that temporal agency can be found in diverse societies. To what degree is the content of time work shaped by one's cultural location?

From a strict grammatical standpoint, the six dimensions of time listed above constitute a confusing mixture of nouns and verbs. "Duration," "frequency," and "allocation" are nouns. "Sequence" and "timing" can be nouns or verbs. And "stealing" is a present participle, a verb that functions as a noun. This is how the dimensions of time were formulated in the original conceptualization of temporal agency (Flaherty 2011: 12). Arguably, it is problematic terminology. "Time" is most often a noun, but "time *work*" entails effort, action, and intervention. There is nothing objectionable about "duration" and "frequency" as dimensions of time, but these terms seem less appropriate when referring to dimensions of temporal agency. We have elected to retain this terminology in this volume. Looking forward, however, it is worth thinking about the refinement of these terms as forms of action, which would be more in keeping with the meaning of temporal agency.

A portion of our temporal experience appears to be determined by our circumstances, whereas another portion seems to reflect our desires and self-determination. Reluctantly, a prison inmate is thrust into solitary confinement. Elsewhere, an individual eagerly enters a sensory deprivation tank; indeed, this person may have paid for the privilege. Both of these individuals will perceive time to pass slowly, but only one of them will do so voluntarily. If we conceive of these scenarios as the opposite ends of a continuum, then it makes sense to ask whether there are gradations of temporal agency between them. Moreover, how are these intermediary cases distributed across the continuum? Is one endeavor more or less agentic than another? With regard to temporal agency, at least, is determinism or self-determination more prevalent?

Success or failure at time work is contingent on one's *temporal intelligence—* knowledge concerning what a person can and cannot do with time. A busy schedule is valorized in some circles, but failure is inevitable if one assumes too many responsibilities during a given period. To what extent is this problem exacerbated by a cultural environment that is characterized by acceleration? The further study of temporal socialization would help us understand why certain individuals and groups have (or lack) the necessary skill and motivation for particular genres of time work. In any society or subculture, specific types of time work will be valued while others are considered deviant. By whom? Why? What role do various resources play in temporal agency? Having the requisite power is especially relevant. It is often the case that we must realize our temporal desires in the face of opposition.

The social distribution of temporal preferences has not been subjected to systematic scrutiny. What conditions bring about predilections for specific types of temporal experience? Why is it that people need a particular past in order to realize a coveted future? How do we use time work to maintain our relationships, and how do these relationships erode with failure to engage in temporal agency? Like prison inmates, we devote considerable effort to making the time we have a bit more interesting. What are the unintended consequences of this temporal agency? How is agency accomplished in the diverse ways that we talk about time? Time work can guide the practical redesign of our physical settings and interpersonal processes. When we are temporal architects, is this beneficial and admirable or intrusive and manipulative?

Time is life, and life is time. Temporal experience is a facet of self-consciousness in social interaction. When we modify temporal experience, we do so by altering our own consciousness and conduct, or that of others. We decide to intervene and, in so doing, change our subsequent temporal experience. This agency is a characteristic feature of human interaction, which means that time work is ubiquitous. By the same token, however, it can be hard to see because it concerns nothing less than the full panoply of human existence in all its fascinating diversity.

Michael G. Flaherty
Professor, Department of Sociology
Eckerd College and University of South Florida, USA

REFERENCES

Auyero, Javier. 2011. "Patients of the State: An Ethnographic Account of Poor People's Waiting." *Latin American Research Review* 46 (1): 5–29.

Bengtsson, Tea Torbenfeldt. 2012. "Boredom and Action—Experiences from Youth Confinement." *Journal of Contemporary Ethnography* 41 (5): 526–53.

Bohannan, Paul. 1953. "Concepts of Time among the Tiv of Nigeria." *Southwestern Journal of Anthropology* 9 (3): 251–62.

Bourdieu, Pierre. 1984. *Distinction: A Social Critique of the Judgment of Taste.* Cambridge, MA: Harvard University Press.

Buetow, Stephen. 2004. "Patient Experience of Time Duration: Strategies for 'Slowing Time' and 'Accelerating Time' in General Practices." *Journal of Evaluation in Clinical Practice* 10 (1): 21–25.

Carr, Tracey, Ulrich C. Teucher, and Alan G. Casson. 2014. "Time while Waiting: Patients' Experiences of Scheduled Surgery." *Qualitative Health Research* 24 (12): 1673–85.

Christensen, Dorthe Refslund, and Kjetil Sandvik. 2013. "Sharing Death: Conceptions of Time at a Danish Online Memorial Site." In *Taming Time, Timing Death: Social Technologies and Ritual,* edited by D. R. Christensen and R. Willerslev, 99–118. Surrey, UK: Ashgate.

Demetry, Daphne. 2013. "Regimes of Meaning: The Intersection of Space and Time in Kitchen Cultures." *Journal of Contemporary Ethnography* 42 (5): 576–607.

Fine, Gary Alan. 2012. "Time to Play: The Temporal Organization of Chess Competition." *Time & Society* 21 (3): 395–416.

Flaherty, Michael G. 2002. "Making Time: Agency and the Construction of Temporal Experience." *Symbolic Interaction* 25 (3): 379–88.

———. 2003. "Time Work: Customizing Temporal Experience." *Social Psychology Quarterly* 66 (1): 17–33.

———. 2011. *The Textures of Time: Agency and Temporal Experience.* Philadelphia: Temple University Press.

Fleming, Crystal Marie. 2017. *Resurrecting Slavery: Racial Legacies and White Supremacy in France.* Philadelphia: Temple University Press.

Garfinkel, Harold. 1967. *Studies in Ethnomethodology.* Englewood Cliffs, NJ: Prentice-Hall.

Giddens, Anthony. 1979. *Central Problems in Social Theory: Action, Structure and Contradiction in Social Analysis.* Berkeley: University of California Press.

Goffman, Erving. 1959. *The Presentation of Self in Everyday Life.* Garden City, NY: Anchor Doubleday.

Hassan, Robert. 2009. *Empires of Speed: Time and the Acceleration of Politics and Society.* Leiden: Brill.

Husting, Ginna. 2015. "The Flayed and Exquisite Self of Travelers: Managing Face and Emotions in Strange Places." *Symbolic Interaction* 38 (2): 213–34.

Idler, Ellen L., and S. V. Kasl. 1992. "Religion, Disability, Depression, and the Timing of Death." *American Journal of Sociology* 97 (4): 1052–79.

Iutcovich, Mark, Charles E. Babbitt, and Joyce Iutcovich. 1979. "Time Perception: A Case Study of a Developing Nation." *Sociological Focus* 12 (1): 71–85.

James, William. 1890. *The Principles of Psychology*. Vol. 1. New York: Dover.

Jensen, Steffen. 2014. "Stunted Future: *Buryong* among Young Men in Manila." In *Ethnographies of Youth and Temporality: Time Objectified*, edited by A. L. Dalsgård, M. D. Frederiksen, S. Højlund, and L. Meinert, 41–56. Philadelphia: Temple University Press.

Jurkane-Hobein, Iveta. 2015. "When Less Is More: On Time Work in Long-Distance Relationships." *Qualitative Sociology* 38 (2): 185–203.

Klingemann, Harald, Arne Scheuermann, Kurt Laederach, Birgit Krueger, Eric Schmutz, Simon Stähli, Minou Afzali, and Vero Kern. 2018. "Public Art and Public Space—Waiting Stress and Waiting Pleasure." *Time & Society* 27 (1): 69–91.

Kramer, Robin S. S., Ulrich W. Weger, and Dinkar Sharma. 2013. "The Effect of Mindfulness Meditation on Time Perception." *Consciousness and Cognition* 22 (3): 846–52.

Last, Murray. 2013. "Dying on Time: Cultures of Death and Time in Muslim Northern Nigeria." In *Taming Time, Timing Death: Social Technologies and Ritual*, edited by D. R. Christensen and R. Willerslev, 247–64. Surrey, UK: Ashgate.

Leshan, Lawrence L. 1952. "Time Orientation and Social Class." *Journal of Abnormal and Social Psychology* 47 (3): 589–92.

Levine, Robert. 1997. *A Geography of Time*. New York: Basic Books.

Lois, Jennifer. 2010. "The Temporal Emotion Work of Motherhood: Homeschoolers' Strategies for Managing Time Shortage." *Gender & Society* 24 (4): 421–46.

McCoy, Liza. 2009. "Time, Self, and the Medication Day: A Closer Look at the Everyday Work of 'Adherence.'" *Sociology of Health and Illness* 31 (1): 128–46.

Mead, George Herbert. 1932. *The Philosophy of the Present*. Chicago: University of Chicago Press.

———. 1934. *Mind, Self, and Society*. Chicago: University of Chicago Press.

Mead, Margaret. (1951) 1966. *Soviet Attitudes toward Authority: An Interdisciplinary Approach to Problems of Soviet Character*. New York: Schocken Books.

Meanwell, Emily. 2013. "Profaning the Past to Salvage the Present: The Symbolically Reconstructed Pasts of Homeless Shelter Residents." *Symbolic Interaction* 36 (4): 439–56.

Meinert, Lotte, and Nanna Schneidermann. 2014. "Making a Name: Young Musicians in Uganda Working on the Future." In *Ethnographies of Youth and Temporality: Time Objectified*, edited by A. L. Dalsgård, M. D. Frederiksen, S. Højlund, and L. Meinert, 153–74. Philadelphia: Temple University Press.

Melbin, Murray. 1969. "Behavior Rhythms in Mental Hospitals." *American Journal of Sociology* 74 (6): 650–65.

Molstad, Clark. 1986. "Choosing and Coping with Boring Work." *Urban Life* 15 (2): 215–36.

O'Rand, Angela, and Robert A. Ellis. 1974. "Social Class and Social Time Perspective." *Social Forces* 53 (1): 53–62.

Phillips, David P., Gwendolyn E. C. Barker, and Kimberly M. Brewer. 2010. "Christmas and New Year as Risk Factors for Death." *Social Science & Medicine* 71 (8): 1463–71.

Phillips, David P., and Kenneth A. Feldman. 1973. "A Dip in Deaths before Ceremonial Occasions: Some New Relationships between Social Integration and Mortality." *American Sociological Review* 38 (6): 678–96.

Radcliffe-Brown, A. R. (1922) 1964. *The Andaman Islanders.* New York: Free Press.

Raymond, Chase Wesley, and Anne Elizabeth Clark White. 2017. "Time Reference in the Service of Social Action." *Social Psychology Quarterly* 80 (2): 109–31.

Rosa, Hartmut. 2003. "Social Acceleration: Ethical and Political Consequences of a Desynchronized High-Speed Society." *Constellations* 10 (1): 3–33.

———. 2013. *Social Acceleration: A New Theory of Modernity.* New York: Columbia University Press.

Scarce, Rik. 2002. "Doing Time as an Act of Survival." *Symbolic Interaction* 25 (3): 303–21.

Schegloff, Emanuel. 1968. "Sequencing in Conversational Openings." *American Anthropologist* 70 (6): 1075–95.

Schulz, Amy, Faye Knoki, and Ursula Knoki-Wilson. 1999. "How Would You Write about That? Identity, Language, and Knowledge in the Narratives of Two Navajo Women." In *Women's Untold Stories: Breaking Silence, Talking Back, Voicing Complexity*, edited by M. Romero and A. J. Stewart, 174–91. New York: Routledge.

Stein, Karen. 2012. "Time Off: The Social Experience of Time on Vacation." *Qualitative Sociology* 35 (3): 35–353.

Thompson, E. P. 1967. "Time, Work-Discipline, and Industrial Capitalism." *Past and Present* 38 (1): 56–97.

van Eerde, Wendelien, Flora Beeftink, and Christel G. Rutte. 2016. "Working on Something Else for a While: Pacing in Creative Design Projects." *Time & Society* 25 (3): 676–99.

Part II

Temporal Afflictions

Chapter 2

Repetition Work
Healing Spirits and Trauma
in the Churches of Northern Uganda

Lars Williams and Lotte Meinert

⬥

Who are you? What do you want?
Who are you? What do you want?
Who are you? What do you want?

A middle-aged woman dressed in white robes is shouting out repeatedly while a young man kneels in front of her. Behind the woman a wooden table serves as an altar, with buckets of water, a straw basket of stones, and bowls of shea butter. Behind the table is a large pile of rocks. The young man is praying. His eyes are closed and he is holding a large calabash in his hands. The calabash has rocks in it. The woman is walking around him, speaking out loud. "Who are you?" she is asking again and again. "What do you want? Why are you here?" His body begins to shake. First his hands quiver, and the sound of the rocks rattling in the calabash fills the small room. He is praying softly to himself, while the woman's voice takes over the room. "Who are you? Why are you here? Show yourself!" She is shouting now. The man is sweating, eyes closed, the rattling sound of the rocks increasing in volume. "Who are you?" she yells. No one answers. But she is not talking to the young man. She is talking to the spirits who have possessed him, the spirits of the past, called *cen*.

The room stirs with people coming in. It is early morning, but the séance has been going on for a while, and the young man is not the first one today to kneel in front of the altar. We are seated on the floor among the church participants, observing and recording the ritual as it unfolds. This kind of ritual takes place every day in the New Jerusalem Tabernacle Church, often several times a day. People are praying in designated areas around the small concrete room, most of them in front of the large rock pile. The young man is nodding in violent spasms now, as another man from the congregation joins the woman and starts to read passages from the Bible. Short passages. Sentences. "Lord Jesus, Lord Jesus," he shouts down at the shaking young man. He begins again, the same passages, saying "Lord Jesus, you will be free through Jesus!" repeatedly. The woman is still asking the spirits to show themselves. The young man starts to cough. His whole body is shaking, and it is hard for him to catch his breath. The woman gives him water from a small calabash to drink. "It is holy water," a man behind us explains. "Lord Jesus," the congregation member shouts, "Lord Jesus, come and take away these bad spirits!" The woman gives the young man water several times, and pours it over his head. He looks like he is having a full seizure: even his face is twitching as he falls to the ground. The calabash falls from his hands, the stones roll around him. The woman throws water on him as she draws crosses in the air. "Jesus will set you free!" the other man shouts down at the young man, who is curled up in cramps on the floor. The woman pours the holy water over the stones that have fallen from the calabash to the floor, brings them to the altar, and throws them on the large rock pile. She then helps the young man to his knees and hands him a long stick, a shepherd's staff, to pull himself up. The congregation member reads the same Bible passage again and prays out loud for the young man. They are passages from the Book of Daniel, chapter twelve, about water and blood, about prophets, about how a new world will come. She leads the young man to the pile of rocks. He collapses in front of the rocks and prays, face down. "He is now reborn," the man behind us whispers.

When we later interview the woman leading this ceremony, she explains, "It was the spirits of the dead from the past, it was *cen* that was haunting the boy. But those spirits are now turned into stones," she explains, pointing to the large pile of rocks on the floor of the altar area. "When we were fighting the government, sometimes we would use stones," the woman continues. "Often, we would run out of ammunition for our guns, so we would bring stones to throw at the government soldiers. Those stones have killed many people. But that was times of war, and now are times for peace and healing, so we are bringing the stones back." She points to the large pile of rocks on the altar, where the young man is praying. "The stones are alive, they are not dead things, and now they are used to heal our people from the bad spirits of the dead."

After our conversation, the woman leads the crowd in praising, singing, and dancing. During the dancing, she starts to march like a soldier. The congregation follows her. It is the spirits of the soldiers that make her march, we are told. It is the spirits of the soldiers that are conducting the ceremony now. They have returned from their violent past and become present in the marching bodies of the living.

The marching and the stone rituals form a way of dealing with a violent past. The ceremony is orchestrated, we suggest in this paper, to deal with structures of violence from the years of war and to gain a sense of agency over that past, which keeps presenting itself in the form of haunting spirits and madness. The ghosts from the past beckon their victims to go back in time, to live in the past. If we understand *cen* or trauma in this way as a loss of agency over (and in) time, the rituals of the New Jerusalem Tabernacle Church may be conceptualized as forms of time work (Flaherty 2003)—efforts to manipulate temporal experiences, rewrite a violent history, and regain temporal agency.

This chapter is based on empirical material from our anthropological fieldwork in northern Uganda between 2010 and 2017. Lars was conducting his PhD fieldwork on spirits and trauma, and he lived with a pastor and his family, following his pastoral work with the village community after years of war. That pastoral work included collective work with the congregation in rituals and ceremonies, as well as individual praying and counseling for church members. Lotte had been doing studies of trauma and spirits in the region, in collaboration with Susan Whyte, since 2010. These studies included nineteen families, two health clinics, and interviews with traditional healers, NGOs, and church leaders. In June 2017, we (Lars and Lotte) initiated a case study of prayer and repetitive practices at a small charismatic church in Gulu Town called New Jerusalem Tabernacle Church. In this chapter, we draw mainly on the case study from this church, but we contextualize this with our other studies in the area.

BACKGROUND: THE WAR AND THE LEGACY OF VIOLENCE

The New Jerusalem Tabernacle Church, where the séance just described took place, is located in a slum in Gulu Town. Congregants are cleansed and reborn on a daily or weekly basis, again and again, in repetitive ceremonies to rid them of "whatever happened to you in the past," including bad spirits and sins. "Whatever happened to you in the past" varies greatly, but the legacies of violence and disruption from the recent twenty-year-long war between the rebel movement Lord's Resistance Army (LRA) and the government forces, which forced 1.5 million people into internally displaced persons (IDP) camps, are an implicit reference. The societal and mental wounds are still healing from the extremely violent killings and mutilations carried out by both the LRA and government forces. Children and young people were abducted and forced to become soldiers. As part of rebel strategies, they were often ordered to kill members of their own families. In the aftermath of the war in the Acholi subregion, families and communities are in a long-term transition process of rebuilding their lives. Despite the remarkable resilience in the community, significant trauma still exists. A study from 2006 found one of the highest measured concentrations of depression and post-traumatic stress disorder (PTSD) in post-conflict zones (Roberts et al., 2008). According to this study, 67 percent of the population in Gulu and Amuru districts meet the criteria for depression, and 54 percent for PTSD (measured with Hopkins Symptom Checklist-25 and the Harvard Trauma Questionnaire; Meinert and Whyte 2017). These numbers—and the checklists themselves—should probably be taken with a grain of salt. Yet there is no doubt that since the war very many people and families are struggling with problems that may be categorized as trauma and depression or as disturbances by spirits or the devil. In 2012, there were still twenty-five NGOs present in the region focusing on trauma treatment. A very large number of *awjaki*, local healers, were also present, involved in helping people deal with traumas and spirits after the war (Meinert and Whyte 2017). So far, less scholarly attention has been paid to the work of religious institutions in relation to healing since the years of war, despite the vast variety and importance of these religious institutions in everyday life in the Acholi region (Apuuli 2011; Finnegan 2013). The Catholic and Anglican churches have a long and dominant presence in the region, but a stable and growing Muslim community also exists, and the call to prayer in local mosques can be heard on Fridays in some of the most remote areas. In recent years, communities of Pentecostal and charismatic churches have been growing rapidly and are attracting increasing numbers of congregants. But for all these ecumenical categories, many of the churches in northern Uganda can be hard to classify, and one such is the New Jerusalem Tabernacle Church. It seems closest to a charismatic or Pentecostal church, yet its members put in a great deal of effort to explain how they are not *Balokolé*, meaning "saved ones," the Acholi term for charismatic or Pentecostal churches. Furthermore, in the text readings and rituals, the ceremonial leaders integrate almost equal amounts of Quranic and Biblical text, as well as traditional spirit beliefs. In this respect this church seems almost like a type of New Age religion (Heelas et al. 2005).

At the end of the war in 2006, the religious and traditional institutions were certainly crucial in securing a peace agreement between the parties of the war. But their importance goes far beyond that role. These institutions also provide relatively stable frameworks and tools for people to deal with the various legacies of violence. Having followed families dealing with problems of trauma and spirits since the war ended, we have found it noteworthy that many try—but then discontinue—medication, treatment with traditional healers (*ajwaki*), and NGO therapy initiatives, whereas more seem to stick to the help they find in churches and other religious institutions. Giving up biomedical treatment may partly be due to the relatively unstable provision and expense of medicine and other forms of therapy, whereas the religious institutions are constantly present in most areas and are relatively inexpensive or even free to attend. We will argue, however, that another reason why the religious institutions attract people and why they continue to go there to deal with problems of trauma lies in the healing potential of the prayer practices that these institutions initiate. A part of the potential of these prayer practices helps to support the experience of temporal agency.

In this paper, we argue more specifically that trauma/PTSD can be conceptualized as a form of time disturbance, and that the intrapersonal and interpersonal repetitive time work conducted in rituals, praying, and the repetition of text passages from the Bible and the Quran are significant in dealing both with spirits and with traumas from the past. Apart from the ritual time work carried out in churches, the religious communities organize everyday practical work groups and prayer meetings, and in this way they establish rhythms and routines in everyday life. We explore these prayer practices using Michael Flaherty's (2003, 2011) ideas of time work as ways of gaining temporal agency in dealing both with spirits and with trauma. With this approach, we would like to contribute to the growing anthropological literature on trauma and life in post-conflict areas. Because the practices used by our interlocutors are prayers and the context is a charismatic church, our discussion of temporal agency also contributes to the anthropology of Christianity and the literature on prayer. We see these areas becoming empirically connected in the lives of the people in the New Jerusalem Tabernacle Church, and in the ways they go about ritual practices to heal the wounds of the past and gain temporal agency.

TRAUMA AS A DISTURBANCE OF TIME

Ever since the American Psychological Association incorporated post-traumatic stress disorder (PTSD) into their diagnostic manual in 1980, temporal dimensions have been implicit in the illness concept. In 1980, the third edition of the manual was published, the DSM-III, and the definition of PTSD included "intrusions" or "flashbacks" as symptoms and criteria for diagnosis. In 2013, the present edition of the manual, the DSM-V, came out, and temporal aspects are still central elements in the diagnosis. In fact, the temporal aspects have their own cluster of criteria (Criterion B), which include intrusive thoughts, nightmares, and flashbacks as symptom criteria (Forman-Hoffman et al. 2018). Nevertheless, notions of temporality seem not to be explicated in the official diagnostic language and clinical assumptions of PTSD.

In the Acholi region of northern Uganda, the symptoms of trauma as we know them from the DSM-V diagnostic system (with flashbacks, nightmares, avoidance behavior, etc.) are often conceptualized in a spiritual idiom called *cen*, meaning the vengeful spirits of the dead. The word *cen*, besides denoting spiritual pollution, is also the verb for "to return," which is in itself a temporal signifier. The causality is perceived to be mostly moral, in the sense that if a person kills another person unjustly, the dead person will come back and haunt the killer, making him or her aware of the injustice and eventually driving the killer mad unless action is taken to right the wrongs (see also Meinert and Whyte 2017, forthcoming; Williams and Meinert 2017). Within some of the Pentecostal-charismatic or nondenominational churches, this will be referred to as *catan*, or the devil, but the basic idea of spiritual contamination or possession is very similar. In some ways, this differs from the Western diagnostic conception of trauma, which is less of a moral concept and more about mechanistic causality. However, we argue that what both have in common is an experiential disturbance of time.

Other scholars have discussed temporal aspects of trauma and traumatic time in various ways. Anthropologist Allan Young, in his influential monograph *The Harmony of Illusions* (1997) on American Vietnam War veterans, notes the paradox in the fact that in clinical conceptualizations of trauma (e.g., as PTSD) the idea of time flows forward, from the traumatic event to the symptoms. Yet in the phenomenological experience of the traumatized person, time flows backward, back to the traumatic event. Young (1997: 135) quotes Roger K. Pitman and S. P. Orr (1990: 169–70):

> One of the striking features of post-traumatic stress disorder (PTSD) is the degree to which a past event comes to dominate the patient's associations. As all roads lead to Rome, all the patient's thoughts lead to the trauma. A war veteran known to us cannot look at his wife's nude body without recalling with revulsion the naked bodies he saw in a burial pit in Vietnam, cannot stand the sight of children's dolls because their eyes remind him of the staring eyes of the war dead. . . .

The ultimate gravitational attraction in the physical universe is represented by the black hole, a place in space-time that has such high gravity that even light cannot pass by without being drawn into it. . . . [Similarly] PTSD patients struggle to avoid thoughts, activities, or situations associated with the trauma . . . , not only because they are so painful, but also because they are so absorbing.

Young (1997) argues for an image of trauma that embodies a dual flow of time. One is a clinical conception of time, more experience-distant in its understanding of symptoms as a reaction to a traumatic event and thus involving a forward flow of time (a conception that, according to Young, prevails because of the technologies and institutions upholding modern diagnostics). Another is an experience-near time flow, in which the traumatized persons keep on involuntarily returning to the past, away from the present moment. They relive experiences—that is, they have "flashbacks" of the horrors of the past. Sometimes this occurs for short moments or flashes, as in Pitman and Orr's (1990) example above, but sometimes also for longer periods. It is this reversed conception of the temporal aspects of trauma that interests us in this paper.

The psychoanalyst Robert Stolorow (1999, 2003) has developed the thesis, based in the philosophy of Heidegger (1962), that the breaking of the unifying thread of temporality is an essential dimension of psychological trauma (Stolorow 2003: 158). Stolorow argues that clinical features that are commonly described as dissociation and multiplicity can be understood in terms of the traumatic events' impact on disrupting the sense of being-in-time. The shattering of one's experiential world that characterizes traumatized experiences is partly constituted by the breaking up of one's sense of temporality. This alteration in the experience of temporality in trauma may be understood with reference to discussions of the phenomenology of time in the work of Husserl and Heidegger. In the thinking of Husserl ([1905] 1991), phenomenological time is fundamental to all lived experience. As pointed out by Stolorow (2003) and Dostal (1993), the experienced present is normally "thick" in the sense that it contains both the past and the future. Heidegger ([1927] 1962: 337) developed this further and understood past, present, and future as "ecstases of temporality." Under normal conditions, all three dimensions are united in experience: every lived experience is always in the three dimensions of time, and in this way our experience of time stretches along between birth and death (Heidegger [1927] 1962: 425). Stolorow (2003: 160) contends that it is the ecstatic unity of temporality—the sense of stretching along between past and future—that is devastatingly disturbed by the experience of psychological trauma: "Experiences of trauma become freeze-framed into an eternal present in which one remains forever trapped, or to which one is condemned to be perpetually returned."

A clinician and colleague of ours who has worked for many years with traumatized refugees at a clinic in southern Denmark told us about a man he had in treatment who worked in a factory at night. This man's employer eventually grew dissatisfied with his work because when he showed up in the morning, the employee had not got much work done. Eventually, the employer put up security cameras in his factory building. When he watched the tapes, they revealed that the employee sometimes would drive a fork-lift into the wall repeatedly for hours; he was not able to remember this afterwards. The clinician explained that the man was "not there," that he was back in time to the war in the Balkans, and that this sometimes could last for hours (Sodemann 2016, personal communication). Or, as one of our Ugandan interlocutors put it (in the local idioms of distress), "When you become mad (*apoya*) because of *cen*, you are often not really there. You wander around because of your madness (*lak ataa ataa*), you are not there in the head, and therefore you don't remember what you do or where you go." In other words, you are somewhere else in time.

What we argue is that trauma (or *cen*) is a form of time disturbance, and that when you suffer from it, you are brought out of the here-and-now and taken back in time. You are taken back to the traumatic events, reliving them for shorter or longer periods of time. We go on to argue that certain practices in northern Uganda, such as those of the New Jerusalem Tabernacle Church, create both personal and collective spaces and practices for treating these disturbances of time, through repetitive ritual practice of prayer and scripture reading. This we conceptualize as a form of time work, drawing on Flaherty's ideas. Flaherty (this volume, 20) writes that, "One's temporal experience will not be altered by wishing for it; something must be done. For this reason, time work is typically laborious. It entails deliberation, effort, and execution. With time work, one aims to revise problematic circumstances." Here, we explore repetition as one form of time work, initiated by rituals and praying in church, that alters the experience of time, perhaps by stitching together the ecstatic unity of temporality so as to recreate the sense of stretching along between past and future (Heidegger [1927] 1962), which is so profoundly disturbed by the experience of trauma (Stolorow 2003). An important aspect of repetition, when it is frequent enough and the duration long enough, is that it brings the subject back to the present moment and "contains" him or her there. Furthermore, repetitive praying and recitation establish a rhythm that can be felt and followed, which helps to create (or recreate) the ordinary feeling that time moves forward and that events can be anticipated, which diminishes the risk of flashbacks. Both of these aspects create an experience of temporal agency. We move on now to describe individual prayer as one of the practices characterized by repetition work.

PRAYING AS REPETITION WORK

Okot is a tall, thin man in his late thirties. He smiles a lot, and talks a lot about his new cassava garden. Apparently, it is growing very well these days. As we walk on a windy road through the tall grass, he points out where his land begins and talks in an almost constant flow of words. He is a cheerful man with an unusual amount of energy. But he was not always like that, he tells us. Okot used to be a mad person (*lapoya*). He would wander around, forget where he was, get aggressive, and beat his wife and children. He "was not really there" (*rom ma peke*), as he puts it. He tells a story similar to so many converts. Eventually he was brought to the New Jerusalem Tabernacle Church in Gulu Town and cured through prayer. Okot went through the same cleansing and rebirth that we saw the young man go through at the beginning of this chapter. But that was just the beginning of his healing process. Now his life revolves around a vigorous and repetitive practice of daily prayer. He explains, "Now that I am born again, I pray a lot. I pray when I get up in the morning, before breakfast, before going in the field, after being in the field, before dinner, before I sleep. I pray all the time. When I get to the field with the others [the congregation members] we pray all along during the day." He will also meet with the other church members several times during the week for collective prayers and the cleansing of evil spirits.

When we reach his house, Okot shows us his altar outside, and the extra hut in his compound, which he has arranged like a small version of the church in town. In sleepless periods and times when he "thinks too much" (*tam ma dwong*), he will sleep in his church hut or pray through the night there. When we asked him to explain his prayer practice, Okot begins a very long description of all the different practices he employs (the passages below are just excerpts from our field notes).

"I begin with the Muslim prayer,"[1] Okot explains. "It's a good one, because you have to stand up, and prostrate and move your body. So, I turn in this direction [supposedly toward Mekka] and I begin." He shows us the bodily movements, moving his hands up to his head, then to the stomach, bowing down in prostration. He goes through the movements in solemn silence. "Then, after the Muslim prayer, I will pray the [Catholic] rosary," he says. He takes out a small string with rosary beads on it and explains:

First you count ten [beads] while you are saying the beginning prayer. After ten [beads] you make a cross [he makes a cross in the air with his arms] and say "Glory be to the Father and Son and Holy Spirit, as the world we will be without end . . ." I say it in our language. It means that I glorify God. I do this every morning, every evening, and then I go here at night and do it if I cannot sleep.

Okot says the prayers out loud: "Hail Mary, be with grace . . . Kikum wrot, kikum tipu maleng. . . ." As he switches between English and the Acholi language, you can hear the rhythm and how he has repeated this so many times. It almost flows out of him, effortless, thoughtless. The rhythm in his words and speech seems to make his movements and words melt together as he repeats it over and over again. He tells us, "There are fifty beads on the rosary so I do this fifty times, and then call the Hail Mary again. . . . Then I finish with these two big ones [he shows us the larger beads on the rosary strings] and then I start from the beginning again." When Okot is not in his context of prayer, in the church or in his prayer hut, he talks very fast and hectically; he stumbles over words, and it seems like he is floating away in his own speech. But when he returns to his prayer, his speech gets a rhythm, a steady tempo: "Glory be to the Father, and to the Son and to the Holy Spirit. As it was in the beginning, is now and ever shall be, world without end . . ." And then back to Acholi language, where the rhythm seems to flow even more smoothly while Okot's fingers count through the beads. And once again, from the beginning: "Kikum wrot, kikum tipu maleng, Maria maleng, Lubanga, Jeso Christo tye . . . Christo Melta, Lubanga, Kikum wrot, kikum tipu maleng . . ." Okot continues in English: "Glory be to the Father and the Son . . ." The intonation of his voice almost becomes a humming, and it seems like the words themselves become less significant as his body rocks slowly back and forth. And he begins again: "As it was in the beginning, is now and ever shall be . . ." The flow of language synchronizes with his slow, bodily rocking, and he begins again repetitively, rhythmically: "Glory be to the Father . . ." He makes a cross in the air with his fingers. His fingers find the beads again, and he starts over once more. "After this," he says, "I will pray for other people if they need it or if there is something I want . . . like, God, you show the sick people where you are so they can come to you—and you change the heart of the political leaders, so they will not bother us in our church and they will let us reach the sick and poor." Okot shows us how to hold the rosary, and he begins praying again, almost automatically: "Glory be to the Father and the Son and the Holy Spirit, Amen, hallowed be your name, your kingdom come, give us our daily bread, forgive us our trespasses, as we forgive our brothers . . ." As he goes on, he starts mentioning people from the church, the leaders, the ones in need. He continues in repetition almost as if we had started him by pushing a prayer button.

What characterizes the speaking and bodily movements in Okot's prayer, apart from the world religion they traditionally belong to, is repetition and rhythm. Okot practices repetition of movement, repetition of words. He repeats these movements and these words every day, in the same order. He repeats them alone, and he repeats them with his fellow congregants. They are repeated daily, weekly, monthly, and for several years now, again and again. They structure his days, his relations with other people, his life at home—they structure his life. There is something about this vigorous repetition of movements and words that seems to also structure his mind and his sense of being-in-time, to keep it together, intact. Perhaps the repetition can be said to contain his madness by stitching together the unifying thread of temporality and nurturing a present relationship with his past and his future—bringing him back, moving him forward.

DISCUSSION: REPETITION WORK, PRAYERS, TRAUMA, AND TIME

Picking up a classic debate in social psychology between pragmatists' and behaviorists' different views on agency, Flaherty (2003: 18) argues that this debate has not sufficiently considered temporality and its importance for understanding human experience. He recasts this discussion within the theoretical frame of time work and asks what role temporality plays in relation to agency for human experience (Flaherty 2003: 17–18). Here, we would like to build on the discussion by bringing in repetition as a central concept, posing it in the context of trauma and prayers in the lives of our Ugandan informants.

Flaherty (2003: 21) categorizes five features of time work among the participants in his research: duration, frequency, sequence, timing, and allocation. In his book, *The Textures of Time* (2011), one new dimension is added, namely "stealing time." In the present chapter, we do not directly apply all of these categories. As a beginning, we employ the basic notions from this framework when thinking about how people manipulate their temporal experiences and gain temporal agency, as Okot and others in northern Uganda do through repetition, prayer, and ceremony. That said, the repetitive speech and movements that Okot and his fellow congregants use to structure their daily life could be seen as a type of sequencing of time. Okot resists his disturbed temporal experience by sequencing time through prayer practice in a way that makes his temporal experience manageable. Okot also sequences his different prayer practices in particular ways: as he says, "It is good to start with the Muslim prayer because you have to stand up, and prostrate, and move your body." The repetitive sequencing of prayer practices brings about the re-emergence of a normal sequencing of temporal experience (i.e., that he is "here right now" when he prays and not "not really there" as he used to be when he was "mad"). Like the people in Flaherty's (2003: 25) study, who apply sequencing of time for the purpose of reaching certain goals and creating certain temporal experiences, Okot sequences his time for the purpose of mending his ruptured temporal experiences (in our words, not his). The sequencing of prayers, beginning with Muslim prostrations, then praying the rosary, then going to the field and saying more prayers there and so forth, creates a structure throughout the day. It works toward a sequencing of time that moves forward in normal fashion and works to counter ruptures in temporal experience–that is, to counter being pulled back in time, back to the traumatic events of the war or "being not really there."

The sequencing of time also takes place on another level, as we saw in the stone ritual. Here, the stones that were once used as weapons to kill are now brought back to heal. Past deeds of violence are in this way "overridden" because the materiality of harm–the stones–are now being used to alleviate the harm from the past (the spirits of the dead returning). This is a form of temporal sequencing that brings the past to the present to manage it through rituals and prayers. By these means, the past can then be left once again in the past. Through this sequencing process, the returning past (in the form of haunting spirits) can be placed where it should be, in the past, rather than hovering as a disturbing feature of the present. This enables the congregation to reform itself through a manipulation of past events in the present. The congregants manipulate time through ritual in order to be reborn by means of healing practices. "Overriding" the practices of killing that the stones used to represent, they create new meaning for the stones in the course of current healing practices, thereby changing what the stones symbolize in the present. And as the meaning of the stones is changed through repetitive ritual practices, the meaning of the past is also changed.

Okot and his fellow congregants also gain temporal agency through allocation of time. Flaherty (2003: 28) writes that "allocation [of time] seems to represent identities, emotional commitments, and strongly held beliefs rather than duty narrowly defined." When Okot sets time aside for his elaborate prayer practices, he is not simply fulfilling a duty. He is managing an identity through the repetition of his prayer practices: he is becoming a devout and righteous man, someone who practices because of particular values in the church and particular moral ideas about people and the world. By allocating time to pray in the way he does, he is becoming the person he wants to be, rather than the traumatized and mad person he used to be. The prayer practices may be conceptualized as technologies of the self in a Foucauldian sense (Foucault 1988) or, alternatively, as a set of skills to manage his mind (Luhrmann 2012; Haeri 2013); but before they can work toward this virtue, time must be allocated for their practice. A premise for this identity management and the management of temporal experience and agency is the allocation of time to practice what is required to reach these goals.

Principally, however, we suggest that our informants are using a new kind of time work, one that was not conceptualized by Flaherty (2003, 2011). We find two types of repetition in our data. One of them is the troubling reoccurrence of traumatic memories that is characteristic of post-traumatic stress disorder. Over and over again, the individuals in question return mnemonically to the horrors of the past. This was what was troubling the young man going through the cleansing ritual we presented at the start. This debilitating pattern is involuntary, and it represents the failure of agency over an ordinary temporal flow. The second type of repetition in our data is found in the prayers and religious rituals embraced by the congregants of the New Jerusalem Tabernacle Church. The ceaseless repetition of their prayers and religious rituals is a healing process because it distracts them from—indeed, replaces—the repetition of horrific memories of the past. Their prayers and religious rituals primarily concern the present and the future. This was what Okot was showing us in his home. Thus, the congregants reestablish the normal flow of temporal experience (from the past, through the present, toward the future) by substituting a healing form of repetition for a pathological form of repetition. By the same token, by means of this time work, they reestablish agency over their own temporal experience. With this line of analysis, we can account for the effectiveness of their prayers and rituals.

Taking Flaherty's (2003) concept of time work as a point of departure, we identify a few studies within the anthropological literature on trauma and on prayer where temporality seems to play a significant role in healing, institutionally or otherwise. In their study on Native American experience of trauma and indigenous ways of healing, Ball and O'Nell (2016: 334) employ the concept of "historical trauma." They argue that this is a more precise term for characterizing the trauma of the Native American communities than post-traumatic stress disorder. This is not unlike the experience of the population in northern Uganda, where trauma was not caused only by a single event or discrete events but was also a prolonged phenomenon concerning a whole people and their recent history. By referring to these problems as "historical trauma," we argue for an explicit focus on temporality and a perspective on trauma as a phenomenon that develops through time in a prolonged fashion. The suffering of these communities can only be understood and healed, Ball and O'Nell (2016) suggest, if this prolonged temporal dimension is brought into the conceptualization of trauma. Experiences of trauma in northern Uganda are both historical and recent, individual and collective. It is hard to establish a beginning to the violent history in northern Uganda, as this reaches back beyond colonial times to periods of slave trade and uprisings (see Meinert and Whyte 2017, forthcoming). Periods of violence have continued to mark the history of northern Uganda up to the recent conflicts. Even though peace has now been established, it is in a sense also difficult to pinpoint an end to violence and traumatic experience because they often transform into various types of domestic violence, suicide, and various kinds of mental illness (Meinert and Whyte 2017, forthcoming).

Another perspective on trauma and church practices comes from Tankink's (2007) study of Pentecostal churches in southwestern Uganda. She argues for the therapeutic functions of prayer practices in relation to the traumatic experiences of civil war and violence in these communities. Tankink asserts that a new perception of the past can be cultivated by orienting people toward the future through prayer and Bible study. This is, in Flaherty's (2003, 2011) terms, an example of how temporal experience is customized through the practice of time work, and it is in this respect similar to how Okot and his fellow congregants rewind their past in order to manage troubled and disrupted temporal experiences. These studies offer powerful evidence that temporal dimensions are at the heart of a people's traumatic experiences, and it follows that healing calls for a focus on various dimensions of time.

Yet it is not only in these particular contexts that issues of temporality are moving to the foreground, but more broadly within the literature on the anthropology of Christianity. According to Robbins (2007), the anthropology of Christianity as a distinct subfield has largely failed to develop due to misconceptions about two main dimensions of Christian life, time and belief (here, we focus only on the first of these). Robbins argues that ruptures, and the transcendence of these same ruptures, lie at the very heart of much of Christian life, and that this can only be properly understood if we consider what models of belief and time are at play. This is relevant to our study in northern Uganda because the congregants of New Jerusalem Tabernacle Church are so occupied with change and rupture. Okot changes himself through the time work of prayer in his home; the church members manipulate history through the time work of the stone ritual, where history is rewritten. Change is managed both through institutional and individual time work, which is of course only possible, as Robbins (2007: 12) points out, because there are already certain ideas present in the community about what time is ("a dimension where change is possible"). On the misconception of time, he writes,

> Something does not just happen *in* time but rather happens *to* it. One temporal progression is halted or shattered and another is joined. It is this kind of thinking about the possibility of temporal rupture that allows people to make claims

for the absolute newness of the lives they lead after conversion and of the ones they hope they will lead in the millennial future. (Robbins 2007: 12)

In other words, the models of time found within these Christian communities are characterized by open-ended possibilities and radical changes and ruptures, after which new lives become possible. As we saw with the stone ritual, for the congregants of New Jerusalem Tabernacle Church, time is not something that events happen *within*, but rather, as Robbins points out, something that events happen *to*. The stone ritual and Okot's prayer practices do not just happen in time; they *change* time and temporal experience, shift the locus of temporal agency, and in this way nurture healing processes.

The studies mentioned above are examples of scholarly work on trauma and time, and on time and religious practice. A different area of literature deals with religious practices and repetition (but not with trauma). Luhrmann's (2012) studies of Christian prayer (see also Luhrmann and Morgain 2013) and Mahmood's (2001, 2005) and Haeri's (2013, 2017) studies of Muslim prayer are such examples. In these accounts, prayer is understood as a set of skills developed within certain communities of practice to deal with the world in a different way. Luhrmann (2012) shows how the mind is managed and changed through prayer, and Haeri (2013) shows how repetition becomes a vehicle for creativity and new meanings through a kind of temporal "craftsmanship." These studies conceptualize prayer in much the same way as we do here. For Okot and his fellow congregants, prayer is a skill that is developed through repetitive practice; as with the Muslim women in Haeri's (2013: 25) study, repetition is not something that makes prayer practice stiff and formalized, "but is more like the craftsmanship of the musician," where continuous repetition gradually develops the skills necessary to manage a small part of the world. And as with Luhrmann's (2012) American informants, Okot and his fellow congregants also practice the management of their minds through repetitive praying. They become better equipped at dealing with the violence of the past. In Hannah Arendt's (1958) words, they create "islands of security" for themselves and each other through their repetition work. This conceptualization of repetition and prayer does not necessarily distinguish between words and movement as analytically distinct features, but sees repetition as a single corporal and pragmatic process.[2] An older, yet valuable contribution to discussions on prayer that is also relevant here is Marcel Mauss's ([1909] 2003) work on prayer as social practice. According to Mauss, praying is fundamentally social, not simply a single request or an outcry from an individual soul. The primary goal of prayer, according to Mauss, is to bring about changes in sacred beings even if they also affect the persons praying. Mauss's work has influenced much current work on prayer, from studies of Scottish Pentecostalism (e.g., Webster 2017) to analyses of speaking in tongues in Ghana (e.g., Reinhart 2017). This understanding of prayer as fundamentally social makes it all the more important to understand how people learn to pray in a social setting, how and by whom they are taught to pray, and how their prayers take form in social life.

CONCLUSION: STRUCTURES OF VIOLENCE AND REPETITION AS HEALING

The long history of civil war in northern Uganda has left significant structures of violence and trauma afflicting the population. These are expressed as evil spirits, domestic violence, and various mental and social problems. We have argued with Stolorow (2003) and Young (1997) that an important part of these structures of trauma has to do with disturbance of the normal unity of temporal experience. Religious practices such as the repetitive praying and rituals at the New Jerusalem Tabernacle Church are, among other things, tools with which to enact temporal agency and modify temporal experience. Moreover, religious systems such as Christianity function, among other things, as systems of temporal manipulation that incorporate the development of skills for the management of mind. In making these claims, we have drawn on Robbins's (2007) discussion of time in Christianity, as well as Luhrmann's (2012) and Haeri's (2013) studies of prayer practice. Building on these insights, we have explored practices of everyday individual and collective prayer mainly from micro perspectives through Flaherty's (2003) conceptual frame of time work. We have argued that the repetitive practices of prayer and ritual help traumatized people to regain a sense of temporal agency by stitching together the structures of time that have fallen apart. Developing the ability to pray, together and alone, have for our Ugandan interlocutors become a way to manage temporal experience and to deal with the traumatic embodiment of the horrors of a violent past.

Lars Williams
PhD, Department of Anthropology
Aarhus University, Denmark

Lotte Meinert
Professor, Department of Anthropology
Aarhus University, Denmark

NOTES

1. The "Muslim prayer" is the daily *salat* prayer.
2. Here, we follow a Wittgensteinian notion of language and practice being two aspects of the same process (Wittgenstein 1953).

REFERENCES

Apuuli, Kasaija Phillip 2011. "Peace over Justice: The Acholi Religious Leaders Peace Initiative (ARLPI) vs. the International Criminal Court (ICC) in Northern Uganda." *Studies in Ethnicity and Nationalism* 11 (1): 116–29.

Arendt, Hannah. 1958. *The Human Condition.* Chicago: University of Chicago Press.

Ball, Tom, and Theresa O'Nell. 2015. "Square Pegs and Round Holes: Understanding Historical Trauma in Two Native American Communities." In *Culture and PTSD: Trauma in Global and Historical Perspective,* edited by D. E. Hinton and B. J. Good, 334–58. Philadelphia: University of Pennsylvania Press.

Dostal, Robert. J. 1993. "Time and Phenomenology in Husserl and Heidegger." In *The Cambridge Companion to Heidegger,* edited by C. Guignon, 2: 141–69. Cambridge: Cambridge University Press.

Finnegan, Amy. C. 2013. "The White Girl's Burden." *Contexts* 12 (1): 30–35.

Flaherty, Michael G. 2003. "Time Work: Customizing Temporal Experience." *Social Psychology Quarterly* 66 (1): 17–33.

———. 2011. *The Textures of Time: Agency and Temporal Experience.* Philadelphia: Temple University Press.

Forman-Hoffman, Valerie, Jennifer Cook Middleton, Cynthia Feltner, Bradlyu Gaynes, Rachel Palmieri Weber, Carla Bann, Meera Viswanathan, Kathleen Lohr, Claire Baker, and Joshua Green. 2018. *Psychological and Pharmacological Treatments for Adults with Posttraumatic Stress Disorder: A Systematic Review Update* [Internet]. (*Comparative Effectiveness Review* 207), Rockville, MN: Agency for Healthcare Research and Quality. Table 1, Diagnostic Criteria for Posttraumatic Stress Disorder, https://www.ncbi.nlm.nih.gov/books/NBK525126/table/ch2.tab1/.

Foucault, Michel. 1988. *Technologies of the Self: A Seminar with Michel Foucault.* Amherst: University of Massachusetts Press.

Geertz, Armin. W. 2010. "Brain, Body and Culture: A Biocultural Theory of Religion." *Method & Theory in the Study of Religion* 22 (4): 304–21.

Grøn, Lone, and Cheryl Mattingly. 2017. "In Search of the Good Old Life: Ontological Breakdown and Responsive Hope at the Margins of Life." *Death Studies* 42 (5): 306–13.

Haeri, Niloofar. 2013. "The Private Performance of Salat Prayers: Repetition, Time, and Meaning." *Anthropological Quarterly* 86 (1): 5–34.

———. 2017. "Unbundling Sincerity: Language, Mediation, and Interiority in Comparative Perspective." *HAU: Journal of Ethnographic Theory* 7 (1): 123–38.

Heelas, Paul, Linda Woodhead, Benjamin Seel, Karin Tusting, and Bronislaw Szerszynski. 2005. *The Spiritual Revolution: Why Religion is Giving Way to Spirituality*. Malden, MA: Blackwell.

Heidegger, Martin. (1927) 1962. *Being and Time*. Translated by J. Macquarrie and E. Robinson. New York: Harper & Row.

Husserl, Edmund. (1905) 1991. *On the Phenomenology of the Consciousness of Internal Time*. Translated by J. B. Brough. Leiden: Nijhoff.

Luhrmann, Tanya. M. 2012. *When God Talks Back: Understanding the American Evangelical Relationship with God*. New York: Vintage.

———. 2013. "Making God Real and Making God Good: Some Mechanisms through which Prayer May Contribute to Healing." *Transcultural Psychiatry* 50 (5): 707–25.

Luhrmann, Tanya. M., and Rachel Morgain. 2012. "Prayer as Inner Sense Cultivation: An Attentional Learning Theory of Spiritual Experience." *Ethos* 40 (4): 359–89.

Mahmood, Saba. 2001. "Rehearsed Spontaneity and the Conventionality of Ritual: Disciplines of Ṣalat." *American Ethnologist* 28 (4): 827–53.

———. 2005. *Politics of Piety: The Islamic Revival and the Feminist Subject*. Princeton: Princeton University Press.

Mauss, Marcel. (1909) 2003. *On Prayer: Text and Commentary*. Edited by W. S. F. Pickering. Postscript by Howard Morphy. New York: Berghahn Books.

Meinert, Lotte, and Susan Reynolds Whyte. 2017. "These Things Continue: Violence as Contamination after War in Uganda." *Ethos* 45 (2): 271–86.

———. forthcoming. "Legacies of Violence: The Communicability of Spirits and Trauma in Northern Uganda." In *Biosocial Worlds: Anthropologiy of Health Environments beyond Determinism*, edited by Jens Seeberg, Aandreas Roepstorff, and Lotte Meinert. London: UCL Press.

Meyer, Birgit. 1998. "'Make a Complete Break with the Past': Memory and Post-Colonial Modernity in Ghanaian Pentecostalist Discourse." *Journal of Religion in Africa* 28 (3): 316–49.

Nielsen, Mikka. 2016. *Experiences of ADHD in Adults: Morality, Temporality and Neurobiology*. Doctoral dissertation, Aalborg University, Aalborg, Denmark.

Pitman, R. K., and S. P. Orr. 1990. "The Black Hole of Trauma." *Biological Psychiatry* 27 (5): 469–71.

Prager, Jeffrey. 2006. "Jump-Starting Timeliness: Trauma, Temporality and the Redressive Community." In *Time and Memory*, edited by J. Parker, M. Crawford and P. Harris, 229–45. Amsterdam: Koninklijke Brill.

Reinhardt, Bruno. 2017. "Praying until Jesus Returns: Commitment and Prayerfulness among Charismatic Christians in Ghana." *Religion* 47 (1): 51–72.

Robbins, Joel. 2007. "Continuity Thinking and the Problem of Christian Culture: Belief, Time, and the Anthropology of Christianity." *Current Anthropology* 48 (1): 5–38.

Roberts, Bayard, Kaduce Felix Ocaka, John Browne, Thomas Oyok, and Egbert Sondorp. 2011. "Alcohol Disorder amongst Forcibly Displaced Persons in Northern Uganda." *Addictive Behaviors* 36 (8): 870–73.

Stolorow, Robert D. 1999. "The Phenomenology of Trauma and the Absolutisms of Everyday Life: A Personal Journey." *Psychoanalytic Psychology* 16 (3): 464.

———. 2003. "Trauma and Temporality." *Psychoanalytic Psychology* 20 (1): 158.

Tankink, Marian. 2007. "'The Moment I Became Born-Again the Pain Disappeared': The Healing of Devastating War Memories in Born-Again Churches in Mbarara District, Southwest Uganda." *Transcultural Psychiatry* 44 (2): 203–31.

Vandborg, Sanne Kjær, Tue Brost Hartmann, Birgit Egedal Bennedsen, Anders Degn Pedersen, and Per Hove Thomsen. 2014. "Memory and Executive Functions in Patients with Obsessive-Compulsive Disorder." *Cognitive and Behavioral Neurology* 27 (1): 8–16.

Webster, Joseph. 2017. "Praying for Salvation: A Map of Relatedness." *Religion* 47 (1): 19–34.

Williams, Lars Hedegaard, and Lotte Meinert. 2017. "Traumer og ånder efter krig i Uganda: Konfigurationer af vold og behandling [Trauma and spirits after war in Uganda: Configurations of violence and treatment]." *Tidsskrift for Forskning i Sygdom og Samfund* 14 (26).

Wittgenstein, Ludwig. 1953. *Philosophical Investigations*. Oxford: Basil Blackwell.

Young, Allan. 1997. *The Harmony of Illusions: Inventing Post-Traumatic Stress Disorder*. Princeton: Princeton University Press.

Chapter 3

ADHD and Temporal Experiences
Struggling for Synchronization

Mikka Nielsen

⟨◇⟩

It is just not there. The sense of time. It is now, now, now. It is about being present.
That is how we are. I just recently learned about time. Well, not watching the clock
and seeing what time it is, but I mean sense of time and having an idea about how
long things take. How long it takes to do grocery shopping and knowing when I
will be back home again. Like getting a sense of it.

—Judith, forty-four years old

Judith was diagnosed with attention deficit hyperactivity disorder (ADHD) seven years before I interviewed her as part of my research on adults' experiences of being diagnosed with ADHD. Her statement illustrates a central finding from my fieldwork: that timing—losing track of time, being on time, and tolerating the slow passing of time—was the subject of many concerns and frustrations among my informants. Somehow my informants always seemed to be running out of time. They had difficulties finishing assignments in time, showed up late for appointments, and sometimes needed extra time to feel comfortable in social settings. However, they also often experienced time as passing too slowly, as if they were unable to wait for the future. Misunderstandings and experiences of being different and of not being able to follow the expected track of time therefore imbued the narratives about living with ADHD. During interviews and while spending time with my informants, I also often felt confronted with the feeling of restlessness, misconnection, and misinterpretation, and I experienced being at a different pace from the person in front of whom I was sitting. Restless movements sometimes overshadowed the interviews. My questions were interrupted whenever new thoughts struck my informants, and our staccato conversations often took surprising directions.

ADHD is described in the DSM-5 (standard classification of mental disorders) as a neurodevelopmental disorder involving symptoms of inattention, hyperactivity, and impulsivity—all symptoms somehow related to time. Patterns of behavior are characterized by a failure to pay attention to details, difficulty organizing tasks and activities, excessive talking, fidgeting, and an inability to remain seated in appropriate situations. That ADHD and timing are connected is well described in clinical and psychiatric research, and even the diagnostic criteria for ADHD disclose the connection. For example, the DSM-5 lists some of the complications connected to ADHD as having "poor time management" (American Psychiatric Association [APA] 2013: 59) and notes that the individual "is unable to be or uncomfortable being still for extended time" (APA 2013: 60).

Within the social sciences, ADHD tends to be explained as a consequence of the medicalization of deviant behavior and social control (Conrad 2007; Timimi and Leo 2009), leaving very little space for investigating how people experience living with symptoms of ADHD or how ADHD unfolds within specific contexts and relations. In this chapter, I wish to contribute an alternative, phenomenological analysis of ADHD by examining ADHD as a certain way of temporally being in the world. I argue that ADHD is characterized as a disruption in the experience of time and a state of desynchronization and arrhythmia, and I explore how experiences of time are customized to resynchronize with the surroundings. My informants all use different strategies for synchronizing with the rhythm of everyday life and with other people. I do not propose to explain whether the arrhythmia that I identify as part of the experience of ADHD is either a cause or effect related to certain neurological processes. My aim is rather to offer a framework for understanding ADHD as an embodied and relational phenomenon and to describe some of the many strategies people struggling with ADHD make use of to navigate a world of various time regimes.

The chapter is a further development of a previous article (Nielsen 2017) that draws on a two-year fieldwork in Denmark in which I examined adults' experiences of being diagnosed with ADHD and living with symptoms of ADHD.[1] I interviewed, spent time with, and had informal conversations with people diagnosed with ADHD in adulthood; I followed some of my informants to doctors, and I participated in several public seminars and conferences about ADHD for patients and professionals to investigate aspects of how ADHD unfolds. This chapter is based on the analysis of twenty-one interviews (ranging from one to four hours) with thirteen adults (five men and eight women, aged twenty-six to forty-five years) diagnosed with ADHD, using a semistructured interview guide and observations made during the interviews.

STUDYING EXPERIENCES OF TIME

Based on a large collection of empirical examples, sociologist Michael Flaherty (1999) offers an important contribution to the study of time and presents different circumstances under which discrepancies between clock time and subjective experience of time occur. In everyday life, perceived time is synchronized with the intersubjective time measured by clocks and calendars, and we rarely think about time passing at a certain tempo. Only in extraordinary situations do we notice that time passes irregularly. When we are either bored and experiencing very little or experiencing an extraordinary many things within the glimpse of a moment, time feels stretched out. In his later works, Flaherty (2011: 11) expands the analysis of time, and he emphasizes that time is not something "'out there,' cosmic, coercive, unchanging, and unchangeable." A central question in research when examining people's experiences of time is whether temporal experience is a product of "determinism," meaning situated factors beyond our control, or whether temporal experience is the outcome of "self-determination," referring to the individual's arrangement of circumstances (Flaherty 2011). We are not passively observing time. Rather, we engage with time, and we experience variations in how time passes in different situations and due to different intentions. Therefore, Flaherty (2011) argues that we need to investigate the interplay between the self and the situation by looking into how people actively customize their experience of time when wanting to either stretch time out or make time pass faster. The concept of "time work," which Flaherty (2011: 11) defines as "intrapersonal and interpersonal effort directed toward provoking or preventing various temporal experiences," points to the activity of trying to influence how we experience time. According to Flaherty (2003: 22), if our circumstances make for the perception that time is passing slowly, "we 'act' in such a way that it seems to accelerate." We therefore customize our temporal experiences to make time pass faster or slower by, for example, doodling in a notebook or thinking of places we would rather be (Flaherty 2003: 22).

How individuals experiment with and manipulate their experience of time is also the subject of this chapter. I show examples of how time is experienced as an intolerable burden and what strategies my informants use to cope with the obstacles of time. However, before describing how people with ADHD perform different kinds of time work, I first outline how I understand ADHD as a disorder of temporal being in the world. My analysis points to the central question: does everyone have the same preconditions for experiencing time? If individuals experience time differently, research on time might need to examine not only the relation between determinism and self-determination in experiences of time but also various individual preconditions for experiencing and assessing time. In this chapter, I investigate time work as an act of provoking or preventing certain temporal experiences based on the intention of synchronizing with and socially adapting to the environment.

My analytical approach when studying experiences of time and practices of time work is, besides the work of Flaherty, inspired by Fuchs's (2005, 2013, 2014) theories of temporal experiences and states of desynchronization as well as by Lefebvre's "rhythmanalysis" (2004), which offers "a new field of knowledge [*savoir*]" (Lefebvre 2004: 13), focusing on rhythm as both object of study and tool of analysis. Fuchs (2014) emphasizes that our experience of time is not a solipsistic phenomenon but happens in reference to others. There is an intersubjective element to time as we engage with and are ordinarily temporally synchronized with others (Fuchs 2014: 81). Understanding time as relative is also the focus of Lefebvre (2004), who argues that time, space, and everyday life are interrelated and we therefore need to think of these concepts together. He further states that "everywhere where there is interaction between a place, a time and an expenditure of energy, there is rhythm" (Lefebvre 2004: 25). Whether they are thought of in relation to societal rhythms of working hours, biological rhythms of sleep, or social rhythms of interactions, rhythms always exist in reference to something or someone. In the case of ADHD, the organization of a meeting, the anticipated routine of reading bedtimes stories to your children, and the expected proceedings of a conversation represent different kinds of temporal structures that may cause experiences of unease and inadequacy to people with ADHD due to difficulties adhering to these structures. Performing time work is the individual's agentic response—with or without the use of artifacts—to navigating in and adapting, to varying degrees, to the temporal structure of the situation.

ADHD AND THE COMPLEX ART OF SYNCHRONIZATION

Citing a famous Danish model diagnosed with ADHD, a Danish newspaper published an article with the headline, "They do not understand what I am saying, because they do not think as fast." The article was shared on the

Danish ADHD association's Facebook profile and was intensely debated by members of the group, who commented on the model's hypothesis that people with ADHD think faster than others and discussed how this difference in speed often creates misunderstandings. Many agreed that people with ADHD have a speediness to their way of thinking and talking and that their thinking is sometimes faster than they are able to communicate. A famous standup comedian with ADHD also joined the debate on Facebook, proposing the following: "The trick is to be able to express yourself in a way that is understandable to others. Even if you have to put yourself in a slower tempo than your thoughts. And then lower your expectations to others' tempo."

I start my analysis by illustrating ADHD as a specific way of temporally being in the world and explore some of the consequences of this alternative way of being. I argue that rhythmically integrating in interactions and following a certain rhythm of society is expected, and that people with ADHD often collide with this norm. When the body is restless, the speech is too fast, or the thoughts accelerate, then clashes of temporal orientations occur. Psychiatric literature on ADHD offers various perspectives on the discussion of temporal experiences. Clinical experiments indicate that people with ADHD have an impaired sense of time and a diminished ability to evaluate temporal durations (Barkley et al. 1997, 2001; Gilden and Marusich 2009). Owing to a different brain structure in temporal processing and "an internal clock that runs with a higher rate" (Walg, Oepen, and Prior 2015: 756), people with ADHD tend to perceive time intervals differently, which may cause, for example, symptoms of impulsivity. A study measuring children's perception of time suggests that children with ADHD perceive time intervals as longer than do others (Walg, Oepen, and Prior 2015). These studies illustrate, from a clinical perspective, the impairment of timely coordination and assessment in ADHD.

Fuchs, a leading researcher in phenomenological investigations on psychopathology and experiences of time, makes an analytic comparison between different temporal orientations in states of mania and depression. What characterizes mania, according to Fuchs (2014: 411), is "an *acceleration* and finally uncoupling of the individual from the world time. . . . The manic person is constantly ahead of himself, addicted to the seemingly unlimited scope of possibilities. Interest in the present is always distracted in favour of the next-to-come. The future cannot be awaited and expected, but must be assailed and seized immediately" (Fuchs 2014: 411; italics in the original). Further, Fuchs (2014: 405) emphasizes that the body is a "resonance body" in which "interpersonal and other 'vibrations' constantly reverberate." Referring to Merleau-Ponty's concept of "intercorporeality," Fuchs (2014: 405) argues that the body interacts with other bodies in a continuous interplay of reciprocal understanding. Everyday contact with others implies a "fine-tuning of emotional and bodily communication and intercorporeal resonance" (Fuchs 2014: 409) to establish a feeling of being in accord with others. This fine-tuning or social synchronization, however, can be challenged in various ways by either "a retardation or acceleration of inner time in relation to external or social processes" (Fuchs 2013: 75), causing a state of desynchronization. We are not always synchronized with our environment; we can be either "too late" or "too early" (Fuchs 2005: 196). Waiting, for example, imposes on us a slower time structure to which we may respond with patience or impatience (Fuchs 2013: 81).

That people with ADHD experience themselves as thinking faster resembles the feature of acceleration mentioned by Fuchs. Waiting for others to follow a line of reasoning causes misunderstandings, and the constant acceleration of inner time complicates the fine-tuning of communication. To "put yourself in a slower tempo" to adapt to the tempo of social interactions, as one of the contributors to the Facebook discussion advised, is not an easy task but requires continuous training and specific strategies. Moreover, the hasty thinking may cause frustrations when the rhythm of a conversation is disturbed. One woman describes how she perceives too much of what is happening around her as her thoughts runs wild, which calls for her "to cool down and pull over" and ask herself how to get back on track. When your attention is caught by the sound of a radiator or a clock ticking, resources for creating resonance with the other are limited, and maintaining a flow of interaction becomes insurmountable. An acceleration of thoughts, leading to information overload, produces poor conditions for engaging in relations and connecting with others.

While the acceleration of thoughts creates situations of desynchronization, the speediness also manifests as bodily discomfort. My informants describe themselves as restless, unable to find inner calmness, and they explain how the feeling of restlessness produces a craving for movement. Kenny is in his mid-thirties and was diagnosed with ADHD seven years before I interviewed him. He explains that ADHD sometimes makes his thoughts race too fast and his limbs move almost autonomously. In the following, Kenny elaborates on the bodily feeling of ADHD and how he copes when ADHD strikes:

Kenny: Mostly, I can feel the tensions here [he points at his head] and it is like . . . it is like trembling electricity through the brain—"bizzzz." Those are the physical symptoms. And then I realize that I start shaking my legs [he is moving one of his legs restlessly].
Mikka: What is up with that leg?

Kenny: Well, it is nothing now, but it is because the energy accumulates and it has to come out somehow. When I go to a meeting, for example, where we have to sit on our butts and are being taught from the blackboard—then my legs start moving. I fiddle with something. It is like carbonic acid all over and that energy needs to be released. So, I will sit and jump a bit.

Mikka: So, that is the valve?

Kenny: Yes, it is. It brings calmness.

During his interview with me, Kenny moved restlessly on the chair, waving his arms to underline his arguments, and he had tics in his left eye. He spoke almost nonstop with great enthusiasm, gesticulating to emphasize his points. The experience of restlessness and the need for "calibrating" the body or letting the energy out is consistent in my data. The body is speeding, and the thoughts are racing.

According to Lefebvre (2004: 30), "The body consists of a bundle of rhythms, different but in tune. It is not only in music that one produces perfect harmonies. The body produces a garland of rhythms, one could say a bouquet." The rhythm of the body refers to the beat of the heart, the repetition of breathing and to the circular element of rest, sleep, and work. The body is a polyrhythmic subject producing and containing different rhythms that need to correspond or resonate to maintain health (Lefebvre 2004: 78). Lefebvre (2004: 25) continues: "Rhythms unite with one another in the state of health, in normal (which is to say normed!) everydayness; when they are discordant, there is suffering, a pathological state of which arrhythmia is generally, at the same time, symptom, cause and effect." Like other phenomenological philosophers who argue that the body becomes the center of attention in times of disturbance or illness, Lefebvre (2004: 31) claims, "Normally we only grasp the relations between rhythms, which interfere with them. However, they all have a distinct *existence*. Normally, none of them *classifies* itself; on the contrary, in suffering, in confusion, a particular rhythm surges up and imposes itself: palpitation, breathlessness, pains in the place of satiety" (italics in original). From a rhythmanalytic perspective, we can understand the restlessness connected to ADHD and the feeling of speediness as a kind of rhythmic disharmony. Thoughts race too fast, blood runs too fast, limbs move too much. Falling asleep becomes difficult, concentrating on reading bedtime stories is almost impossible, and sitting still in meetings leads to fidgeting with pencils and movements of the legs to let some of the accumulated energy loose. Feeling inner restlessness draws attention to the physical body, attention that is normally not present, and the bodily arrhythmia is experienced as disturbing and pathological. What Leder (1990:

84, 91) calls a "dys-appearance" or an "absence of an absence" of the body, which we normally ignore, Lefebvre (2004) describes as a rhythm surging up and imposing itself. When it feels to Kenny as though carbonic acid or electricity is running though his body, his limbs call attention to them, revealing a disharmony.

For Kenny, attending a meeting is a confrontation with a specific time set. In a meeting, there is an agenda to follow and a specific rhythm to the interaction. Following the argument that people with ADHD have "an internal clock that runs with a higher rate" (Walg, Oepen, and Prior 2015: 756), as illustrated by experimental studies, we can understand Kenny's impatience. Kenny is confronted with another rhythm, a time other than his own. The feeling of the energy accumulating in his body, as Kenny describes it, reflects the continuous accumulating time difference between his internal time and worldly time. Seen as matters of desynchronization, Kenny's impatience at the meeting opens up a new way of understanding ADHD as a phenomenon that is not just located in the individual but is also intersubjective. Kenny's portrayal of accumulating energy illustrates how the temporal structure of the meeting challenges Kenny and how confrontation with others creates a desynchronization that results in discomfort.

DEVELOPING TIME WORK STRATEGIES

Flaherty (2011: 2) argues that modifications of our own temporal experiences are "realized through subtle and guarded practices." He is concerned with the doing of time—whether consciously or unconsciously practiced. According to Flaherty (1999: 35), our sense of time is described as a temporal habitus, and synchronicity "is part of the underpinning for interpersonal coordination and social order." Participating in appointments structured around schedules, calendars, and seasons, we develop a correspondence between the flow of experience and the flow of the clock; socially, we adapt to "the managed pulse of social interaction" (Flaherty 2011: 47) as we tend to establish a rhythm to our activities. Time work, however, refers not only to our social habitus and ability to internalize the temporal regimes imposed upon us, but also to the "agentic practices that are meant to control or customize temporal experience" (Flaherty 2011: 149), which people typically practice to "resist external sources of temporal constraint or structure" (Flaherty 2011: 3). When circumstances are considered problematic, we strategically perform time work that alters our experience of the situation.

States of acceleration, restlessness, and experiences of uncoupling from the surroundings may cause some difficulties. According to my informants, the consequences of deviating from the norm are dispiriting, and the feeling of being different sometimes leads to withdrawal from social settings. To adapt to the surroundings, my informants make use of various strategies— some involving different devices, and some learned by carefully crafting new practices. As a psychiatrist said at one of the seminars about ADHD I attended during my fieldwork, "To people with ADHD, it is about finding the brake pedal." In the following, I present examples of how my informants perform different kinds of coping practices to manage their symptoms of restlessness and speeding thoughts, and, by examining these practices as time work, I argue that they are driven, to varying degrees, by an ambition of synchronization.

Some tools are used for structuring daily activities: doctors' appointments, children's activities, time for taking medicine, and laundry time slots are listed on whiteboards and scheduled in apps on smartphones to manage the frequency of activities and allocation of time. The tools offer a visual overview of weekly activities, and alarms on the phone insistently remind the user of the right time for taking the daily three, four, five, or even more pills. But efforts of managing time also include more radical methods. When restlessness dominates, concentration weakens, and thoughts seem chaotic, one specific remedy helps. Here, Susan explains how medication changed her body—or as she puts it, the "tempo" of her body:

> I get an inner calmness. I guess that is the best way to describe it. For example, when reading bedtime stories to my kids, they are too big for that now, but when I did, it was almost like . . . I did it, but it was not the nice experience that I had wanted it to be—before I got the medication. Because my head was speeding 180 [km/h] while I was reading. I did not have the calmness to do what I was doing. I also tended to be really short-tempered and everything just shot out of my mouth and maybe sometimes inappropriately. The medication helps with that as well. It is a kind of general calmness in the body. I have so much more calmness in my body. But I have to get used to it; driving in a lower gear, if you can say it like that, and accept it. I find it quite hard realizing that my body feels drowsy in my world. But I guess that is just because I am in a normal tempo now. But compared with previous-me, this is drowsy to me and I have to accept that it is okay and not feel guilty about not running around all the time.

The drugs help Susan find "a normal tempo," and even if the current tempo seems drowsy to her, she appreciates the benefits. When taking Ritalin, Susan manages to generate the expected focus and rhythm needed for dwelling in the moment of reading bedtime stories. A bodily sensation of calmness enables her to find interconnectedness with the situation and her children's need for attention. The setting demands focus, attention, and presence from Susan, but without the drugs, her thoughts accelerate, and she disconnects from the situation. Kenny makes use of a similar strategy, but since Ritalin had more negative than positive effects on him, Kenny sticks to alcohol as a calming remedy. When his brain "runs amok," he empties two bottles of wine, waits for the effect to kick in, only to throw it all up to avoid the hangovers and then go to sleep. Kenny is well aware that the technique is unsustainable, and he usually tries to shield himself from situations that may trigger his head to overload. But once in a while, he resorts to alcohol.

Another strategy for managing bodily sensations of restlessness and the accumulation of energy may be movement, as Kenny's case from the meeting showed us. Most of my informants describe movement, whether it be fidgeting with things, walking, or other kinds of bodily stimulations. The opposite strategy, however, may also suppress the unwanted restlessness—or at least mask it. During an interview with Karen, a forty-five-year-old woman who was diagnosed with ADHD four years earlier, she told me how she sometimes locks her body in order to stay calm. According to Karen, life with ADHD is a constant encounter with clashes and misunderstandings when different ways of thinking and acting collide. Sometimes she manages to fit in and live up to the expectations of others. "I seem calm to you, right? But I can damn right promise you, I am not," Karen said, explaining how she twists her legs around the legs of the chair and keeps her arms crossed in front of her chest to keep herself restrained: "The whole body is locked." She knows that her restless movement, when she tries to ease her "craving for being hyper," is disturbing to others, and thus instead of moving her legs and fidgeting with her hands, she limits her cravings for movement by locking her body. The use of ball blankets and ball vests among people with ADHD for restraining the body similarly points to a strategy for bodily stimulation. These blankets and vests have small balls sewn into them that, due to their heavy weight, have a calming effect on the user.

Understanding temporal experiences as corporally embedded, I find these practices of managing bodily symptoms of ADHD as techniques for experimenting with temporal experiences. Time work can be a means for resisting temporal constraints, but time work may also, as the above examples illustrate, consist of techniques for enduring, responding to, and accommodating certain temporal structures. Anthropologist Marc Goodwin (2010: 15) has analyzed practices of body rocking and similar kinds of self-stimulation practices related to ADHD as instances of "becoming the moment." To become the moment, Goodwin (2010: 15) claims, means to "inhabit time without concern for the future (the main criterion of impulsivity), and thus to live differently in the present." Rituals of self-stimulation enable the body to become the moment—a body that "accrues time as a penalty in the form of understimulation, and that perceives this time as a burden" (Goodwin 2010: 19). Body rocking, in this sense, holds a special relation to time because it consumes time. By performing body rocking, the individual is immersed in a world he or she controls, and time is made entirely one's own, at least momentarily. In the same way that new technologies such as iPods and videogames shelter us from the surrounding world, body rocking provides instant gratification and an affective regime of becoming the moment (Goodwin 2010: 50). Goodwin's (2010) analysis points to a central aspect of time work. Becoming the moment means slowing down the acceleration of inner time, insisting on the present through movement, and attempting to synchronize with the surroundings by consuming time.

When in a meeting, as Kenny describes, the absence of stimulation makes time unbearable, but moving the legs and letting the energy out is an act of inhabiting the body and connecting with the outside—and thereby becoming the moment. Karen also experiences a desire for movement in order to accept sedentary situations. However, knowing how others perceive her restless movements, she abstains from fidgeting with her hands and feet. She does her best to tolerate the unendurable stillness, to "find the brake pedal," and to inhabit the present time. Consciously and unconsciously, my informants experiment with time work strategies as they struggle to fit in, bear with their differentness, and somehow rhythmically adapt to their surroundings. Opportunities for performing time work depend on the context, and while movement, body rocking, and fidgeting may be suitable in some settings, these practices are not always appropriate or sufficient, and other kinds of techniques are needed.

THE NORMATIVITY OF TIME WORK

Modern society demands rhythmic synchronization in social interactions as well as in engagements with institutional, occupational, and domestic life. From a rhythmanalytic perspective, bodies are trained to follow the rhythms of calendars, institutional work hours, and interactions as part of a "dressage" of the body (Lefebvre 2004: 48). Lefebvre and Régulier (2004: 83) speak of work as "the reference to which we try to refer everything else back." We organize the day according to our work. Our bodies are expected to adapt to the temporal regime of society and follow the rhythm of a seven-day week and eight-hour job. These disciplining practices, this dressage of the body in both social and institutional perspectives, require that individuals are capable of multitasking and managing time, and there is a normative expectation of the individual to rhythmically integrate into interactions without noteworthy effort.

One might think that a speedy being would be an advantage in a continuously accelerating society (Rosa 2015). If the time of a speedy individual is met by accelerating world time, we might expect synchronization, and the impatience and restlessness of the person might be neutralized as the world catches up. However, as I have argued elsewhere (Nielsen 2017), research contradicts this perspective, claiming that the complexity of modern society accounts for the increasing number of individuals who experience symptoms related to ADHD. For example, critical research on ADHD points to changes in the educational system as one of many explanations for the emergence of ADHD. New teaching methods focusing on self-regulation may be a key reason that children who have problems with organizing and attention are struggling in school (Timimi and Leo 2009: 139). In an accelerating society, where time and self-management have become central values for children as well as adults, temporal deficits are intensified and exhibited.

As demonstrated in this chapter, synchronization is both a complex intercorporeal exercise, when individuals establish resonance through the fine-tuning of emotional and bodily communication, and a practice of aligning with the temporal regimes of society. So, what is learned from understanding ADHD as a certain way of temporally being in the world? And how can the creative and pragmatic strategies used in everyday time work by people suffering from ADHD be used to inform and develop the treatment of ADHD? Growing literature focuses on the benefits of physical activities and mindfulness for children in general as well as for children and adolescents with ADHD (Månsson et al. 2017). Asking my informants about experiences of practicing mindfulness, however, often led to explanations of how they found the practice almost unbearable and exhausting in its insistence on doing nothing. In contrast, one woman told me she enjoyed a body awareness program she was offered by the municipality because it taught her new techniques for using her body. Whether mindfulness or other meditation practices reduce symptoms of ADHD is not to be determined here, but the potentiality of alternative practices when treating ADHD is noteworthy. One specific study is particularly interesting when discussing alternative approaches to managing impatience, hyperactivity, and inattention because the study finds that employing target-shooting sports for mental and bodily training increases the ability of children diagnosed with ADHD to calm down and focus on specific tasks (Månsson et al. 2017). Using breathing techniques and practicing the ability to balance mind and body while shooting, children with ADHD were able to enhance their attention toward an object (Månsson et al. 2017). As target shooting offers immediate feedback (have you hit the bull's-eye or not), the exercise is motivating for children with ADHD, who specifically struggle with waiting for the results of their efforts.

From an analytical perspective focusing on temporal experiences, the target shooting research points to the benefits of "adapting the environment to provide a clear and concise structure, in regards to routines, time and space" (Månsson et al. 2017: 5). Structuring activities in ways that consider different challenges with temporal management and that assist strategies for focusing on the here and now may be an alternative or supplement to pharmaceutical treatment of ADHD. The complex art of "being in the moment," as Goodwin (2010: 15) puts it, can counteract the acceleration of inner time and ultimately contribute to synchronization with the surroundings. According to Lefebvre (2004: 48), "To enter into a society, a group or nationality is to accept values (that are taught) . . . , but also to bend oneself (to be bent) to its ways" (parentheses in the original). Whether it concerns breathing, movement, or other bodily practices, people need to "learn to hold themselves" as part of the dressage of the body (Lefebvre 2004: 48). The imperative of following the rhythm of society is unavoidable; however, the potential of not only individuals to adapt to society but also institutions to organize activities and learning environments that facilitate such rhythmic correspondence shows new ways for creating synchronization.

What is learned, then, from examining ADHD as a disorder of temporal impairment and as a certain temporal way of being in the world is how people with ADHD use multiple techniques and creative strategies for managing symptoms of the disorder. To think of these bodily techniques—people's choices to take drugs or children's increased concentration and satisfaction with shooting games—as time work allows for an alternative interpretation of people's deficiencies and struggles and their agentic coping practices when adapting to norms for interaction. We experience time differently, and we therefore encounter different challenges in life related to adjusting and navigating in time. Some individual time work practices may compensate for temporal discrepancies, but developing environments that facilitate concurrence and synchronicity might as well be part of eliminating experiences of temporal derailment.

CONCLUSION

Experiencing time in unconventional ways may cause professional and social complications, and the consequences of living with an impaired sense of time can be extensive. In this chapter, I have offered an alternative perspective on how to understand ADHD and how to examine strategies for managing symptoms of the disorder. I have illustrated a connection between differences in the perception of time, bodily restlessness, and the experience of speedy thoughts, and I have suggested that these can be understood within the frame of rhythmic integration. This aspect of temporal experiences contributes to the literature on time with its specific focus on practices, and to include this perspective invites new ways of examining time work strategies. The analysis suggests that we all have different preconditions for experiencing time and that these diverse temporal ways of being in the world bring about various challenges and opportunities. Time work, or the practice of customizing our temporal experiences, may be a strategy for managing experiences of time as an intolerable burden and for synchronizing with and socially adapting to the environment.

Mikka Nielsen
Postdoctoral Fellow, Department of Anthropology
University of Copenhagen, Denmark

NOTE

1. Nielsen, Mikka. 2017. "ADHD and Temporality: A Desynchronized Way of Being in the World," *Medical Anthropology* 36 (3): 260–72. Reprinted by permission of Taylor & Francis Ltd.

REFERENCES

American Psychiatric Association. 2013. *Diagnostic and Statistical Manual of Mental Disorders: DSM-5.* Washington, DC: American Psychiatric Association.

Barkley, Russell A., Gwenyth Edwards, Margeret Laneri, Kenneth Fletcher, and Lori Metevia. 2001. "Executive Functioning, Temporal Discounting, and Sense of Time in Adolescents with Attention Deficit Hyperactivity Disorder (ADHD) and Oppositional Defiant Disorder (ODD)." *Journal of Abnormal Child Psychology* 29 (6): 541–56.

Barkley, Russell A., Seth Koplowitz, Tamara Anderson, and Mary B. McMurray. 1997. "Sense of Time in Children with ADHD: Effects of Duration, Distraction, and Stimulant Medication." *Journal of the International Neuropsychological Society* 3 (4): 359–69.

Barkley, Russell A., Kevin R. Murphy, and Mariellen Fischer. 2008. *ADHD in Adults: What the Science Says.* New York: Guildford Press.

Conrad, Peter. 2007. *The Medicalization of Society: On the Transformation of Human Conditions into Treatable Disorders.* Baltimore, MD: Johns Hopkins University Press.

Flaherty, Michael G. 1999. *A Watched Pot: How We Experience Time*. New York: New York University Press.

——. 2003. "Time Work: Customizing Temporal Experience." *Social Psychology Quarterly* 66 (1): 17–33.

——. 2011. *The Textures of Time: Agency and Temporal Experience*. Philadelphia: Temple University Press.

Fuchs, Thomas. 2005. "Implicit and Explicit Temporality." *Philosophy, Psychiatry, & Psychology* 12 (3): 195–98.

——. 2013. "Temporality and Psychopathology." *Phenomenology and the Cognitive Sciences* 12 (1): 75–104.

——. 2014. "Psychopathology of Depression and Mania: Symptoms, Phenomena and Syndromes." *Journal of Psychopathology* 20: 404–13.

Gilden, David L., and Laura R. Marusich. 2009. "Contraction of Time in Attention-Deficit Hyperactivity Disorder." *Neuropsychology* 23 (2): 265–69.

Goodwin, Marc. 2010. "On the Other Side of Hyperactivity: An Anthropology of ADHD." PhD dissertation, Department of Anthropology, University of California, Berkeley.

Lefebvre, Henri. 2004. *Rhythmanalysis: Space, Time and Everyday Life*. London: Continuum.

Lefebvre, Henri, and Catherine Régulier. 2004. "The Rhythmanalytic Project." In *Rhythmanalysis: Space, Time and Everyday Life*, edited by H. Lefebvre, 71–83. London: Continuum.

Månsson, Annegrete G., Mette Elmose, Søren Dalsgaard, and Kirsten K. Roessler. 2017. "The Influence of Participation in Target-Shooting Sport for Children with Inattentive, Hyperactive and Impulsive Symptoms—A Controlled Study of Best Practice." *BMC Psychiatry* 17 (1): 1–6.

Nielsen, Mikka. 2017. "ADHD and Temporality: A Desynchronized Way of Being in the World." *Medical Anthropology* (36) 3: 260–72.

Rosa, Hartmut. 2015. *Social Acceleration and the Theory of Modernity*. New York: Columbia University Press.

Timimi, Sami, and Jonathan Leo. 2009. *Rethinking ADHD: From Brain to Culture*. Basingstoke, UK: Palgrave Macmillan.

Walg, Marco, Johannes Oepen, and Helmut Prior. 2015. "Adjustment of Time Perception in the Range of Seconds and Milliseconds: The Nature of Time-Processing Alterations in Children with ADHD." *Journal of Attention Disorders* 19 (9): 755–63.

Part III

The Politics of Time

Chapter 4

Hacking Time and Looping Temporalities in the Identification of the Adult "Living Disappeared" in Argentina

Noa Vaisman

In mid-1999, a few days after her twenty-first birthday, Mercedes Landa received a subpoena to appear at Federal Criminal Court number 4 in downtown Buenos Aires. There, in the quiet office of Justice Gabriel Cavallo, she was told that her filiation was in question and that she would have to undergo a DNA test. This would be the only way to find out who her parents were and who she might be. At the time, Mercedes was living with those she knew to be her parents—Mercedes Beatriz Moreira, a homemaker, and Ceferino Landa, a retired army officer. She had no suspicions about her origins, and it was only after the official court document arrived on the doorstep of her family's home that she was told, for the first time, that she was not Moreira and Landa's biological daughter. A few days later, she gave a blood sample at the National Bank of Genetic Data (located at the time in the Durand Hospital), and a number of months later, on 10 February 2000, she received the news that she is the biological child of Gertrudis Hlaczik and José Poblete Roa. Both biological parents are among the estimated thirty thousand forcibly disappeared persons who were abducted, tortured, and assassinated during the last civil-military dictatorship that ruled Argentina between 1976 and 1983.

Judge Cavallo was conscious of the delicate situation. After receiving the information from the Bank, he waited fifteen days before inviting Mercedes to his office. In the meantime, he arranged two other events: the arrest of Mercedes's supposed parents, which took place while she was being told about her true genetic origins, and a meeting with her biological family, which took place only shortly after the young woman was provided with the information about her genetic origins and shown a picture of herself when she was a few months old.

Based on extensive interviews, Analia Argento, a journalist and the author of the book *Home Again: Histories of Restituted Children and Grandchildren* [*De Vuelta a Casa: historias de hijos y nietos restituidos*] writes of this moment:

> Although what she heard [from the judge about the genetic test] reassured her, she felt that there was no need for the DNA test in order to know that the baby girl in the picture was her [the picture was placed on the cover of the large file Judge Cavallo had on his desk]. She turned white . . . and only paid attention when the judge told her that at that very moment a police car was being sent to her house to arrest Landa and Moreira . . . she felt angst and sadness . . . her worrying was interrupted by Judge Cavallo.
> —your family is here, you must meet them.
> —can't it wait for another moment?
> —they are all outside, in the hall. They have waited long and it would be appropriate to meet them now.
> —fine [Está bien].
>   The door to the office opened and in entered around twenty men and women of all ages . . . . The Poblete and Hlaczik [families] feared that, like other young persons, she would not want to meet her true family. There is no law that can force [someone] to care [for another] according to blood ties. This could be the first and the last time that they would see her. (Argento 2009: 20)[1]

Mercedes was told her name was Claudia Victoria Poblete and that her real date of birth was 25 March 1978 and not 13 June 1978 as her falsified birth certificate stated. She was forcibly disappeared with her mother when she was eight months old and had been held, according to testimonies of survivors, in the clandestine camp "El Olimpo" for a few days before being appropriated by Landa and his wife. Raised in a strict but warm environment, she did not question her origins, even though she had been aware that her parents were much older than her friends' parents and that there were no photos of the pregnancy. Thus, the revelation of her genetic kinship ties had caught her by surprise. However, by then, as she explained in her testimony,[2] she had been told by Moreira and Landa that when she was very young (at the age of five or six) she underwent a DNA test because at that time she was already suspected of being one of the disappeared children (Guthmann n.d.: 111).

Claudia Victoria is also the first appropriated individual, of the now 130 identified "living disappeared," who declared in an oral trial against her appropriators (*Clarín*, 23 June 2001). Although she kept living with them for quite some time after her identification, and continued to do so even after the verdict and specifically after she gave testimony in the trial stating her true name, her real date of birth, and the names of her genetic parents, she has also been cultivating ties with her biological family. Over the years these relations with the biological family have developed, she explained in her testimony, saying, "Today, I feel they are part of me and I feel like part of them as a family" (Guthmann n.d.: 112).

I begin with this story of Claudia Victoria Poblete because I believe it brings forth many of the ways in which the experience of time is worked upon, managed, and manipulated in the process of locating and identifying adult living disappeared. Working through artistic representations and published testimonies of these adult living disappeared, as well as extensive interviews I conducted on the topic with those who have dedicated much of their lives to the search (specifically, human rights activists, judges, lawyers, artists, psychologists, and psychoanalysts), in this chapter I explore the different forms, sites, and processes by which time is worked upon before, after, and in the process of genetic identification. Inspired by Michael Flaherty's concept of "time work," I examine how time is redirected but also how it is manipulated and resisted in complex situations where choice, freedom, and desire may not coincide. In doing so, I propose the term "hacking time" as a way to explore the varied ways in which time, history, and kinship are worked upon in the lives of the living disappeared. But before I get ahead of myself let me first explain how I understand the concept of "time work."

"Time work," the term coined by Flaherty to explain "one's efforts to promote or suppress a particular temporal experience" (2003: 19), "reveals human effort to intervene in the trajectory of events," and involves our attempt to "control, manipulate, and customize our own temporal experience or that of others" (Flaherty, this volume: 13). But how this manipulation actually happens in different cultural contexts and in complex situations like the one described above is less clear. Flaherty offers a detailed analysis of the different forms of time work, including work on duration, frequency, and sequence among others. In this chapter, my analysis of time work is paradoxically both broader and more limited. On the one hand, I explore the experience of biographical-chronological time and the way it is fashioned through DNA identity tests; on the other hand, I examine the management of the moment of identification and the different tactics that identified individuals and others employ to shape their temporal experience. In doing so, I introduce the notion of "time hacking," which highlights not only the way in which others—in this case the state and its judicial system—hack an individual's experience of time, but also how individuals recode and rewrite their own temporal existence.

HACKING TIME: DECODING, REWRITING, AND TEMPORAL STRUCTURES.

> Hackers change and rewrite codes, their "politics are geared toward re-ordering the technologies and infrastructures that have become part of the fabric of everyday life." (Coleman 2011: 515)

Writing on the everyday politics and ethics of hackers, Gabriela Coleman explains that, like geeks, hackers shuffle and rearrange the underlying direction of computer programs and consequently the structure of (at least some) worlds. Their ethics is much broader than the dichotomy often used to describe them or their acts: malevolent criminals or freedom fighters. Instead, their positions and struggles vary but many times include struggles for privacy on the one hand and freedom of information on the other (Coleman and Golub 2008; Jordan and Taylor 1998; Powell 2016). Their acts "reveal as well as transform culture and technical products" (Powell 2016: 602). In bringing the term "hacking" into our discussion of time, I am interested in thinking through the ways in which certain actions in the world—specifically, uncovering and rewriting code—can "work on" or, more broadly, "rearrange" both the *sequence* and the *experience* of time. To develop this point, I will need to go in a somewhat roundabout way by first exploring the relationship between DNA and code.

In popular discourse, DNA has been described as the code of life, and while it is clear that the metaphors we use, or the various analogies we make, in describing DNA, such as "the 'secret of life,' the book, the alphabet . . . the blueprint . . . the map, software" (Roof 2007: 7; see also Nelkin and Lindee 2004), import particular values and meanings that are not necessarily part of DNA's material structure, it is also clear that these metaphors have effects in the world (Lakoff and Johnson 2003). The common belief that DNA is a code or a book implies that it can be read, deciphered, and rewritten (Roof 2007). Paternity tests, prenatal genetic testing, and other new and ongoing interventions in human genetic makeup are all ways in which this map is interpreted and worked upon (Gammeltoft 2004; Dickenson 2007). In fact, it is exactly the fear of changing the code—the human genome—that has generated extensive ethical debate in current biomedical research (Konrad 2005; see also Vaisman 2018). Second, considering DNA to be a blueprint or a map gives rise to a particular form of thinking that divides the world into internal structures and external manifestations. Thus, ideas about internal materials (i.e., genetic structures) are translated into assumptions about surface appearances. A key example in this context is the search for genetic ancestry and the surprises some people encounter when they discover that their racial and ethnic origins are quite different from their external manifestations and hence from their culturally informed expectations (Sommer 2010).

In the case of the living disappeared, these two dimensions of DNA, as a blueprint that can be uncovered and decoded, and as a map for external surfaces, are particularly revealing. The unveiling and decoding of DNA can provide answers to lacunas that (sometimes) exist on the outer/social surface. For example, in numerous cases of identified living disappeared, the genetic identification opened up the possibility of identifying and bonding with the biological family through the discovery of similar traits (hair and skin color, height, but also interest in political activism). These physical or personality characteristics are also sometimes what differentiated the identified individual from the family that raised him or her. In many cases, these revelations on the material level (DNA) become nodes of entanglement through which a "new" identity is "revealed" or constructed. Take, for example, the case of Ezequiel Tauro Rochistein, who resisted DNA identification for close to a decade. Once identified, and after having met his biological family, it was his ability to see the similarities between his biological mother and his daughters that facilitated his acceptance of his new identity. He described it thus: "It was very revealing. It was really crazy to see photos of my (biological) mom when she was two years old, it was a copy of my daughters" (*Rio Negro*, 20 October 2012). Leonardo Fossati Ortega has a different story. For him, the question "who do I resemble?" was one of the motivations for his own search for identity. As he explained to Angela Pradelli over numerous interviews, he wanted to be similar to someone. "Who do I look like, who am I similar to?" he asked and added, "I wanted to find that my nose is similar to one of my family members', that I was similar to them in a gesture or in our way of talking or walking, in the things that they said. Whose hands are like mine?" (Pradelli 2014: 123). Once Leonardo found out about his origins, he also found some answers to those inquietudes: "I saw pictures of my mother and I found out that I looked like her. We were very similar when we were young" (Pradelli 2014: 139).

But the deciphering of codes and the attempt to reconcile external surfaces with internal structures also have implications for a person's experience of time. Specifically, in the case of the adult living disappeared this identification (or "decoding") undoes the common experience of linear-biographical time that clearly marks a past, present, and future and introduces instead other forms or experiences of time, which I will discuss further below.

Rearranging Time and Temporal Reckoning

What does it mean to think of temporality as code? How are the linear (past-present-future) biographical structures hacked when genetic identification takes place? One way to think about this is to consider that, through the identification, time moves back toward a past that, while not lived, was always there lurking as a potentiality or as a source of uncertainties. But even if time moves back, it does not stay still; rather, it loops, returning to merge with the present.[3] Once the past reappears (i.e., the person is identified as the abducted child or the outcome of a birth that took place in the clandestine camp), both the experience of linear temporal structures and personal life course are thrown into turmoil. This movement into the past and looping into the present is not only an outcome of the state's decision to identify the living disappeared; rather, it can also be the result of a personal decision taken by the identified individual to return to a past that was somehow possible but at the same time is, even after the identification, still an unknown. In this act of turning to the past, the subject may recuperate traces of his or her former life (particularly if abducted and appropriated as a young baby), or rescue alternative personal as well as familial and political histories from oblivion. Below, I give a few examples of this very complex process.

Leonardo Fossati describes what happened once he was told of his genetic identity:

> The judge brought the certainty, the absolute certainty. The first thing I felt was great joy that I was able to resolve the matter. So first there was the encounter. After that appeared the loss. Because in the beginning it was my history but it [also] was not. I was getting to know my origins, yes, but until that moment I thought that my life started on the 20 March 1977 when I arrived at the home of the family that raised me. I took that date as the first day of my life. And now I was learning, through various testimonies, that it was the 12 of March. I found out something that was mine, like my date of birth, but this information still felt distant from me. (Pradelli 2014: 137)

In this case, Leonardo attempts to make sense of a past that belongs to him but is also remote, something that is both his and not his at the same time.

It is this encounter with a past, which also implies an encounter with his biological origin, that further marks the loss—that is, the understanding that this potential past and all that is entwined in it cannot be fully captured or lived. His sense of discomfort with the past that erupted into his present is not uncommon among identified living disappeared. The past (and the potentiality that it holds of both loss and belonging) changes the experience of time because it becomes part of, or is integrated into, the present, producing an intertwining of temporal modes, which is experienced as awkward and unsettling.

The case of Victoria Donda reflects a somewhat different way of considering the looping of the past into the present. Once the results of the DNA test confirmed that she was a child of disappeared, Victoria had to confront many contradictions, some of which she felt incapable of handling as one big whole. Instead, as she explains in her autobiography, she compartmentalized and attempted to take on her new identity: "At first my main goal was to reposition myself in the universe without regard to other people or relationships. This meant figuring out what it meant to be Victoria Donda, which also meant finding a place for Analía [her name when she was appropriated], whom I couldn't allow to disappear on the grounds that her whole life had been built on lies" (Donda 2010: 165). This attempt to accommodate both an unknown but also a very intimate past that emerges through the DNA test, and a present that exists in tremendous flux, is illustrated in numerous passages in Victoria's autobiography. There she describes her need to find out more about her parents as a way to make sense of their presence in her life as well as to explain some of her own idiosyncrasies. In other passages, she refers to another challenge, also a result of the looping of the past into the present: specifically, her attempts to come to terms with the fact that an unbridgeable emotional and ideological gap exists between her biological sister (who was raised by their uncle, a military official who was involved in their parents' disappearance) and herself.

In both Leonardo's and Victoria's cases, we see individuals who are struggling with the looping of the past into the present—a process that shatters the experience of chronological-biographical time. The newly identified living disappeared must find ways to assimilate, or develop mechanisms to confront the unsettling information, which includes not only information about their own past that is revealed to be false, but also the certainty that there was another possible life for them had they not been appropriated. To elaborate on this point, let me turn to a text written by the dramaturge and author Mariana Eva Perez.

Mariana was raised knowing that her mother had been pregnant when she and Mariana's father were disappeared. Growing up with the figure of the disappeared brother, who was later found and identified, she writes to him in a now well-known dramatic text "Instructions for a Butterfly Collector":

> Dear Rodolfito, colon. Today it is the 2nd of June and another week ends without us knowing the result of the genetic test that can change everything, and when I say everything, I say [mean] *everything*. I am writing to you, as always, but now I don't know who I am writing to. There is a very tall guy who sells hotdogs at the station in San Miguel, who smiles with a smile that moves me inexplicably, clumsy, like me, with great feet, like me, who has a swirl in his hair, exactly like me, who was born a few days after you did, my Rodolfito, my little brother, who is a child of a milico [military officer] of the same force that took our parents, who for over a month I ask myself, is he my brother, if you are you. I wake up: you are? You are not? (Perez 2014: 8)

Toward the end of the text, Mariana writes,

> You are not Rodolfito, simply because Rodolfito is no one other than myself, me when I only knew how to be your sister. It is not easy, but I must let Rodolfito move away and make room for you, the tall guy of the thousand scars of a past without me.
>
> I told you once that you were my life. Rodolfito, my little brother, the stolen child of mom and dad who was my life when my life was your absence. (Perez 2014: 10)

Mariana's dramatic text, which was first performed in Buenos Aires in 2002 as part of the cycle *Theater for Identity* and later revised in 2010 to its current and final form, demonstrates an alternative past and an alternative biography that the living disappeared—in this case her biological brother—might face once genetic identification is effectuated. This other past may inform others' attempts at shaping the identified living disappeared's temporal experience. It seems to me that in recognizing the gap between the desired brother and the biological brother, Mariana is also gesturing toward the incommensurability of two pasts living in the present. And while they may not sit nicely with each other, they nonetheless coexist (see Vaisman 2013).

In addition to looping, other kinds of time work may emerge in the identification process. First and foremost, the decision of when to do the DNA test is a form of time work enacted by either the individual or the state, or both. The variety of responses to this demand is great, and it is hard to generalize, but in broad terms it seems that many individuals who did not themselves actively search for their origins take some time to undergo the test. Psychologists working with these individuals describe it as "personal time" and explain that each individual has his or her own process of elaboration and that these processes should be respected. Judges, although informed by the work and experience of psychologists, may have a different approach, and in recent years they have tended to order a house search on the same day or only a few days after the individual was offered a voluntary blood test and refused to undergo one.[4] In the case of Claudia Victoria Poblete mentioned above, the test was conducted soon after her first meeting with the judge and seems to have been an outcome of the legal process rather than a personal agentive decision, although it must also be recognized as such, particularly when compared to the many who refused the test (see Vaisman 2019).

The next period in the identification process where time work is most prominent is while the DNA is being compared to the stored DNA of the families that are looking for their missing kin. Most individuals find themselves powerless during this interval, and time seems to stretch endlessly. Again, it is very hard to generalize because both the identification technologies and the context have changed dramatically over the years, but two responses are noteworthy. Leonardo, whose story of restitution I narrated above, decided after many months to stop waiting for the results and to go on with his life. When the news finally came, he was tremendously surprised. Similarly, Claudia Victoria attempted to continue her life as if nothing had happened. She continued to live with her appropriating parents while she waited for the news from the Bank. In both of these cases, the inability to effectuate time as one waits for the results generated a closing off of the potential for looping—that is, they both demonstrate an active attempt to continue on the linear path of biographical time while resisting, at least for a while, the potentiality of a past that may arise from the genetic test itself.

A third moment of time work is evident in the text describing Claudia Victoria's response to the test results. Here is the first time that the looping effect described above emerges. It is the instant when the past leaps into the present, throwing into great disarray the experience of chronological time. In Claudia Victoria's case, this moment was tightly tied to a fourth one: the judge's insistence that she meet her biological family at that very instant. In that situation, Judge Cavallo held the reigns of time and directed them with great speed toward a deeper form of looping the past into the present. It is in this event, where lives collide and recognition through small gestures happens—Claudia Victoria seeing her biological family members for the first time and her biological family seeing her as an adult for the first time— that time is experienced differently for her. She describes it as a moment of shock, where she found herself standing still and accepting the gifts she was given: pictures, segments of newspapers, and some cassettes with recordings of interviews conducted with family members and friends of her biological parents. A short while later, and after they had all left, she was still standing with all these artifacts in her hands, unsure of what to do. Judge Cavallo, watching her stand there, suggested she call a friend who could accompany her home. She was then driven to the central train station only a few blocks away, but on the way she asked the driver to stop behind the building where her appropriating father was waiting in his car and spoke to him:

> —go home. The police is going [is on its way] to detain you and mom— she warned him.
> —what did the judge tell you? What family do you belong to?
> —I do not remember well. Poblete Chamorro stated the DNA test. (Argento 2009: 21)

In this short interaction, it seems to me, time is suddenly condensed. An appropriating "father" asks about an event, which took place twenty-two years earlier, and to which he was an active accomplice. In the act, he exposes his own doubts and the lingering questions he must have lived with throughout Claudia Victoria's early life. In other words, we can only imagine that the past, in the form of unanswered questions, and maybe even fantasized alternative lives, was always present as a backdrop to all familial interactions. We can also only assume that extensive work was needed to push the coexistence of lived and imagined lives and pasts repeatedly into oblivion.[5]

Why Hacking *Time?*

I began this discussion by claiming that we should understand the experience of time in the case of the adult living disappeared as a form of hacking time. However, there are many ironies in using this term to talk about identification and temporal experience. Hacking ethics is framed in many instances as struggles for freedom, privacy, and the free circulation of knowledge. Moreover, it is often described as a counter-institutional act that upholds individual as well as collective rights. In recent years, however, the identification process of adult living disappeared displays assumptions about freedom and privacy as well as the counter-institutional nature of hacking that must be understood in a somewhat different manner.

For the past four decades, the search for the living disappeared has developed in different directions, due mainly to obstacles in the process of locating and identifying individuals. One of the central challenges over the years was the refusal of some of the suspected living disappeared to undergo a blood test and to provide a DNA sample. In 2003, the Supreme Court of Argentina ruled that the state could not take a blood sample by force from a suspected living disappeared, but in 2005 judges found a new way of confronting this situation: they began ordering house searches where personal objects, including clothes, linen, and hair and tooth brushes were collected. These personal objects were used to extract DNA (what I term "shed-DNA"; Vaisman 2014). While it seemed at first that this solution was productive, it also met with some resistance, both in the courts and on the ground. In some cases, individuals who were tipped about a future house search succeeded in manipulating the objects (planting objects with foreign DNA) so as to complicate the process of identification. Others searched for recourse within the judicial system, reaching the Supreme Court with their request not to be identified using their DNA. In 2009, the Supreme Court of Argentina ruled in the case of a shed-DNA test, stating that, although blood tests may not be carried out by force, a shed-DNA test based on materials collected from a house raid is valid (for further elaboration on this point and the historical process, see Vaisman 2019). Today, more often than not, even those individuals whose houses are raided choose to give a blood sample rather than have their personal belongings collected. In this way, they both resist the state's intrusion into their personal belongings and the privacy of their home, and assert their agency in matters of identity and identification.

It seems, then, that some of the cases of shed-DNA identity tests fly in the face of individual rights and privacy concerns. The ironies, however, are not lost on the courts. In fact, they are very much present when discussions about the rights of individuals to privacy versus the rights of society and the family to the truth (that is, the right to find out if the person in question is their kin) are debated (Vaisman 2012). Similarly, human rights declarations, which are very much about individuals and their rights, are used to argue for and against these forms of identification, raising many questions and ironies that I have discussed in other parts of my work (Vaisman 2014).

These ironies notwithstanding, I believe that the cases of shed-DNA tests have particular resonance with time hacking. Here, it seems that the full meaning of hacking is exposed. In *The New Hacker's Dictionary*, hackers are described as "1. A person who enjoys exploring the details of programmable systems and how to stretch their capabilities . . . 7. One who enjoys . . . overcoming or circumventing limitations. 8. [deprecated] A malicious meddler who tries to discover sensitive information by poking around" (Jargon File 4.4.7; also in Raymond 1996).[6] Hacking in the context of shed-DNA tests is, one could claim, reversed because it is not the individual but rather the state that is poking around to discover sensitive information. But hacking can also help us make sense of how time is experienced by these individuals who do not want to be identified or who are unwilling to undergo a DNA test. My reading of the various accounts available through court testimonies, extensive media reports, and films is that, very literally, their life course—their temporal experience of linear-biographical time—has been hacked.

A vivid example of this experience can be gleaned from the response of Evelyn Karina Vazquez Ferrá, whose case was debated in the Supreme Court in 2003, to the process of identification and the final revelation, based on a shed-DNA test, that she is, in fact, a child of disappeared.[7] In numerous media appearances dating to the time when her case was debated in the Supreme Court, she explained that she is not interested in learning about her biological origins. When she finally met members of her biological family, an event that took place before the shed-DNA test confirmed her filiation, she was reserved. She could not understand how they might like her without knowing her. "It is not automatic, maybe if a relationship is established but I do not push a button and say my sister is not my sister or my nephews are not my nephews. That is craziness" (Argento 2009: 179). When the gendarmerie came knocking on her door in the very early hours of 14 February 2008 requesting to enter the apartment and carry out a search, Evelyn was beside herself. Listening to the court's order, which was read aloud, she realized there was no way she could refuse them entry. They took both hers and her husband's toothbrushes, and began looking through her laundry basket for a used pair of panties. This is how, based on her interviews with Evelyn, Argento describes the situation that ensued:

> —It's OK but the panties no. Take the hairbrush, see how my hair is falling out you have tons.
> —Señora, we are going to take the panties.
> —It is an embarrassing spectacle [papelón], I am sorry that I am saying this to you, I know you are doing your job but if the [Supreme] Court wanted to preserve my privacy, how are you going to take my dirty nickers? . . . Please I ask you, I will cut a finger and you can collect the blood, but not the nickers. (Argento 2009: 181)

The scene that unfolded at Evelyn's apartment that morning is a violent form of hacking, of changing the course of everyday life and chronological-biographical time (among other things)—that is, there is a before and after for this event. Hacking here takes place on numerous scales: hacking the DNA through shed-DNA tests, hacking the legal process by offering an alternative to compulsory blood tests (and in that way opening new possibilities for legal investigation), but also hacking temporal experience and a sense of chronology since through the genetic identification test the past was looped into the present. Evelyn, however, kept resisting. She appealed the house raid and the potential past that could emerge from the DNA test collected from her personal belongings, and she has not searched for information about her biological parents. We could speculate that in her attempt to refuse the looping of time—the entering of the past into the present as a dynamic and vibrant experience—she has resisted the eruption of information following her identification, and has attempted to fold the past back on itself so as to recreate a single experience of chronological temporality that would allow her to continue her planned life course. But we may also question whether this form of resistance to time hacking can ever be successful (see Vaisman 2019 for a detailed discussion of resistance and the impact of kinship information on an individual's experience of self).

CONCLUSIONS

Hacking and looping time are forms of manipulating temporal experience from within and from without. In concluding this chapter, I would like to return to Flaherty's formulation of time work as "temporal agency" to consider how choice and agency may play into time work in the context of genetic identification of adult living disappeared. Flaherty's model for time work assumes that our temporal experiences are guided by our particular personal circumstances and local norms and habits, as well as by the "temporal desires or dictates of others" (Flaherty, this volume: 15). Time work in his formulation, then, is often a matter of *choice* and *desire* (whether that of the individual or of others), and, while this formulation may be appealing, I believe that it may be productive to broaden it so as to include the unpredictability of both the experience of time and the work that shapes this experience. In many situations and particularly in the cases I discuss in this chapter, choices and desires are less straightforward or clearly defined, and, more importantly, they may have very unpredictable effects.

In some of the cases I presented here, individuals chose to undergo a DNA identity test or searched for their origins. Yet, in undergoing genetic identification, they also opened themselves up to many forms of time work that they could not have anticipated nor have the tools to control. These may include, for example, experiences of time that arise from the demands of biological families, the public narratives that circulate about one's life, or even an encounter with a surviving parent. Similarly, when the state is the initiator of the search, the experience of time is shaped by others and is even less under the control of the individual in question. Here again, it is not only the undesired act of hacking, but the unpredictable consequences of the search that can generate very different experiences of time. There are many instances where the search does not lead to identification as a living disappeared. That is, the individual learns that the people who raised him are not his biological parents, but there is no indication that he is a child of disappeared. As a consequence, the looping of the past into the present is complicated by the fact that there is no clear past that emerges out of the DNA test (see Vaisman 2019). We can only assume that time work in these situations is challenging and unpredictable, even more so than in the case of the identified living disappeared.

To recap, similar to computer hackers who decode and sometimes re-write programs, time hacking in the context of the search for the living dis-appeared decodes or unveils a past, and in the act may also (if the result is successful identification) rewrite biographical time. Looping may, with time, slowly come under one's control, but in some cases it might not, leaving the individual in a state of flux for years (as some cases of identified living disappeared illustrate). In this context, then, it seems that time work is an emergent practice that, while sometimes an act of desire and agency, can also be hard to predict and control. This is true not only for the individual in question but also for the state, the appropriating family, and the social net-works that are challenged to reincorporate an individual whose experience of time is one marked by both looping and hacking.

Noa Vaisman
Assistant Professor, Department of Anthropology
Aarhus University, Denmark

NOTES

1. This and all other texts in Spanish are translated by the author.
2. This was in the trial against her appropriating parents, see Guthmann n.d.
3. I am thinking here of a loop of time, although it might be worth considering whether instead of a single loop it might be better described as a Mobius belt where time is both inside and outside, in the present and the past simultane-ously. A further layer can be added to the notion of looping if we consider the "looping effects of human kinds" (Hacking 1996), a discussion that for lack of space I will not develop here.
4. This, and the information presented below, has been collected through inter-views with a number of lawyers and judges who have handled cases of living disappeared.

5. In fact, many of the psychologists and psychoanalysts working with the living disappeared talk about the secret that shapes the identity of these individuals. Some of them argue that these secrets are worse than living with the truth—as painful as it may be. Moreover, to date I am unaware of any available testimonies of appropriating parents and their experience raising a living disappeared. Like many of the perpetrators of human rights crimes in Argentina, they have chosen not to give a full account of their experiences in the courts, nor tell their story to the media.
6. http://www.catb.org/jargon/html/H/hacker.html.
7. In the first instance, Evelyn was requested to undergo a DNA test. She appeared in Judge Servini de Cubría's office, and the following interaction ensued:

    —you will need to do the DNA test
    —I am not going to do it
    —what do you mean you are not going to?
    —for now I will not. Let's let time pass until I understand what is happening . . .
    —I am not going to do the DNA [test], my dad already confessed, I am not going to use my body so you can have him arrested. (Argento 2009: 165–66)

REFERENCES

Newspapers

Clarín, 23 June 2001.
Rio Negro, 20 October 2012.

Argento, Analía. 2009. *De Vuelta a Casa: historias de hijos y nietos restituidos*. Buenos Aires: Marea.
Coleman, Gabriela. 2011. "Hackers Politics and Publics." *Public Culture* 23 (3): 511–16.
Coleman, Gabriela E., and Golub Alex. 2008. "Hacker Practice: Moral Genres and the Cultural Articulation of Liberalism." *Anthropological Theory* 8 (3): 255–77.
Dickenson, Donna. 2007. *Property in the Body: Feminist Perspectives*. Cambridge: Cambridge University Press.
Donda, Victoria. 2010. *My name is Victoria: The Extraordinary Story of One Woman's Struggle to Reclaim Her True Identity*. New York: Other Press.
Flaherty, Michael G. 2003. "Time Work: Customizing Temporal Experience." *Social Psychology Quarterly* 66 (1): 17–33.
———. 2020. "The Lathe of Time: Some Principles of Temporal Agency." In this volume.
Gammeltoft, Tine. 2014. *Haunting Images: A Cultural Account of Selective Reproduction in Vietnam*. Berkeley: University of California Press.
Guthmann, Yanina. n.d. *El Caso Simón: Discurso Jurídico, legitimidad y Derechos Humanos*. Teseopress.com.

Hacking, Ian. 1996. "The Looping Effects of Human Kinds." In *Causal Cognition: A Multidisciplinary Debate*, edited by Dan Sperber, David Premack, and Ann James Premack, 351–394. New York: Oxford University Press.

Jordan, Tim, and Paul Taylor. 1998. "A Sociology of Hackers." *Sociological Review* 46 (4): 757–80.

Konrad, Monica. 2005. *Narrating the New Predictive Genetics: Ethics, Ethnography and Science*. Cambridge: Cambridge University Press.

Lakoff, George, and Mark Johnson. 2003. *Metaphors We Live By*. Chicago: University of Chicago Press.

Nelkin, Dorothy, and Susan Lindee. 2004. *The DNA Mystique: The Gene as a Cultural Icon*. Michigan: University of Michigan Press.

Perez, Mariana Eva. 2014. "Instrucciones para un coleccionista de mariposas." *Kamchatka* 3: appendix 3–10.

Powell, Alison. 2016. "Hacking in the Public Interest: Authority, Legitimacy, Means and Ends." *New Media & Society* 18 (4): 600–16.

Pradelli, Ángela. 2014. *En Mi Nombre: Historias de Identidades Restituidas*. Buenos Aires: Paidós.

Raymond, Eric S. 1996. *The New Hacker's Dictionary*. 3rd edition. Cambridge, MA: MIT Press.

Roof, Judith. 2007. *The Poetics of DNA*. Minneapolis: University of Minnesota Press.

Sommer, Marianne. 2010. "DNA and Cultures of Remembrance: Anthropological Genetics, Biohistories and Biosocialities." *BioSocieties* 5: 366–90.

Vaisman, Noa. 2012. "Identity, DNA and the State in Post-Dictatorship Argentina." In *Identity Politics and the New Genetics Re/Creating Categories of Difference and Belonging*, edited by Katharina Schramm, David Skinner, and Richard Rottenburg, 97–115. New York: Berghahn Books.

——. 2013. "Shedding Our Selves: Perspectivism, the Bounded Subject and the Nature-Culture Divide." In *Biosocial Becomings: Integrating Social and Biological Anthropology*, edited by Tim Ingold and Gisli Pállson, 106–22. Cambridge: Cambridge University Press.

——. 2014. "Relational Human Rights: Shed-DNA and the Identification of the Living Disappeared." *Journal of Law and Society* 41 (3): 391–415.

——. 2018. "The Human, Human Rights and DNA Identity Tests," *Science, Technology and Human Values* 43 (1): 3–20.

——. 2019. "Kinship, Knowledge and the State: The Case of the Adult 'Living Disappeared' of Argentina." In *Cambridge Handbook of Kinship Studies*, edited by Sandra Bamford, 279–305. Cambridge: Cambridge University Press.

Chapter 5

Temporal Front and Back Stages
Time Work as Resistance

Lisa-Jo K. van den Scott

I ease open the door and slip inside the house. Quietly, I take off my shoes in the entryway. In Arviat, Nunavut, a small Inuit hamlet in the far north of Canada, people pride themselves on not knocking on doors. Knocking is for the police and those not versed in Inuit practices. After having lived there for five years, I am back for a research trip. First, however, I want to say hello to Heidi, an Elder in the community. We were close when I lived in town, and I know she will love being surprised. I have a gift for her, a printout of a picture I took of her and her best friend.

I tiptoe into the main room and lean against the door frame. Her daughter sees me first and laughs. Then Heidi turns, and when she recognizes me, she leaps up, claps her hands, and starts laughing as she rushes to hug me. Not only am I following through on a promise to come back after moving away, but I am also performing knowledge of the temporal practices in Arviat. I dropped in, rather than calling. I did not knock and wait at the door. Western formality around doors takes time. I did not make them conform to my Western temporal expectations, but rather I conformed to theirs.

Heidi generously agrees to participate in my formal interviews, which complement my ethnographic data. We set a time, an odd practice for her, and I return on the appointed day and hour. Heidi, however, does not keep a planner. She has no cell phone prompting her to keep appointments and to be here or there. She is where she is. People come to her. She is an Elder. Within Inuit time, as well as within Western time, position and power matter. I am the first to arrive that evening. As I read through my brief transcript I find the following:

(someone comes in to visit, we decide to keep going) . . . (another comes in to visit) . . .

(another arrives with a gift for her.)

The interview stops so she can, essentially, hold court. We try the next evening, but radio bingo got in the way, so she tells me to come back after bingo the next night. I do, and stumble upon an illicit poker game. I sit with Ruby on the floor to the side and we eat frozen, raw caribou from cardboard on the ground, slicing off shavings with an *ulu* [traditional curved knife]. (Heidi's interview)

There is a relaxed coming and going all evening, into the early hours of the morning. No one is rushing and no one is talking about work. These are the back stage hours, when Inuit practice Inuit time, in defiance of encroaching Western cultural paradigms about time, which are implicitly ideological.

In this chapter, I discuss temporal resistance as a form of political time work using the case study of Inuit in Arviat, Nunavut, Canada. An individual or group performs time work when they put effort into shaping their temporal experience, either suppressing or encouraging particular temporal experiences (Flaherty 2011). Inuit face many forms of encroaching Western cultural paradigms in their everyday lives, and foremost among them, though often overlooked, is a colonizing time regime. The state imposes Western systems of work, economics, and bureaucracy, which amount to a time regime, one which rational time inhabits. Westerners in town uphold Western cultural ideals around time and time management. I use Goffman's concepts of "front stage" and "back stage" to discuss how Inuit engage in agentic time work to resist the structure of an imposed time regime by enacting and protecting temporal back stages in which they perform "Inuit time." These back stages may or may not intersect with spatial back stages in how Inuit allocate time in spaces and for particular practices, duration of time in spaces, and timing.

After introducing the setting, this chapter begins with a discussion of the participation in time regimes as acts of belonging, and resistance as acts of nonbelonging. Next, I examine the temporal front stage in Arviat and the role of the nine-to-five workday and rational time. I proceed to ways Inuit create and maintain a temporal back stage and conclude with the role of space in these temporal realms.

SETTING AND METHOD

Arviat, Nunavut, is a small, northern Canadian hamlet with a growing population of roughly 2,400 at the time of my research. It is located on the west coast of the Hudson Bay, accessible primarily by airplane. Geographically well-removed from the bulk of Canada's population, it was among the final Inuit areas to be colonized, a process that began in the 1920s and that saw Inuit forcibly settled into the Arviat hamlet by the early 1960s. At this time, the Canadian government implemented an aggressive housing plan. The Inuit of this area had been living nomadically in family groups. Their dwellings had consisted of *iglus* in the winter and tents in the summer. Permanent structures were not present in this area before colonization sedimented this group into the hamlet now called Arviat. The housing plan, begun and concluded within mere decades, shifted Inuit "indoors" into permanent spaces constructed by their colonizers.

Thomas and Thompson (1972) saw the walling-in of Inuit into houses as an attempt at rapid cultural change. The government opened schools, a health center, and offices, all of which implemented and taught the nine-to-five work paradigm. The citizens of Arviat, called Arviammiut, agentically work to bring their culture indoors, into spaces increasingly dominated by Western influences and the Western gaze. Walls and doors restructured everyday life at profound spatial and temporal levels, creating anomie. As Inuit struggle to establish their culture in a community context, they focus their attention on their cultural identity as Inuit, performing Inuitness. For example, as van den Scott (2016) describes, Arviammiut particularly value the ability to use everything, as well as creativity. When Marge takes a worn spatula and glues lace around it, the thing that makes that spatula attractive on the wall is that it enacts Inuit values. Abigail tells me during an interview about the stickers her mother put on the range hood of their stove, saying "my mum's pretty creative" and that "whatever she finds, she finds a way to use it." Life within houses means living life with Western spaces. This is one way in which Arviammiut perform Inuitness inside the new houses.

I lived in Arviat for five years and made two return research trips in the following three years. I learned Inuktitut and took part in community events. I was privy to conversation among imported Westerners in town about their views on the work practices of local Inuit, as well as to conversation among Arviammiut workers and nonworkers about their workplaces and their views on the nine-to-five paradigm. My research primarily examines the forced relocation of Inuit into houses and the ways in which they navigate the current landscape of their everyday lives, particularly around matters of identity, space and place, and time. In addition to ethnographic field notes, I also collected fifty formal interviews and photographed the walls inside homes as part of my broader work on space and time. My findings emerged through reading and rereading for themes, as well as conclusions gradually realized through years in the field. I rely heavily on my ethnographic experience and reflexive memos. All names of participants are pseudonyms.

TIME REGIMES AND BELONGING

Political resistance, in general, manifests itself within temporal domains for two reasons. The first is that temporal practices demonstrate group membership. By the same token, violating or resisting temporal practices becomes an effective way to perform nonmembership. The second reason is that temporal practices carry ideologies. These shape practices and beliefs so fundamentally that time regimes emerge. Pushing back against a time regime is a potent way to resist the imposition of a dominant social group's cultural arrangements.

Participating in temporal practices and norms expresses group membership in thought communities, or mnemonic communities (Zerubavel 1997); it defines who is "your kind" (Zerubavel 1979a). Arviammiut, as a marginalized group subjected to rapid colonization, routinely perform practices that express where the boundaries lie between and among groups to demonstrate not only how Inuit they are, but also that they are a separate and distinct group within the Canadian landscape. Participating in temporal practices established by Western culture results in Inuit pushing back against the idea that they are members of this group. For example, my field notes and interviews are replete with the phrase "us Inuit," such as when Melanie answers a question about plastic flowers decorating her walls, "yeah, us Inuit, the men hardly decorate the house" (Melanie's interview).

Temporal coordination that expresses membership ranges from deciding when a book club will meet to acknowledging a particular calendar and recognizing the time as a specific year, month, day, and to naming the correct hour according to the time zone and whether it is daylight savings time or not. Without aligning temporal practices, one cannot participate fully in group life. Think, for example, about how we consider certain sufferers of mental illness to be offbeat from the rest of society (Zerubavel 1997), or how we deem older people who are not aware of the day of the week to be incompetent, despite how challenging it would be for anyone with unstructured time to keep track of the days of the week. On vacation one loses track of time, and is indeed removed from the everyday world.

Phillip Vannini (2011) found that residents of an island in British Columbia, Canada, agentically worked on "island time" as a way to differentiate themselves from mainlanders. Engaging in temporal practices (or not) demonstrates deep-rooted expressions of belonging (or not belonging) and identity. This makes time work and the temporal arena an especially effective domain for resistance (van den Scott 2017b). Resisting temporal practices demonstrates "I am not part of your group." It is an effective arena for Arviammiut to practice being "us Inuit."

The temporal practices with which we enact membership are socially constructed and historically contingent. As such, they embody ideologies and social organization (Beidelman 1963). Calendars not only define insider and outsider status according to one's practices (Zerubavel 1982), but they also carry with them social beliefs concerning hierarchies, moral temporality, and temporal embeddedness (Lewis and Weigert 1981). In short, temporal practices represent cultural identity.

When we have access and to whom we have access carry an implicit belief structure concerning hierarchies in society, reflected in our temporal practices. When can a student reach a professor and who waits for whom? Who gets their religious holy days off work? Calendars support or deny group practices and establish hierarchies of importance and belonging. We can see the hierarchical arrangement of professions in how it is more natural to pose how a student reaches a professor than vice versa. Certainly, weekends are not the best time to access a faculty member. The rhythm of the week and weekend carries with it related expectations around access, which are unequally distributed across groups. Weekends are couples' time, when single people often find themselves alone.

Position and power matter not only within groups, but among groups. Groups with more power, such as Western colonizers, are able to impose a moral temporality over groups such as the Inuit, but not without resistance. Calendars and religion have a long, interconnected history. In Canada, for example, you get Christmas off whether you are celebrating or not. Whether or not you have a Muslim or Jewish holy day off work depends on the generosity of your employer and local employment laws. Even if you get the day off, few others have that day off, and you may be held responsible for catching up when you return to work or school. This example demonstrates a hierarchy of religions related to calendrical practices.

There is a strong moral component to time, particularly in regard to time management. How many of us have scoffed at the friend who is always late? For marginalized groups, however, such as indigenous groups, lateness can be met with more than an eye roll; their behavior may be interpreted through a lens of historical judgment and stereotypes. Their lateness may be labeled laziness or a lack of professionalism. This moral interpretation reinforces prejudices around the group as a whole and applies a moral framework of temporality that falls like a net over people's actions, allowing those who fit through the gaps to receive eye rolls, while others are tangled in assumptions and judgments.

Temporal practices also include ideologies around being temporally embedded in cross-cutting social realms, such as work and home, and offer norms that place those realms into a particular hierarchy. Our responsibilities toward work often come first in practice, despite prevailing narratives about how nothing matters more than family. People draw on ideologies and norms that are tied to group temporal practices when managing conflict among and within social realms. Yet the social realms themselves are relatively newly defined, even in the Western context, emerging with the rise of industrialization and the fetishization of the nuclear family.

Calendrical arrangements impart, establish, and reify group boundaries as well as ideologies, accentuating social contrasts along both lines. While we may engage in talk of ideologies with pleasant conversation about theory on peaceful white pages inviting us to pontificate, the ideologies associated with temporal practices can create harsh time regimes that can be used as weapons, tools of colonization, or political instruments. Populations may have their time controlled to exclude them from dominant social processes (Melbin 1978).

Goffman (1959) takes a dramaturgical approach and studies behavior as performances across various scenes. The "front stage" is the public performance, the show. The "back stage" is where one relaxes the formality and publicly oriented performance, although one is always still performing. These regions are defined in relation to each other, as the back stage is often when and where an individual performs in direct contradiction to their own front stage performance, such as when a sales person goes to the staff room and complains about a customer.

Inuit perform political time work (Flaherty 2011) to create temporal front and back stages. During the temporal front stage, Inuit demonstrate that they are capable of Western time practices—that they are able to participate in the world at large. During the temporal back stage, Inuit practice "Inuit time." They adjust how they attend to time, along with their temporal norms and expectations. Creating this back stage allows Inuit to agentically involve themselves in their own temporal experiences and to perform resistance, decolonizing as much as possible their back stage times. In this way, they emphatically state, "I am not a member of your group." They make it apparent that they do not ascribe to Western hierarchies of work and power. They exercise their own temporal morality. Inuit time provides the temporal place to practice and enact Inuit ideologies, in spite of attempts to erode Inuit culture. Pierre Bourdieu (1977) argues that doors are thresholds across which worlds are reversed: public to private, home to community, and so on.

Bourdieu tantalizingly suggests that doors are not the only thresholds, however. Thresholds can be temporal as well as spatial. By creating a temporal threshold, Arviammiut have constructed a barrier, a floodgate, with which they agentically close the door to as much of Western culture as possible.

FRONT STAGE: WORKIN' NINE TO FIVE

While time work is a generic social process (Prus 1987), the experience of time is socially mediated—we learn how to experience time from our mnemonic communities (Zerubavel 1997). The experience of time, therefore, falls into the epistemological realm. Inuit experience the implementation of rational Western time, and especially nine-to-five jobs, as an institutional assault (Goehring and Stager 1991). While time and space are deeply interwoven, Coulthard (2010) finds that indigenous people's experience privileged moving through space, while Western cultural paradigms privilege moving through time. A time regime that forces Inuit attention to be on temporal, rather than spatial, elements of social experience profoundly undercuts traditional ways of being and knowing (Goehring and Stager 1991; Stern 2003). The collective memory of the community is pushed beyond the historical horizon (van den Scott 2017a). The past is transformed, as an artifact interpreted through the present (Flaherty and Fine 2001). Thus, colonizing regimes affect perceptions of time and have implications for memory over and above establishing temporal delineations of group membership and imposing ideological frameworks.

In the late 1950s and early 1960s, the Canadian government resettled nomadic Inuit of the area into the hamlet of Arviat, Nunavut. As part of the colonization process, they introduced a time regime that included a new annual and monthly calendar, the seven-day week, the concept of working from nine-to-five (Stern 2005), clocks (van den Scott 2017b), and the redefinition of work and home as two temporal and spatially segregated realms—and thus ideologically segregated (Engel-Frisch 1943). Stern (2003: 74) points out that Inuit of Holman, much like those of Arviat, superficially accepted "town-based temporal rhythms," which include the standard full-time workday as the norm.

Evelyn, an Elder who lived nomadically on the land until her early adulthood, has experienced the full transition into community life. Here, her translator relays Evelyn's account:

When they were out on the land, they always had something to do, always, productive. Being productive. There was no noon hour, like, lunch hour, there were no coffee breaks, nothing. . . . She's saying she was, she was living like this, from nothing, living off the land, and now working at the school. . . . When she started, like, when she was on the land, she didn't even know that there, other things would have existed. . . . She's seen two, Inuit way and *Qablunaaq* [Western] way. Her parents were very able people. Very able. And they helped her when she was a child and now she, because they're no longer around, she's now living in modern world. Modern today. *Ii.* [Yes.] She knows what she thinks is two worlds. [laughter] Two life. . . . She's lived in two worlds.[1]

Evelyn sees the encroaching Western practices as another world, although she is able to see herself as of both worlds at the same time. To her, the Western world is a world of work, located primarily in the work realm. The Inuit world of traditional practices is located primarily in the home realm (Stern 2003), in the off-work times. The nine-to-five workday stands out as definitive of the changes Evelyn has experienced.

The most salient aspect of the invasive time regime is the introduction of the nine-to-five workday. This workday is Western in nature. Control of normative temporal practices, such as work, is a central component of social control (Zerubavel 1977, 1981). Rational, mathematical time represents a key part of Western time (Adam 1995; Weber [1905] 1998; Zerubavel 1985). Despite the presence of other, less rationalized forms of time-reckoning, mathematical forms lead the charge under conditions of colonization as a dominant group seizes political control. Goehring and Stager (1991) describe the shift from nonlinear, unregulated time to rational, measured time as an institutional assault. In the past, environmental conditions shaped the rhythms of work for Inuit, rather than mathematically measured time (Moore 1963).

For Inuit, rational time has become symbolic of, and a synecdoche for, their entire relationship with their colonizers. Here is one example from my field notes (8 May 2012):

We also talk about poverty. . . . Oliver tells me about when he and his daughter were eating at a McDonald's [while traveling]. They see a man sitting outside with bags and a newspaper that he had picked up off the street. He says to his daughter "do you think he is really homeless?" She says "yeah, he is homeless." So they go out and he says to him, "sir, have you eaten today?" and he answers that he cannot even afford a cup of coffee. He says that he shook the man's hand and palmed him $20, so that none saw but he and his daughter, to spare the man's dignity. He talked at length about how shocking it was to him that people are just walking by walking by, looking and not helping, not stopping, not caring. Their boss is—and he taps his wrist to indicate the clock. He says over and over how he cannot understand it. Others in the room, including me, are nodding.

When Oliver taps his wrist, he links the Western value system with clock-time. Rational clock-time becomes a synecdoche for the Western paradigms that have swept through the North in the colonizing process.

The nine-to-five job enacts ideologies through its norms concerning hierarchies of groups (employed versus unemployed), a moral temporal framework (who is on time), and the creation of distinct realms of work and family that require prioritization at different times. The new temporal framework disrupts previous norms around achieving synchronicity (Lewis and Weigert 1981). Stern (2003) finds that, among Inuit, the nine-to-five construct disciplines local activities and discourages engaging in traditional activities. Thus, the oppressive time regime seeks to align Inuit practices with Western ones, undermining Inuit culture and ways of knowing and being through assimilation into temporal practices. Working the nine-to-five job severely restricts one's ability to find the time to engage in traditional activities. Thus, the nine-to-five workweek, in all its glory, becomes the ideal target for temporal resistance. The redefinition of home and work as separate realms allows for a superficial acceptance of the nine-to-five workweek by defining a temporal front and back stage.

BACK STAGE: PERFORMING NONMEMBERSHIP

Resistance can take many forms, and Inuit fight fire with fire—or rather temporal ideologies with temporal ideologies. They practice "time work" (Flaherty 2011) by agentically engaging with their temporal experience and with the community's delineation of temporal practices and norms. They work on time and on making time work for them. While Inuit are doing time work as part of their cultural identity, they also are performing Inuit identity in the face of (and at) Western time regimes in resistance to rational time. I will outline below how Inuit do this by practicing backwards time, using the nine-to-five workday against itself, and performing unreliability and loose time. In addition, Bingo becomes a tool in temporal practices. The use of Christian, or business, names at certain times, and Inuit names at other times reinforces front and back stages. For example, Jake is called Jake at work. When I see him at a drum dance, however, people are calling him T—, an Inuktitut name. He is called T— in social situations, in people's homes, and when participating in traditional activities. In essence, his name is Jake from nine to five, and T— outside of that.

Not keeping to a schedule, for those without jobs, is a way to aggressively perform Inuit time and to participate in the back stage time. Goehring and Stager (1991) examine rational time by looking at its introduction to the Inuit, and highlight the shift from what they call polychromatic time (P-time), which is nonlinear and unregulated, to monochromatic time (M-time), which is linear, rational, and measured. Since Arviammiut associate M-time with *Qablunaaq* [Western] ways of knowing and being, performing engagement with P-time becomes a way to showcase an informal, more Inuit, way of being. In addition to performing traditional skills, behaving in ways that are contra *Qablunaaq* practices expresses a reaction against the new temporal rhythms and the representation of power conveyed through the spatial ecology of Arviat.

Sleeping all day and being awake all night on backward time, while a marginalized practice, frequently occurs with the youth. As Stern (2003: 152) notes, citing Brody (1975), "Time weighs heavily on the young." Brody (1975) and Stern (2003) both refer to the meandering restlessness of the youth, Brody referring to the eastern Arctic, and Stern to Ulukhaktok to the west. While unemployed youth may practice backward time in many places, the sociohistorical context in Arviat is one of behavioral judgment of Inuit by Western adults with jobs in the community who adhere to the nine-to-five ideal.

Alice's daughter, Gertrude, in her early 20s and jobless, laughs when she tells me she is on "backwards time." Pamela Stern (2003) calls this being "upside-down" in her study of Holman, Northwest Territories (now called Ulukhaktok). Stern finds that the nine-to-five workweek functions as "time discipline," creating local time norms that marginalize being temporally backwards. Stern's (2003) analysis of temporal practices in Holman leads her to interpret strict adherence to the 12:00pm to 1:00pm lunch break, and the accompanying extremely regular rush to return to work by 1:00 pm, as evidence that people fear disapproval, as well as surveillance into their personal lives, which may include drugs and alcohol.

While Stern observes Inuit being on time when returning to work, I also find notable the prompt departure from work at noon and 5:00 p.m. Goehring and Stager (1991: 677) see the Inuit as having borne an institutional assault on polychromatic time (P-time), which, coupled with their belief in the acceptance of fate, has meant an attitude of "it can't be helped." Although the nine-to-five jobs cannot be helped, the "time discipline" (Stern 2003) incurred can be subversively taken to the extreme both as a form of resistance and a way to protect time for the sake of traditional practices, as I noted in my field notes:

> The community is pretty dedicated to the nine-to-five idea, using it to ensure that there are temporal boundaries considered valid in the South which limit the ability of Southern things to encroach on their time/lives. The few exceptions are water and sewage trucks, which do run after 5, but not all night, and

the grocery stores, which are open to about 7. Government workers, however, teachers, desk jobs, janitors, secretaries, everyone else vacate their post at 5 on the dot. They are free of a sense of pressing urgency when it comes to paperwork once 5 hits. That's it, they are done. They can be part way through an email and they will just stand and leave. An admirable quality and a clever use of the temporal construct suggested by the South as a way to give boundaries to Southern cultural encroachment. (Field notes, 17 May 2012)

Punctuality, then, establishes thresholds that separate Western front stage and Inuit back stage time, and establishes Western time as bounded. Stern (2003) notes that Holman residents, like Arviammiut, base their assessment of doing well at work more around time spent at work, rather than output. Time trumps output. By standing up and essentially walking out on their jobs exactly at noon and five, Arviammiut resist being completely subsumed by clock time.

Paradoxically, they are using clock time to resist M-time and protect (in rational time terms) a temporal space for the performance of P-time. This works to limit the influence of *Qablunaaq* ways of being, temporally creating Inuit space and time. While their homes still create a *Qablunaaq* space, it is more malleable in meaning than the work space. One may perform Inuitness at one's home walls—walls as symbolic of Western eyes (van den Scott 2015). At work, however, performances of Inuitness are dramatically curtailed during the nine-to-five workday. Inuit practice P-time, therefore, either by leaving work mid-email when the bell tolls five, or, for the unemployed, by living in "upside-down" time (Stern 2003). These forms of resistance enable them to negotiate temporal structures and practice Inuit time.

Back stage temporal practices successfully create periods of time that protect Inuit traditionality in particular ways from Western traditions. These practices, however, can be interpreted as representing unreliability by Western workers who have been imported to the North for managerial positions; here is one example from my field notes (14 May 2012): "Next we go to the Elders' Centre. . . . They are full at 8 residents. [The manager] said that they need to hire many support staff because many don't show up reliably, especially if it is bingo night or something." I had similar informal conversations with school principals regarding Inuit teachers. Lateness or absence, however, is not accidental. It is agentic time work. During hunting season, many prioritize hunting over their jobs. Occasionally, children will be withdrawn from school for time on the land. Allison tells me about the importance of time on the land for learning Inuit ways of knowing and being: "That's why, since—what?—April, they've been not going to school every day 'cause we're back here and forth. Just to know how it is. Illa, I want them to learn their education, but part of my other thing is how to be out in the land" (Allison's interview).

Many families maintain cabins on the land, often close to town, within a half-hour ATV (all-terrain vehicle) trip. The land is the locus of Inuit knowledge and culture (Takano 2005). Time spent on the land, therefore, represents time spent learning and expressing Inuit culture, which becomes even more important when living in *Qablunaaq* spaces. Sandra works from nine to five, but on weekends she spends all her time at her cabin once the weather warms. Many, like Gemma and Lucia, will zoom out to their cabins immediately after work and stay for hours in the long days of summer.

Lateness and absence perform "loose time" (van den Scott 2017b), a loose adherence to schedules, such as having no specific bedtime for children or being late or absent for a scheduled meeting. Sometimes this is the only way that Arviammiut can control their participation in Western practices. The Inuit's consent practices and cultural stance toward making mistakes make it difficult for them to say no in ways that make sense from the perspective of Western consent models (Damas 2002; van den Scott 2017b). I note an instance of this problem in my field notes:

> I am about to leave when Emily calls to say she is ready to be interviewed. I head over. I am relieved and impressed. When she had not been home the first few times she said she would be, I assumed she was dodging me. Several who have not been able to say no to being interviewed get out of it by making scheduling virtually impossible, despite my flexibility of being free anytime at all. One did say flat out that she was busy all week. I am fine with this because I know that it is hard to say no here and it is important for them to have these ways to get out of something they don't want to do. After I try a couple of times to set up an interview, I usually give up, not because I am not tenacious, but because I know how hard it is to say no for them and I need to respect that this might be their way of communicating that (or at least effectively getting out of it). I am glad Emily genuinely had other things come up and I head over there. (Field notes, 9 June 2012)

Those who, unlike Emily, wanted to be nice to me but not be interviewed could perform time work to alter their experience and flow of the day, ensuring avoidance or lateness for an interview. What looks like unreliability to Western eyes is actually agentic time work, a profound form of resistance.

Loose time extends into temporal practices expected of children: "[The mother] does not feel the need to wrangle her child into a set sleeping pattern, or eating pattern, which takes away the idea of sleepless nights. [The child] can sleep anytime. The idea of worrying when your child does not eat or sleep [evaporates]. The constant battles over bedtimes and foods one may or may not like are non-existent" (Field notes, 9 June 2012). This mother, as is the norm, carries her infant child in her *amoutik*. This is a form of women's traditional clothing and has a hood structure in which to carry a child through its toddler years. The child can sleep in the hood against the mother's back, but the *amoutik* can also be turned forward for breastfeeding. The child can wake and sleep in the hood according to her or his needs. When visiting, the *amoutik* can be folded to provide a soft sleeping space for the child, as well.

While loose time fits with traditional Inuit time, it can present challenges to adaptation to the Western temporal regime:

> In terms of sleeping, [the toddler] has no bedtime. He falls asleep when he is tired. This works very well and indeed he does not continue to push and get overtired, but just falls asleep when he needs to. Sleep has not become a fight for him. At the same time, I can see how challenging the school regime will be for him, as for others here. To be there at a specific time means keeping a sleeping schedule, which he does not and his family only partly does. They sleep eventually at night, but mostly crash when they are tired, whatever time of day. (Field notes, 17 May 2012)

Performing Inuit time undermines Western ideologies, but it can also make it difficult for children to figure out their own relationships to work and school mentalities. I observed a class difference: those of higher social economic status tended to perform less resistance and consequently their children were more able to cope with the nine-to-five temporal framework. There are significant economic and social rewards for adaptation to the Western temporal regime. Families with whom Western traders, in the early to mid 1900s, initially worked, and who served as guides for traders, have often had a longer exposure to Western frameworks. They find themselves better placed today, and their lessened resistance can facilitate socioeconomic adaptation to the Western temporal regime. This is not always desirable: if they embrace all facets of the Western regime, they risk being seen as having turned their backs on the community in some way.

Bingo as Tool

Bingo is an anomaly in terms of punctuality and Inuit time. Arriving and leaving work punctually is a form of work-to-rule, protecting 5:00 p.m. until 9:00 a.m. the following day, along with weekends, for practicing Inuit time. Lateness for social arrangements performs Inuit time. Bingo is popular in the community, however. Games are sometimes organized at the community hall, but radio Bingo is more frequent. At times during my research, there were up to three evenings of Bingo a week on the radio, plus once a week at the hall. Groups, especially women, get together and play—silent during the rounds, socializing before, after, and during breaks in the game.

Arviammiut tend to be on time when it comes to Bingo. Radio Bingo came up frequently when I tried to make arrangements to interview someone. Often, it turned out to be a Bingo night and neither of us had realized this until I showed up. In other instances, the interview would be shaped around Bingo, such as this example in my field notes (9 June 2012): "As we get started, the 50/50 Bingo starts, for which she has two cards. She asks if I want to daub one and hands it to me. We do the 50/50 and hold off on the interview for those 10 minutes or so and then get started." Bingo could also cut an interview short. Melanie had been on the land and, having forgotten about our interview, only came back into town to play Bingo. We began an interview before Bingo started. Toward the end, she started looking at the clock, and I was compelled to say, "Last one, I know it's getting close [to Bingo]." When visiting, I would either be invited to daub as well, or I would be left to my own devices, sipping tea and hanging out with the kids while the women hunkered down around the radio and played.

Bingo can be contentious within the community. Occasionally there is a push within the community to turn away from Bingo, as this form of gambling has become addictive for many. At one point, I attended a summer-long women's sewing group whose statement of purpose was to offer an alternative activity on Bingo nights. Occasionally someone posts on Facebook urging people not to spend their money on Bingo (Field notes, 3 June 2012). Some, like Evelyn and Emma, play alone, but most play with family and friends, such as Deborah, who has a regular group of six who get together, and Abigail's sister, whose friends come over to play.

Western managers who cope with extreme punctuality, such as school principals, expressed to me frustration concerning employees who would show up at 9:00 a.m. when the bell rang, rather than being ready to work (or, in the case of teachers, in their classrooms ready to teach) when the bell rang. They would comment on the ability of these same employees to always be on time for Bingo. Arviammiut are not unaware of these criticisms. Indeed, they may foster them. Bingo becomes a tool used to demonstrate an ability to be early or on time outside of the workday, but on Inuit terms. It also acts as a tool to push back unwanted activities, particularly extracurricular activities, which may be expected at work. Other things must shape themselves around the timing of Bingo.

Names

Names are a way in which Inuit enact behaviors that distinguish between a temporal front stage and back stage. Names signal formality and participation in rational, bureaucratic temporalities and ideologies. Christian names accompanied colonization as a feature of Western bureaucratic practices. In an act of bureaucratic violence (R. Collins 1974), the Canadian government assigned Inuit identifying numbers, which were stamped—along with a crown and the words "Eskimo Identification Canada"—on leather discs for Inuit to wear around their necks or sew into clothing. The individual assigned numbers were preceded by either an "E" or a "W," noting a geography east or west of the settlement of Gjoa Haven. I would regularly hear people talking about these disc numbers in everyday conversation, such as when Abigail and Gerald got into a conversation about what each other's disc numbers were (Field notes, 21 August 2016). A group of Arviammiut, working in collaboration with researchers on Nanisiniq: Arviat History Project, exhibit the absurdity of this system by making a video of how one would try to board an airplane if discs were still in use (Nanisiniq 2010). Christian names sometimes accompanied disc numbers, also as a bureaucratic tool (van den Scott 2017a). Elizabeth reports to me her being denied medical care by the church until she took a Christian name.

Today, last names are hardly ever used. Many Arviammiut are known back stage, within the Inuit community, by their Inuktitut names. In business dealings or in dealings with *Qablunaaqs*, particularly during the nine-to-five workday, however, they use their Christian name, as was mentioned about Jake. At any formal events, such as weddings, their Christian name will be given first and their Inuktitut name given as a middle name. Taxes, bills, and paychecks all use an individual's Christian name. By invoking an extra layer of naming and enacting Inuktitut naming practices back stage, the Inuit further protect an informal culture among themselves and find a way to keep the formality of Western culture at arm's length without using the formality of Western culture to accomplish this task. In schools, government, and other business situations, Arviammiut insist on first names, asserting their belief in informality. By using their Christian names, however, they are still successfully creating barriers of access to their back stage and establishing, through lack of access, back stage time as private time (Zerubavel 1979b)—private *Inuit* time. It was deeply significant for my close friends, as well as the children from my after-school program, that I would learn and remember their Inuktitut names, and that people would often call me by my Inuktitut name, *Saimaniq*, especially the Elders.

SPACE AND TEMPORAL FRONT STAGE AND BACK STAGE

There is an obvious and salient spatial dichotomy of work and not work that aligns with front and back stage temporal practices. Temporal front and back stages, however, may or may not intersect with spatial front and back stages. In any case, the performance of informality within the *Qablunaaq* spaces of the hamlet signals Inuit ideologies.

Within their houses, which are imposed Western spaces, Inuit perform Inuit identity to their walls, pushing back against the Western eyes they feel upon them (van den Scott 2015). They do this in how they decorate their walls (van den Scott 2016), consume their food, and practice everyday life. The most dramatic example I saw was in Lily's home, where the family had actually gathered stones from where their family used to roam nomadically, and carved traditional scenes into their wall, shellacking the stones in place to form a mosaic of these scenes. Others referred to Lily's wall so much that she became her own theme in my analysis. In this sense, homes are not fully back stage spaces. These houses are part of the rationalization of time and space introduced by Western cultural paradigms. As such, they support the movement toward more rational temporal constructs as binding on the time of the Inuit. When Inuit negotiate their identity while walled off from the land in these new houses, informality is not only a strategy but it also permits the grafting of Inuit culture into an indoor *Qablunaaq* space. Their traditional culture certainly involves an openness and warmth with others, traits which are threatened by Western, rational formality. The strict temporal formality demanded by the state is contrary to what the Inuit view as appropriate behavior on the land or in their own spaces.

In public spaces, they cannot engage with their walls in the same way, as noted by Lauren in the following extract: "But, like, at, um, the school, like there's a picture of the queen and then there's another display for students' work, and then at the Church there's a cross, there's crosses." Under the gaze of these portraits and crosses, Inuit engage in out-of-time behavior through extreme punctuality, loose time, or backwards time, such as walking off the job at exactly 5:00 p.m., discussed above.

Some spaces commingle Western and Inuit ideologies. The community hall, for example, fluctuates among various uses. Sometimes it is set up as a court from nine to five, when judges and lawyers fly in and conduct proceedings for a few days. Sometimes the hall hosts wedding receptions. Other times, the hall hosts Bingo, dances, or community feasts. At the community hall, the nine-to-five ideology prevails. The temporal threshold is palpable as 5:00 p.m. ticks by and the space is rearranged for evening activities.

I attended court one day, during the workday. In the center of the large room, a long table had been set up for judges, translators, and other officials concerned with the courts. Facing that, folding chairs had been arranged to replicate as much as possible the spatial dynamics of a Western courtroom. Witnesses were called formally, and by their Christian names, to the witness stand. An aura of hushed urgency hung among those of us watching or those waiting to be called on, while the white officials seemed at ease in the space. I also happened to attend an evening event at the hall that weekend. Come 5:00 p.m., the chairs and tables are stored and rearranged to ring the room; the stage at the far end of the room is set to go, and a band plays square-dance music while a half-dozen groups twirl in the center of the room. I hear almost exclusively Inuktitut names now. Behaviors match whether it is *Qablunaaq* time or Inuit time, including the use of Christian or Inuktitut names. Inuit time stretches on into the flexible night hours, populating a time ghetto that is not dominated by the nine-to-five framework (Melbin 1978).

CONCLUSION

Arviat has seen many changes since it was first established by force mere decades ago. As part of these changes, the nine-to-five workday became dominant. Rational time carries with it the ideologies of encroaching Western cultural paradigms. As such, rational time and the colonizing time regime becomes a synecdoche for Western ways of knowing and being.

Inuit resist rational time and membership in Western systems by treating the nine-to-five workday as a temporal front stage, extending the new differentiation of the work and home realms. They maintain a temporal back stage reserved for "Inuit time" in a number of ways. Some without jobs work on "backwards time," where they sleep for most of the day and stay awake all night. Others with jobs use the nine-to-five mentality against itself, essentially working-to-rule by leaving the job promptly at 5:00 p.m. in order to protect time outside of the "regular" workday from rational-time ideologies. Occasionally, Inuit practice lateness or absenteeism as the performance of Inuit time in resistance to rational time. Some non-Inuit interpret this as unreliability, which the Inuit can then use agentically to maneuver through rational time. Additionally, they agentically use Bingo, particularly radio Bingo, and Inuktitut names to further enact temporal back stages.

On these occasions, after work and on weekends, Inuit aggressively practice "Inuit time" *at* the Western time regime in which they find themselves. As such, they decolonize time, as much as possible, by establishing a threshold between Inuit and Western time and their accompanying ideologies and cultural practices. Through processes of subversive and overt resistance, Arviammiut work to establish contemporary identities as *of*theworld, while not being consumed *by*theworld.

Lisa-Jo K. van den Scott
Assistant Professor, Department of Sociology
Memorial University of Newfoundland, Canada

NOTE

1. Although I did speak Inuktitut, when interviewing Elders I would bring a translator with me to make sure I got it right.

REFERENCES

Adam, Barbara. 1995. *Timewatch: The Social Analysis of Time.* Cambridge: Polity Press.
Beidelman, T. O. 1963. "Kaguru Time Reckoning: An Aspect of the Cosmology of an East African People." *Southwestern Journal of Anthropology* 19 (1): 9–20.
Bourdieu, Pierre. 1977. *Outline of a Theory of Practice.* Cambridge: Cambridge University Press.
Brody, Hugh. 1975. *The People's Land: Whites and the Eastern Arctic.* Harmondsworth, UK: Penguin Books Canada.
Collins, Randall. 1974. "Three Faces of Cruelty: Towards a Comparative Sociology of Violence." *Theory and Society* 1 (4): 415–40.
Coulthard, Glen Sean. 2010. "Place against Empire: Understanding Indigenous Anti-Colonialism." *Affinities* 4 (2): 79–83.
Damas, David. 2002. *Arctic Migrants/Arctic Villagers: The Transformation of Inuit Settlement in the Central Arctic.* Montreal: McGill-Queen's University Press.
Engel-Frisch, Gladys. 1943. "Some Neglected Temporal Aspects of Human Ecology." *Social Forces* 22 (1): 43–47.
Flaherty, Michael G. 2011. *The Textures of Time: Agency and Temporal Experience.* Philadelphia: Temple University Press.
Flaherty, Michael G., and Gary Alan Fine. 2001. "Present, Past, and Future: Conjugating George Herbert Mead's Perspective on Time." *Time & Society* 10 (2/3): 147–61.
Goehring, Brian, and John K. Stager. 1991. "The Intrusion of Industrial Time and Space into the Inuit Lifeworld." *Environment and Behavior* 23 (6): 666–79.
Goffman, Erving. 1959. *The Presentation of Self in Everyday Life.* New York: Anchor Books.

Lewis, J. David, and Andrew J. Weigert. 1981. "The Structures and Meanings of Social Time." *Social Forces* 60 (2): 432–62.

Melbin, Murray. 1978. "Night as Frontier." *American Sociological Review* 43 (1): 3–22.

Moore, Wilbert E. 1963. "The Temporal Structure of Organizations." In *Sociological Theory, Values, and Sociocultural Change*, edited by Edward A. Tiryakian, 161–69. New York: Free Press of Glencoe.

Nanisiniq. 2010. "They Don't Accept E-Disks for Flights!?!" YouTube video, 13 August, 1:37. https://www.youtube.com/watch?v=u9_qmGQpk80.

Prus, Robert. 1987. "Generic Social Processes: Maximizing Conceptual Development in Ethnographic Research." *Journal of Contemporary Ethnography* 16: 250–93.

Stern, Pamela. 2003. "Upside-Down and Backwards: Time Discipline in a Canadian Inuit Town." *Anthropologica* 45 (1): 147–61.

———. 2005. "Wage Labor, Housing Policy, and the Nucleation of Inuit Households." *Arctic Anthropology* 42 (2): 66–81.

Takano, Takako. 2005. "Connections with the Land: Land Skills Courses in Igloolik, Nunavut." *Ethnography* 6 (4): 463–86.

Thomas, D. K., and Charles Thomas Thompson. 1972. *Eskimo Housing as Planned Culture Change*. Ottawa: Northern Science Research Group, Department of Indian Affairs and Northern Development.

van den Scott, Lisa-Jo K. 2015. "Geographies of Knowledge and Identity: Everyday Lived Experience and Features of the Home, Community, and Land, in a Post-Nomadic Arctic Hamlet." PhD dissertation, Northwestern University, Ann Arbor.

———. 2016. "Mundane Technology in Non-Western Contexts: Wall-as-Tool." In *Sociology of Home: Belonging, Community and Place in the Canadian Context*, edited by Laura Suski, Joey Moore, and Gillian Anderson, 33–53. Canadian Scholars Press International.

———. 2017a. "Collective Memory and Social Restructuring in the Case of Traditional Inuit Shamanism." *Symbolic Interaction* 40 (1): 83–100.

———. 2017b. "Time to Defy: The Use of Temporal Spaces to Enact Resistance." *Studies in Symbolic Interaction* 48: 137–55.

Vannini, Phillip. 2011. "Constellations of Ferry (Im)mobility: Islandness as the Performance and Politics of Insulation and Isolation." *Cultural Geographies* 18 (2): 249–71.

Weber, Max. (1905) 1998. *The Protestant Ethic and the Spirit of Capitalism*. Los Angeles: Roxbury Pub.

Zerubavel, Eviatar. 1977. "The French Republican Calendar: A Case Study in the Sociology of Time." *American Sociological Review* 42 (6): 868–77.

———. 1979a. *Patterns of Time in Hospital Life: A Sociological Perspective*. Chicago: University of Chicago Press.

———. 1979b. "Private Time and Public Time: The Temporal Structure of Social Accessibility and Professional Commitments." *Social Forces* 58 (1): 38–58.

———. 1981. *Hidden Rhythms: Schedules and Calendars in Social Life*. Chicago: University of Chicago Press.

———. 1982. "Easter and Passover: On Calendars and Group Identity." *American Sociological Review* 47 (2): 284–89.

———. 1985. *The Seven Day Circle: The History and Meaning of the Week.* New York: Free Press.

———. 1997. *Social Mindscapes.* Cambridge, MA: Harvard University Press.

Part IV

Spirituality and Atheism
as Temporal Agency

Chapter 6

Se Deus Quiser

Catholicism as Time Work among the Xukuru of Pernambuco

Clarissa Martins Lima

Can practicing Catholicism be thought of as a form of time work? Is it a way of interfering in a particular experience of the present, populated by ancestors and saints and pregnant with the forthcoming? In the following, I will look at these fundamental questions through the prism of a specific ethnographic case, which is the Catholicism enacted by the residents of Vila de Cimbres, an indigenous village of the Xukuru do Ororubá ethnic group located in Pernambuco, northeastern Brazil. I have been doing ethnographic fieldwork in Vila de Cimbres for the last ten years (Lima 2013, 2017; Lima and Vander Velden 2018), but never with an explicit interest in time. What follows here is thus a reflection, in retrospect, upon aspects of life in the village through the notion of time work as formulated by Michael Flaherty (2011). One could call this an experiment, as explorative and provisional as it may necessarily be. I will argue that the inhabitants of the village work upon time through the agency of a third party, namely God.

As in any other society, time assumes a number of different forms in the Vila. People have to get up in the morning and go to work at specific times, whether it is to work on the gardens, at home, or in some salaried job. One must also be ready to send the children to school before the gates close. Sometimes people have to catch a bus or a lift to the nearby town, Pesqueira, to go to the market square, get paid, or, most of the time, both: payday winds up being the day many people spend shopping. Harvest occurs when the corn is ripe—*embonecado* (stuffed), they say—the beans are *bonito* (pretty), the tomatoes have become red, and so on. Kids are baptized; young people receive first communion in the church; and those who have passed away are commemorated at specific points in time (a week and then one year after death, when the dead are called deceased). Annually, people celebrate at midnight on 24 June–St. John's Day–when the ancestors arrive in the village to dance with their descendants. But it is also possible to find the ancestors every Sunday, when they are called in a ritual. And the most awaited day for everyone is certainly 2 July, the Nossa Senhora das Montanhas Day, the day of the patron saint of the village and the mother of the Xukuru. On that day, the saint, who lies all year round high on an altar inside the church, walks in procession alongside the devotees, who can approach and touch her.

Different times, therefore, combine what we could call traditional and modern, sacred and profane, in the same space, affecting the lives of the same set of people. But above all this time reckoning resides God. It is customary to say "se Deus quiser" (God willing) whenever statements about the future are voiced, just as it is common to say, concerning past or present happenings, "porque Deus quis" (because God wanted). Although similar interjections are common in many social settings around the world (an English speaker may say "God willing," and an Arab speaker "'In shā' Allāh"), I shall argue that at least here, in Vila de Cimbres, these expressions are more than just an interjection. In my understanding of life in the village, to say "porque Deus quis" or "se Deus quiser" is an expression of a profound and all-inclusive trust in God's intervention, an intervention that believers may, through their adherence to Catholicism, affect.

To present my argument, I must start with the Xukuru understanding of God. God is one, people claim all the time in the village. Without intending to deny this statement, I will show how, in spite of the Xukuru's profession of God's unity, the way their conception of God is manifested in everyday life is not always the same. Modulations in imagery cause God to sometimes appear as an immanent being, and other times as transcendent. It is from these modulations that I show how conceptions of God affect conceptions of time, and how adherence to Catholicism can be viewed as a form of time work, one which, through the relationship with God, implies the constant presence of a third party.

THE XUKURU

This chapter is based on ethnographic fieldwork in a Xukuru village located in the poor backlands of the Brazilian northeast. The Xukuru group has a long history of contact with the non-indigenous population. Since the beginning of Brazilian colonization, their land has been invaded by colonists and catechists, and they gradually lost ownership of their territory. They also were not permitted to use their native language or practice their rituals. Finally, the policy at that time encouraged interethnic marriages in order to dilute (and erase) the Xukuru population by integrating them into what at that time constituted the Brazilian people. As a result, the Xukuru went to work for farmers who occupied their land, and they resided in small portions of their territory, speaking exclusively Portuguese. They converted to Catholicism and lost most of the traits that differentiate the indigenous from the non-indigenous population (cf. Hohenthal 1954; Neves 2005; Silva 2008; Souza 1998, for the Xukuru case; for indigenous peoples in Brazil in general, see Carneiro da Cunha 1992).

But it must be made clear that this is the official version of history, formulated from the available documentation on the period, produced mostly by the missionaries and settlers themselves. It was only in the 1990s that the Xukuru began to be heard and could tell their own version of history, with milestones that do not match those of official historiography. Despite the memory of violence they suffered, the Xukuru claim that they never lost their ethnic identity because they were always there, fighting for their land. As it turned out, their struggle was simply ignored by the Brazilian authorities. And, directly relevant to my argument, there is no memory of conversion to Christianity among the Xukuru, as in other groups (Robbins 2003, 2004; Wright and Vilaça 2009). From the Xukuru's point of view, as we shall see, they have always been Catholics—which, according to their accounts, is compatible with practices that could be considered traditional.

It was also in the 1990s that, after a series of internal and external mobilizations, the Xukuru managed to retake their territory. Currently, they inhabit an area spanning just over twenty-seven thousand hectares, which encompasses the group's twenty-four villages, where approximately ten thousand people live. Each of the group's villages has specific characteristics, whether in terms of population, area, the environment, or climate conditions. Despite these differences, the region is very dry, complicating the economic survival of the group, which is based on agriculture. Furthermore, all the inhabitants of the Xukuru's land are recognized as Xukuru for having been *nascido* and *se criado*[1] (born and raised) in the land of Nossa Senhora das Montanhas (Our Lady of the Mountains), the patron saint of the region. For this reason, they are called her *filhos* (children) and the relatives of the ancestors that found her.

Even today, Nossa Senhora das Montanhas remains in the same place where her image was found, in Vila de Cimbres. It is also in this village that her church is located. According to Xukuru legends, it was built by their *antepassados* (ancestors) so that she could live there, since she refused to leave her place of origin. Also according to their narratives, it was as a response to this act that Nossa Senhora granted the Xukuru the right to reside on their land and made them her *filhos*, promising them special attention. It is important to note that there is no equivalence between this legend and historical data—a point which, as we shall see, has fundamental implications for the argument developed throughout this chapter, as I have mentioned above. Specifically, in regard to the topic of religion, the relationship with Nossa Senhora das Montanhas is considered to have been established prior to the group's encounter with non-indigenous society. It is the encounter between Nossa Senhora das Montanhas and the *antepassados* that establishes and defines what it is to be Xukuru and at the same time distinguishes this group from the rest of humanity. In this sense, Catholicism is considered to predate the encounter with non-indigenous society. According to the Xukuru, all of mankind is born Catholic, since this belief system is the fruit of divine intervention. In other words, human beings are the sons and daughters of God, and thus Catholic. But only the Xukuru are the children of Nossa Senhora das Montanhas, and she constitutes their particular medium through which a connection to divine intervention is established.

VILA DE CIMBRES AND TIME

From any one of the winding roads that reach Vila de Cimbres, amid the Caatinga scrublands and potholed roads, the church of Nossa Senhora das Montanhas soon looms large in the landscape. It is also visible from each of the homes of the nearly one thousand people who reside in the village. It is located on a large square, which on most days is inhabited by pigs, a few cars, and lovely children who run in their small flip-flops as if blown along by the wind. Couples take advantage of the darker corners when night falls. Young people congregate to talk there and occasionally to drink. Some people, when passing through the village, seek refuge from the exhausting noonday heat that rules the region in the shadows cast by the church. In the late afternoon, a number of village residents can be found in front of the church, since this place has the best cell phone signal. In short, daily life in Vila de Cimbres takes place under the eyes of Nossa Senhora.

But on 2 July, the feast day of Nossa Senhora das Montanhas, the square is completely different, and what happens on this day imitates what used to be done by the *antepassados* and by the *caboclos velhos* (old *caboclos*, persons of mixed indigenous Brazilian and European ancestry). On the day commemorating Nossa Senhora das Montanhas, the divisions of time that regulate everyday life in the village are suspended. Residents of all the Xukuru villages crowd into Vila de Cimbres and eagerly wait for Nossa Senhora das Montanhas to be brought out. A bonfire made from logs contributed by parishioners is lit in her honor, as a way for the people to get rid of their sins. The *antepassados* are invited to participate in the festival through songs meant to attract them to the living. Everyone who participates in the celebration wears their best clothes and prepares food for the numerous relatives who come to the event. In fact, the feast day of Nossa Senhora das Montanhas is the most anticipated of the year; everyone is excited to find out what finery Nossa Senhora will be dressed in or whether the event will draw even more participants.

But it is not just on her feast day that Nossa Senhora das Montanhas is present in the village. It is not necessary to go into the church to ask for her protection, although some people suffering from more serious misfortunes may ask for the church to be opened so that they can speak with her. People may speak with her when passing by, or just point to the church from their homes (sometimes by simply glancing in that direction) when referring to her or wishing to make a request. In general, Nossa Senhora and the church blend and become one. Moreover, as a background for social life in the village, they represent the continuity behind the divided and punctuated everyday time.

However, even though the Xukuru's relationship with Nossa Senhora das Montanhas is crucial to understanding what they define as being a good Catholic, their definition does not end with her veneration. Even more encompassing than references to Nossa Senhora are references to God, who is present in the speech of the residents of Vila de Cimbres. As the Xukuru say, God first, and then she, the mighty mother. Most, if not all, houses in the village are decorated with plaques and images containing phrases that invariably refer to the presence of God and to the village residents' devotion to him. Images of the Holy Spirit are also widespread, along with many saints. On the one hand, these saints are responsible for the individual trajectories of the village residents, since each spirit is considered responsible for one aspect of the Xukuru universe. On the other hand, as happens in other Catholic areas, the saints connect each resident to God (Brown 1981; Mayblin 2010; Sáez 2009). Exceptions represented by the few evangelicals who live in the village corroborate this point. Of these residents, the Catholics ask, "What kind of person is this, who doesn't have a saint in their house?" In this sense, the saints not only connect people to God, but also are part of how an image of the residents of a particular home is constructed for the other residents in the village. Catholics are seen as good people (see also Mayblin 2010).

Besides the phrases related to God, and the images of saints that show a relationship between the residents and God, a range of activities (from the habitual to the extraordinary) are tied to God's will. From the *até amanhã* (until tomorrow) prayer said every night before a family goes to sleep to a sick person's desire to recover, from planning a simple trip out to the fields the next day to a trip with tickets already purchased, it is up to God to decide and up to God to allow what will happen. The inhabitants of the village always begin or end their sentences with *se Deus quiser* (God willing). This is not just using a simple mode of expression. From their point of view, God not only created but also runs the world. Whether something happened or did not happen is an expression of God's will; this also applies to what will or will not happen. God is responsible for the past; God is responsible for the future. This way of understanding the world, with time as the medium of God, not of human beings, seems essential to understanding the various times that are part of everyday life among the residents of Vila de Cimbres. If there is a right time to go to school, to pay bills, to go to the doctor, which all involve a punctuality that people need to respect (particularly because some of these tasks are connected to the Brazilian government's system of income distribution), ultimately it is God who says whether these deadlines will be respected or not. In other words, these bureaucratic times (so to speak) are subjected to divine will: "Tomorrow I will go to school, God willing"; "Whether I get there on time, it is up to God." Phrases like this fill my field notebook.

This is also true for the seasons, which divide the year into winter, which means rain, and summer, the time of drought. This annual repetition marks the climate and the landscape of the region, and people generally talk about it as an annual repetition of divine will. Some years the summer is dry; in others, rain continues to fall even well into summer. "Who can understand this crazy weather?" many ask, without failing to add, "But God knows" or "It was because God wanted and we should respect." There is a right time for planting and a right time to harvest, which is not the same for all the cultivated crops (Araújo 2011). But it is also God who is ultimately responsible for a good crop and a good harvest. Likewise, there is a right time to be born. I often accompanied women who wanted to get pregnant, and when they told of their desire to have children, they added, "But it is God who knows," or if it was taking a long time for them to get pregnant, they said, "It's not yet God's time." Women who were already pregnant even told me, "The doctor scheduled the Cesarean for [this day], but the child will be born on the day that God allows it, on the day that he scheduled." Finally, as a last example (although I could provide many more), there is a right time to die. According to the inhabitants of Vila de Cimbres, everyone is born with a *destino* (destiny) mapped out by God, which includes their day of death. Therefore, when someone dies, it is said that that person's "time has come."[2]

Each one of these occurrences has its own logic, but they all have one thing in common: all of these events are decided by God. Still, this is a divine sovereignty where space for human activity is also allowed. In fact, as we shall see below, the way in which these times operate are considered a divine response to worldly actions, for better or for worse. It is this dual existence that governs time in Vila de Cimbres, combining transcendence and immanence. In the following, I will show how this dynamic operates in notions of the past, the present, and the future, getting us closer to an understanding of how a particular kind of time work can unfold in the village.

GOD AND TIME

One day, talking to a friend in the village about my research, I asked her if she could describe to me how the world was created. This question was generally received with some amusement by the villagers: "Do not you know? It was God who did"—many simply said, surprised by my question. Others, however, took the time to tell me a story with details that in every way resembles the response my friend gave me that day:

> God made the world in three days. And the man came into the world, you know, and could not do what He did. The science of God is greater. Of every species that God made, he left two for procreation. The big bang was God who created it. Everything that exists in the world is the creation of God. No one is capable of generating a new life on Earth. . . . The world was made through God. He gave himself completely, not one part. We, who live in the world, who do not believe him. All that is alive is of God, it was he who created it.

This statement will be my starting point for exploring the ways God is manifest in Village de Cimbres and his connection with time. From this friend's speech, which brings together in a singular way ideas commonly conveyed by the villagers, I isolate some fundamental points that reveal divine modulations. It must be borne in mind that, ultimately, from the Xukuru standpoint, *God is one.* However, when manifested in different forms, God ends up differing from itself, and I say this without implying a contradiction from the point of view of the villagers.

First, her statement says that God made the world, the whole world: "Everything that exists . . . is the creation of God." She refers to an absolute past, the time of creation; before God, nothing existed. God takes on a very precise image here: a transcendental entity in the Kantian sense of that term, which, through its powers, gives rise to the world, but also, for what interests us here, gives rise to time. In this sense, time has its condition of existence in God. Furthermore, my friend's speech establishes an important difference: in speaking of creation, she also speaks of humans and their inability to reproduce the divine deed. This separation between what is God's work and what is the result of human action is important, as we will see later.

Then, when she affirms that "no one [other than God] is capable of generating a new life on earth," or when she says that "everything that is alive is from God, it is He who created it," the divine creation appears limited. God is no longer responsible for creating all that exists—and the very possibility of human action already implies this—but for creating a specific domain of the world: everything that is alive. The villagers understand "everything that is alive" as everything that is inhabited by a soul or similar principles: people, certainly, but also animals, rivers, rocks, earth, and climatic events such as wind or rain. God is no longer just the past, but also the present, since everything that is born has in it God's condition of existence. And if God is the condition for a past to exist, God is also the condition of the present: everything that is of God comes with a traced destiny. The hour of birth and death, as I have already mentioned, but also when one begins to walk, to speak, to date, to work, or to marry, in the specific case of human existence. All of these things occur according to the will of God, at the hour that God marked.

But there is another aspect of God in the formulation expressed by my friend that should be noted, as well. In spite of the importance of recognizing human action, in general, when people affirm that something is of God, what is implied is another force: the devil. Within this framework, the divine creation appears limited to everything that is alive that is good in this world. But there are also bad things or, as the villagers say, things that have no future (a formulation that also involves time, as I will argue below). And all these things are described as what the devil left in the world in the past, and, like the divine creation, are perpetuated in the present.

In addition, my friend says that in making the world, God "gave himself completely." In giving himself, God is in the world and corresponds to the immaterial dimension that is present in everything created by God, past or present. This immaterial dimension is also considered the vital principle of beings: God made life, God is life. This immaterial dimension is, by definition, invisible to human eyes because of the difference in nature between God and the things of this world. Although human beings have this spiritual dimension in themselves, they are matter, which prevents them from fully accessing it. As I discuss elsewhere (Lima 2017), what is of God, or all that is immaterial, leaves traces, signs, which are subject to *curiar* (spying), but about which one should not make absolute or deterministic statements, precisely because it is part of a domain that transcends the human realm. In this other image, God is also in the present, but immanently. God is the mystery, the secret that is present in everything alive.

Finally, my friend criticizes those who are "in the world" and do not have faith in God, once again showing that there is space in the world for what is *not of God* and, conversely, for the divine judgment of worldly actions. The idea of destiny, therefore, is counterbalanced by this possibility of acting outside of God's plan. On the other hand, a transcendental image of divine existence is evoked. It is possible to deviate from the divine ways, but, as they say recurrently in the village, "no one can do more than God." The recurring example they gave me was the Titanic: "Did not they say that even God could not sink it? He went there and sank it, to show those who doubted Him." No one escapes the divine designs, even if they only materialize in the future. After all, this too belongs to God.

THE PRESENT WITH GOD

It should be remembered above anything else that, in Portuguese, time and weather are the same word (*tempo*). It is this dual meaning that I will use to talk about the present. After all, it does not seem a coincidence that the same word is used to address two things that only appear to be distinct. Many authors have already shown how time is an effect of the changes or differences across the seasons of the year (e.g., Evans-Pritchard 1978; Gell 1996; Munn 1992). But in the case of the Xukuru, this correspondence assumes another shape by connecting time, weather, God, and human activities. This use of one word for two seemingly different phenomena is not happenstance, as I shall argue, and looking further into this usage will help me show how time is lived (and worked upon) by the villagers.

In a dry area like the one inhabited by the Xukuru, periods of drought (such as the recent one in the region spanning seven years) are always challenging. Agriculture becomes nearly impossible, affecting families' food supplies and income. Cattle suffer from the lack of green pasture and many of the animals die, with severe impact on the local economy. People ration the small supply of water they can store and sometimes go many days without any water at all in their homes. Nonetheless, I have never heard a single complaint. "God knows what he is doing, and if he wants to send rain, he will," is the common explanation.

With this in mind, it is not strange that days when the sky is filled with heavy clouds, which are seen in other regions as *tempo feio* (ugly weather),

are described by the Xukuru as the most beautiful. Yet this admiration is almost always scolded, with someone saying "Take your eyes off it," or "Don't
put your eyes on it." Often people told me that the rain sent by God may
be diverted or undone by "human eyes." God is responsible for the rain,
but human eyes may impede it. Why does God, a being described as pure
benevolence, allow drought and take so long to send rain? How can human
eyes drive away what they ultimately desire the most and that which is the
result of divine agency? And how is this connected to the central issue of
this chapter, time?

In fact, the Xukuru conception of personhood (Mauss 2003) opens the
possibility that worldly things do not correspond to divine expectations, as
already mentioned. A person is considered a composite of *alma* (soul) and
matéria (matter), and deep within there is a directive that, if neglected, will
lead an individual away from God. While the *alma* is a naturally good aspect
of a person (since it is understood to be a part of God that dwells in every
human being), the *matéria* is understood to be what possesses a person's own
desires, which is contrary to the idea of a good person, and consequently
must be contained at all times.[3] Most of the time, these desires are related
to food and sex, and they are viewed as problematic by the Xukuru. They
represent sins of the flesh, which corrupt people and alienate them from the
model of divine existence, which is defined by the Xukuru as a necessarily
abstemious existence, and which is therefore the ideal of Catholic practices.

The desires of *matéria* have yet another characteristic manifestation:
human beings are *invejosa* (envious). This envy is precisely how the residents
of Vila de Cimbres explained to me the way *matéria* works. One woman told
me, "It's that thing, you go to someone's house and see something beautiful, you admire it and soon want it for yourself." Relatedly, there are the
numerous complaints I heard in the village that nobody can make a major
purchase in the city, whether of food or household goods, without all the
neighbors looking and wanting it for themselves. In other words, *matéria*
moves people, causing them to act in ways that are deemed inappropriate,
and this happens not only but most often through the *olhos* (eyes), unleash-
ing what the Xukuru call the *olhado* (the look, a concept widespread in the
world, as observed by Herzfeld 1981; Maloney 1976; Queiroz 1980).

The *olhado* is one of the main visible effects of carelessness with the *alma*
or with the *matéria*. The *olhos*, Xukuru people often told me, are an "expression of the soul." In this sense, they are simultaneously *alma* and *matéria*. For
this reason, the *matéria* must be contained and the *alma* must be cultivated
through a series of observances that are directly related to what the villagers
call Catholicism. The daily practice, however, is far from the ideal. People
often fail to attend mass, fail to observe specific diets, have inappropriate

behaviors (such as excessive desire for material goods and consumption of alcoholic beverages), and do not shy away from "calling a name," as the villagers refer to the use of profanity. This behavior is connected, ultimately, with everything that was "left by the Devil" in the world to divert human beings from divine destiny. Worldly existence is, from this perspective, sinful. Even when being a Catholic is strictly followed, this practice cannot override the sinful nature of matter; it remains indelible, although it can be mitigated.

Therefore, the complaints mentioned above concerning eyes placed on the clouds are not coincidental. The placing of one's eyes on something is a way of directing a corrupted and sinful mixture of soul and matter at this divine manifestation. In so doing, one may block what people often want the most: rain. For this reason, one must not look at the clouds that portend rain because this risks manifesting material desire, which has as its main feature the destruction of the object of desire. Rather, the Xukuru encourage using the expression "God bless" in reference to problematic circumstances. If the lack of rain is placed in the key of "it is because God wanted," its continuation is understood and accepted as God's will. In this scenario, what is at stake is recognition of a world in which all is accomplished by supernatural, not human, forces.

Rain is an important aspect of the weather for villagers, especially because of the region in which they live. The times for planting and harvesting, through the ripening of the crops, are programmed according to the rainy season, which corresponds to what the Xukuru call winter. However, in a society that depends on agriculture for survival, the importance of rain does not end in agricultural activity. The time of harvest after the rains is also when people schedule weddings, build houses, or take trips. In this sense, time and weather are coupled or fused, guiding to a large extent—though not exclusively—local temporal experience.

In the Xukuru world, God is responsible for rain. Just like all climatic phenomena, it was created by God in the past, and every current or future instance of precipitation only occurs by divine will. Here, we return to the image of the God-creator, responsible for making everything that is alive and good in the world. The word "time" is understood by villagers to mean the moment chosen by God. But the absence of rain is seen as a divine punishment that results from the way people have led their lives, increasingly prone to yield to the desires of material existence. It follows that the absence of rain has the same explanation: "because of God's will." When it rains, we are before the transcendental God, the primary condition for the manifestation of any phenomenon. When it does not rain, we confront the immanent God of judgment: "no one is higher than God," people affirm repeatedly, and one way God manifests power is justly punishing those who walk outside God's ways.

At the same time, the clouds, the quintessence of rain, are considered a "mystery" or a "secret," signs of the divine presence about to erupt in the world, and they represent an aspect of God itself. Moreover, just as one's destiny can be altered by associating oneself with what is "of the devil," so it is with this other divine manifestation when interpellated by human eyes. Again, what is at stake here is a twofold recognition. There is a God who not only acts in the present, but is also part of the present and can be repelled or turned away by "what the devil left in the world." That is why the expression "God bless" is used; it is another way of trying to mitigate the sinful nature of matter. This understanding does not imply breaking with the transcendental image of divine existence: "God knows what he is doing, and if he wants to send rain, he will." Once again, we arrive at the idea that no one but God can be the ultimate reason for what transpires in the future.

On the face of it, then, there seems to be little space for time work (Flaherty 2011) in the Xukuru world, since even in a scenario where time is composed of people and their actions, God is responsible for determining what will happen. Still, when we look more carefully at how the future appears in the Xukuru universe, a different line of interpretation is apparent. While the future is unknown for humans, because it belongs to God, it is not completely unpredictable. I will show that, by trying to predict and influence God's decisions, the Xukuru engage in time work.

SE DEUS QUISER: INDIRECT TIME WORK

As I said earlier, all action that refers to the future is finished with the affirmation "God willing" (*se Deus quiser*). Thus, people avoid predicting what is going to happen in the future. There will always be a dimension of uncertainty, as the future "belongs to God," but people can influence an outcome by demonstrating piety and humility. Another expression commonly used by the villagers describes this possibility: "All I do is with God in my thoughts." To the Xukuru, practicing Catholicism can be thought of as a form of temporal agency, as a way of interfering in or modifying a specific experience of time.

As previously noted, references to God and Catholic messages are not only evident in people's discourse; they are present in every house, in the church, in the village calendar. They also are present in various local practices. These forms of behavior take place within a specific temporality and morality: those dictated by Catholicism. They include attending mass, respecting the family, relating to the saints (as shown in the countless images of saints present in the houses of this village), and following the Word of God, as well as shunning material goods and doing charity. In concert, these practices produce a good person, a *Catholic* person. They constitute daily acts and attitudes that should be adhered to during one's life. To borrow a term from Foucault (2005), being a Catholic is part of an "aesthetic of existence" that moves the Xukuru universe. It is simultaneously an ideal (one reached only by saints, as they tell me) and a functional way of existing in the world. It is a practice that must be exercised every day and involves ethics, such as knowing how to suffer and how to accept things, as well as an aesthetic appreciation for beauty and everything else that comes from God. Ethics and aesthetics are inseparable concepts in the Xukuru world. If you do what is right, God will do what is good for you and will not punish you.

Each of these possibilities corresponds to the expression "Everything I do is with God in front" or "To catch up with God," another recurrent saying in the village. As they explained to me, everything that is done with God "has a future" (*tem fururo*). In contrast, everything that is done with the devil is described as "having no future" (*sem future*) or "what goes back" (*o que anda para trás*). It will be judged and undone by God. So, everything that is "of the devil" does not last because evil has no future. In this sense, the practices that comprise being Catholic correspond to an attempt to attenuate the sinful nature of matter by means of establishing a daily relationship with God, but they also describe a way of entering into affiliation with God.

It is not a matter of denying God's will concerning future events. What is at stake is just the opposite. They recognize that God is ultimately responsible for what is to come, and that trying to be a good person according to the laws of God (i.e., a Catholic person) is crucial: "Whoever takes God," they say, "by God is worthy" (*quem se pega com Deus, por Deus é valido*). Despite not being able to predict the future because it is beyond their control, the villagers understand that being a good person and following God's will is a practical way to have a future, a good future, even if its exact contents cannot be predetermined. Bake a cake, plow a patch, build a house, anticipate the weather, arrive in a punctual manner; the future of each of these actions is indeterminate. But when each of them is undertaken "with God up front," the possibility of success, even if conditioned by God's intermediary will, is enhanced.

According to Flaherty's (2011: 10) definition, the concept of time work refers to "intentional effort to customize one's own temporal experience." By time work, moreover, he refers to "intrapersonal and interpersonal effort directed toward provoking or preventing various temporal experiences. . . . Time work is the self-selected cause of one's temporal experience" (Flaherty

2011: 11). From this standpoint, time work concerns the possibility of controlling or manipulating one's own temporal experience. In the case of the Xukuru, this would entail the possibility of indirectly altering a time determined by God. It is a self-conscious or intentional endeavor to manipulate God's will through something that, in principle, is in no way subversive: Catholicism.

In other words, by attempting (they are not always successful) to follow the path of God every day through Catholicism, my Xukuru interlocutors are reaffirming one mode of temporal experience, which as Flaherty (2011) reminds us, is a form of time work. Flaherty (2011: 85–86) observes that *"choosing to conform* with normative expectations . . . is only a little less agentic than choosing to resist them. Conformity is a species of agency." What the Xukuru material shows us confirms Flaherty's argument, revealing another dimension of "conforming with normative expectations." My findings suggest that conforming to Catholic practices (and, ironically, accepting one's own lack of direct agency) can be an indirect way of manipulating time. In the specific case of the residents of Vila de Cimbres, they are attempting to control the future, God willing.

Clarissa Martins Lima
PhD, Department of Anthropology
Universidade Federal de São Carlos, Brazil

NOTES

I thank the anonymous reviewers of Berghahn Books. I also want to express my appreciation for the inspirational comments from participants of the Time Work seminar, which were very helpful in the revisions of this chapter. Finally, I am immensely grateful to the organizers for their diligent editorial assistance with earlier versions of this chapter. Their suggestions were extremely valuable. My research project is financed by FAPESP, and I am grateful for this support.
  1. The terms in italics are native expressions; they are followed by approximate translations in parentheses.
  2. But some deaths are said to be *fora do tempo* (off schedule), in other words, they take place outside of the time God planned. We will explore this issue later.
  3. However, this does not involve considering a radical rupture between soul and matter. The transformation of the soul into something bad has a visible effect for the residents of Vila de Cimbres in material excesses; a bad soul certainly cannot contain it. Similarly, a person who chooses a life marked by excesses is viewed as someone who is excessively concerned with worldly pleasures and certainly would not be able to care for the affairs of the soul, creating the op-

portunity to be a bad soul. In this way, *matéria* is not a simple habitat of the soul. There is a relationship of mutual influence between *matéria* and *alma*, and it is in this soul-material connection that people are produced. One can leave a mark on the other, and so both must be continually cared for.

REFERENCES

Araújo, André. 2011. "Una Mirada Agroecológica en la pisada Xukuru do Ororubá: un presente de possibilidades." Master's thesis, Universidad Internacional de Andalucía.

Brown, Peter. 1981. *The Cult of the Saints: Its Rise and Function in Latin Christianity.* Chicago: University of Chicago Press.

Carneiro da Cunha, Manuela. 1992. *História dos Índios no Brasil.* São Paulo: Cia das Letras.

Christensen, Dorthe Refslund, and Rane Willerslev, eds. 2013. *Taming Time, Timing Death: Social Technologies and Ritual.* Farnham: Ashgate.

Dalsgård, Anne Line, Martin Frederiksen, Susan Højlund, and Lotte Meinert, eds. 2014. *Ethnographies of Youth and Temporality: Time Objectified.* Philadelphia: Temple University Press.

Evans-Pritchard, Edward. 1978. *Os Nuer.* São Paulo: Perspectiva.

Flaherty, Michael G. 2011. *The Textures of Time: Agency and Temporal Experience.* Philadelphia: Temple University Press.

Foucault, Michel. 2005. "Une esthétique de l'existence." In *Dits et Écrits*, vol. 2, *1976–1988*, edited by Daniel Defert and François Ewald, 1549–54. France: Quarto Gallimard.

Gell, Alfred. 1996. *The Anthropology of Time: Cultural Constructions of Cultural Maps and Images.* Oxford: Berg.

Lima, Clarissa. 2013. "Corpos abertos: sobre enfeites e objetos na Vila de Cimbres (T. I. Xukuru do Ororubá)." Master's thesis, Universidade Federal de São Carlos.

———. 2017. "Tempo e Qualidade na Vila de Cimbres: uma abordagem etnográfica da (contra)mistura." *R@u* 9(2): 87–107.

Lima, Clarissa, and Felipe Vander Velden. 2018. "The Dead among the Living: Materiality and Time in Rethinking Death and Otherness in Lowland South America." In *Mirrors of Passing: Unlocking the Mysteries of Death, Materiality, and Time*, edited by S. Seebach and R. Willerslev, 166–86. New York: Berghahn Books.

Herzfeld, Michael. 1981. "Meaning and Morality: A Semiotic Approach to Evil Eye Accusations in a Greek Village." *American Ethnologist* 8 (3): 560–74.

Hohenthal, William, Jr. 1954. "Notes on the Shucurú Indians of Serra de Ararobá, Pernambuco, Brazil." *Revista do Museu Paulista* 8: 93–166.

Maloney, Clarence. 1976. *The Evil Eye.* New York: Columbia University Press.

Mayblin, Maya. 2010. *Gender, Catholicism, and Morality in Brazil: Virtuous Husbands, Powerful Wives.* New York: Palgrave-Macmillan.

Munn, Nancy. 1992. "The Cultural Anthropology of Time: A Critical Essay." *Annual Review of Anthropology* 23: 379–405.

Neves, Rita de Cássia. 2005. "Dramas e Performances: o processo de reelaboração étnica Xukuru nos rituais, festas e conflitos." PhD diss., Universidade Federal de Santa Catarina.

Queiroz, Marcos. 1980. "Feitiço, mau-olhado e susto: seus tratamentos e prevenções na aldeia de Icapara." *Religião e Sociedade* 5: 132–60.

Robins, Joel. 2003. "What is a Christian? Notes toward an Anthropology of Christianity." *Religion* 33 (3): 191–99.

——. 2004. *Becoming Sinners: Christianity and Moral Torment in a Papua New Guinea Society.* Berkeley: University of California Press.

Sáez, Oscar. 2009. "O que os santos podem fazer pela antropologia?" *Religião e Sociedade* 29 (2): 198–219.

Silva, Edson. 2008. "Xukuru: memórias e histórias dos índios da Serra do Ororubá (Pesqueira-PE), 1959–1998." PhD diss., Universidade Estadual de Campinas.

Souza, Vânia. 1998. *As Fronteiras do Ser Xukuru.* Recife: Fundação Joaquim Nabuco, Editora Massangana.

Vilaça, Aparecida, and Robin Wright. 2009. *Native Christians: Modes and Effects of Christianity among Indigenous People of the Americas.* Burlington, UK: Ashgate.

Chapter 7

"It Is Just Doing the Motion"

Atheist Time Work in Contemporary Kyrgyzstan

Maria Louw

⟨◆⟩

A PHOTO SHOOT AT THE ETERNAL FLAME OF ATHEISM

On a spring day in 2017 in Bishkek, the capital of Kyrgyzstan, a newly married couple did a photo shoot together with a group of close friends. They went to Prospect Chuy—a major avenue in the city—where, in front of the National Academy of Sciences, a planetary atom model had recently been erected; there, the couple posed together with their friends, unremarked by most passers-by.

The scene, indeed, may not seem very remarkable—and not so different from the scenes in front of the "Eternal Flame" at the Victory Square monument in Bishkek, where one frequently encounters newly married couples who come there to have their picture taken and pray for a happy life. But it was important to Dastan and Gulnara.[1] They had carefully selected the site for their photo shoot, as it was about the only one in the city devoted to the celebration of science and rationalism. An older, Soviet version of the atomic model had previously been dismantled, but unlike other pieces of monumental art from Soviet times—celebrating internationalism, labor, progress in science and technology, and rational knowledge—many of which have been untended and left to decay, a new one had been set up, and it now made the perfect background for the wedding picture: "Well, where else would we go, if not to our 'Eternal Flame' guarding atheism," as their friend Damira wrote when she later posted one of the pictures in a Facebook group for atheists and agnostics in Kyrgyzstan—a group Dastan had created a couple of years

121

ago. Damira also posted other pictures from the group's activities around the wedding, including a parody of Da Vinci's Last Supper painting where Dastan and Gulnara posed with their atheist friends at the wedding banquet, Dastan in the role of Christ and Gulnara in the role of Mary Magdalene.

For Dastan, Gulnara, Damira, and their friends, these playful commentaries on the rituals surrounding marriage in Kyrgyzstan—and their online afterlives—constituted important breathing spaces in a context where atheism has gone from being state-imposed and having a very prominent presence in public space during Soviet times—in art and posters, in political speeches, in school curricula—to being virtually invisible, and where expressing atheist convictions has come to be seen as highly controversial. It is a context where a growing interest in Islam among large parts of the population has made Islam more visible in urban space (Louw 2019; Nasridinov and Esenamanova 2017) and has left its mark on the rhythms of life, and where a narrative that makes life here and now a mere prelude to the afterlife has gained in prominence.

Through the lens of time work—a concept coined by Michael Flaherty (2011) in order to examine how people purposefully alter or customize various dimensions of their temporal experience—this chapter explores how young Kyrgyz atheists struggle to maintain their atheist sensibilities in social contexts that have become marked with religious practices, rituals, narratives, and attitudes: from the five daily prayers and the fast during Ramadan to more local practices related to commemorating and attending to the ancestor spirits, as well as more subtle aspects of daily interaction that add a certain Islamic rhythm to social life and place human life in a larger temporal framework where ancestor spirits interfere with the lives of the living, and where the central telos of human action is to secure one's fate—and the fate of one's relatives—in the afterlife. Although young Kyrgyz atheists find this telos not only irrational, but also fundamentally unethical, they rarely contest it openly and directly. They do not succumb to it, either; rather, they strive to create alternative temporal experiences. They do so through the creation of alternative life-stage ceremonies—which, by their very nature, point at a particular moment of a person's life in relation to a larger temporal structure—and also through the more subtle affective work of ironizing, joking, and embracing playfulness, as well as efforts to empty religious acts and phrases of their eschatological meaning.[2]

FROM STATE ATHEISM TO PRIVATIZED ATHEISM

In the Soviet Union, the promotion of atheism and restrictions against religious practice were central aspects of governmental policies, and the Sovietization of Central Asia involved a massive assault on Islam. Anti-religious campaigns were launched; these included mass rallies where women were encouraged to burn their veils, which for the Bolsheviks were icons of Islamic tradition associated with repression, ignorance, and religious fanaticism (Kamp 2006; Northrop 2004). Religious property was confiscated, mosques and *madāris* (religious schools—the plural of *madrasah*) were destroyed, the *ulamā* (religious authorities) were persecuted, and Soviet Muslims were isolated from contact with the rest of the world. The number of mosques permitted to operate was relatively small, and people were discouraged from attending them (Keller 2001; Ro'I 2000). As a result, for many Muslims the practice of Islam was largely confined to the performance of life-cycle rituals such as weddings, circumcisions, and funerals. To some extent, Islam was rendered synonymous with tradition—a marker of national identity (Khalid 2007).

When the Soviet Union dissolved in 1991, there was a sense among large parts of the population in the region that seventy years of Soviet rule had made them forget what it meant to be Muslim and, correspondingly, there was a great interest in exploring it. During this period, many commentators talked about an Islamic "resurgence" taking place, evidenced by, for example, an increase in the number of mosques and the activities of missionaries from other Muslim countries. While many citizens continued to lead a rather secular life, others began to observe rituals openly, such as the five daily prayers or the fast during Ramadan, or—in the case of women—to wear the hijab. Some began to claim a greater role for Islam in social and political life. Some started following and promoting "universalist" or "scriptural" interpretations of Islam, while criticizing traditional popular practices and beliefs, such as visits to and veneration of sacred places and the importance ascribed to the ancestor spirits. Others would criticize these "new" Muslims for promoting versions of Islam that are foreign to the Kyrgyz, advocating, instead, forms of Islam grounded in local practice (Isci 2010; Louw 2011; McBrien 2017; Montgomery 2016; Pelkmans 2017).

Within this context—dominated by heated debates about what kind of Muslims the Kyrgyz should be, but only rarely any questioning of the idea that the Kyrgyz are in fact Muslims[3]—it is relatively uncontroversial to declare oneself an atheist if one has grown up during Soviet times. In retrospect, it was seen not as a personal choice to become one, but a necessary adaptation to the political situation. However, it is a very different matter to be young—that is, born after, or just before, the dissolution of the Soviet Union—and atheist. Religious life in Kyrgyzstan, as previously mentioned, being closely bound up with family and community events marking important moments in the life of a Muslim (circumcision, marriage, and death, for example), declaring oneself an atheist is not merely seen as a personal rejection of religion, but more broadly as the rejection of community and the values and practices that underpin it.

Most, therefore, tend to live their atheist identity in a relatively discreet manner, playing down their convictions in the company of family, neighbors, and peers. Many, however, are active on social media. New media such as websites, blogs, and online fora have played a large role worldwide in what may be termed a neo-atheist resurgence,[4] creating new forms of interaction and communication between atheists, sometimes across national boundaries. They are particularly important in places where atheism is seen as controversial, and where atheists may feel isolated in their communities (Cimino and Smith 2014: 54). Kyrgyzstan is no exception to this trend. Just as "traditional" ideas about Islam have increasingly been challenged by (mostly) younger Muslims who advocate more universalistic and scriptural versions of religion, new generations of atheists are emerging in Kyrgyzstan whose ideas are not so much informed by Soviet state atheism, or atheism as practiced by Soviet generations, but to a larger extent by globally circulating works of prominent neo-atheists such as Richard Dawkins and Christopher Hitchens, as well as by international communities of atheists—for example, on social media. This younger generation of atheists make up a very diverse group. Some are devoted to a scientific worldview, seeing it as incompatible with a religious worldview. Others are feminists or LGBTQ+ activists and have been led to atheism primarily because of the gender inequality and/or homophobia they see as central to religion, and Islam in particular. Some are highly inspired by neo-atheist literature. Others are primarily led to atheism through personal experiences of ethical transgressions related to religion or representatives of religion. Some identify themselves as "atheists," whereas others prefer the terms "agnostic" (but may nonetheless, at times, refer to themselves as "atheists").

MUSLIM TIME WORK

> I remember one case when I was in high school. And my biology teacher, she was like, "and who in the class does not believe in God?" And I was the only one. And then she was, "ha ha ha—so you believe we came from these monkeys?!"

To Tatiana, a woman in her thirties, this episode during her high school years stood out as a telling case that illustrated how a religious world view, or narrative, had become increasingly dominant in society, and how a sense of loneliness, or isolation, had come to accompany the profession of an atheist worldview. "Oh my god, and you are a biology teacher!" she said, finishing her story and shaking her head in disbelief. If a former bastion of science and rationalism—a biology class in a public school—was no longer free from the influence of religion, if a biology teacher would ridicule evolutionist ideas concerning the origins of human kind and promote, instead, a creationist understanding, were there any spaces left for being atheist at all?

Tatiana was not alone among my atheist interlocutors in pointing out how a religious, and notably Islamic, understanding of time or temporal framework had come to prominence in Kyrgyzstan. Indeed, talking about their experiences being atheists in contemporary Kyrgyzstan, many of them centered their reflections on changing ideas about the past, present, and future and changings rhythms of social life that made them feel out of sync with the communities in which they lived. These are the effects of Muslim time work, as it were. For some, what was most notable was how a religious rhythm had increasingly come to mark everyday life. They would tell of cases where main roads in Bishkek were blocked by people attending the Friday prayer, slowing down the traffic, for example, or of secular events that would be interrupted during prayer time, leaving those who did not pray to sit and wait, feeling that their time was being wasted.

Perhaps most notably, they felt, life would change fundamentally during Ramadan, which, in their experience, was observed by an increasing number of people each year. People's eyes would be set on the Islamic lunar calendar and on the times for sunrise and sunset; those who were able to do so would spend their daytimes sleeping and stay up late; those who could not would work at a slower pace. Dastan recalled how, walking around his neighborhood during the month of Ramadan, he would be met by neighbors with *"Orozonguzdar qabïl bolsun!"* (May your fast be accepted!) He did not fast and had never done so, and the fact that people just assumed that he did—and that people, in this way, identified each other as religious by default—to him was a sign that the city had changed profoundly during the last ten years or so, and that an Islamic temporal order had become the norm. Usually, he just replied, "The same to you," or something like that, dissimulating, but also found himself increasingly refraining from closer engagement with people in the community in which he lived. Instead, he had become more active in online social communities. After a heated discussion about the fast on his own Facebook page, where he had questioned the rationale behind people's fasting during the intense Central Asian summer heat, he created a group for Kyrgyzstani atheists and agnostics in 2014.

Others would point out the difficulties of navigating as an atheist in a world where ancestor spirits are ascribed great importance and are thought to be interfering with the world of the living to a great extent. Among the

Kyrgyz, there is the widespread belief that *arbak*, ancestor sprits, follow the lives of their living relatives and sometimes seek to interfere with them, and that one should remember and attend to them in order not to incur their wrath. These more locally grounded ideas and practices are shunned by some Muslims as incorrect according to Islam but are important to many more traditionally oriented Muslims, and as such are part of the temporal order young atheists navigate. Firuza, for example, told me how once when she visited her native village, her relatives asked her to contribute four hundred US dollars to a new tombstone for one of her ancestors. She did not like visiting the burial ground, and she did not like the idea of spending four hundred dollars of her hard-earned money on a dead person, being much more interested in the living. However, she donated the money in order to ensure that her relatives did not get into trouble due to her improper behavior and was at least happy for her relatively independent life in Bishkek, in which she was not asked to care for the dead on a daily basis.

In Islam more generally, worldly life is seen as a mere prelude to, or preparation for, the afterlife, in which every person will eventually be judged by God and given rewards or punishments according to his or her good and bad deeds. It was not merely what, in their eyes, was the irrationality of this narrative that bothered my atheist interlocutors, but also, and perhaps more importantly, how it influenced people's temporal experience, leading them to devalue and disengage from the here and now and its ethical demands. Several of my atheist interlocutors in Kyrgyzstan expressed a deep-felt indignation toward the eschatology of Islam and the ethics implied in it. In classical Marxist terms, some of them talked about Islam and its ideas about the afterlife as being "opium for the people," providing people with (false) hope and a sense of direction in situations characterized by hardship and the lack of future opportunities. Some emphasized how the attention to one's fate in the afterlife in Islam encouraged people to be unethical, as good deeds toward others were not seen as valuable in themselves, but merely made sense in the context of a temporal order that had to do with one's own salvation and therefore essentially were expressions of selfish concerns. Amir, a man in his early thirties, provides the following example:

> I had a passion for development work . . . but I could not understand why people do not do this really genuinely? Everybody is buying off a ticket to heaven somehow by doing good . . . You are not really doing it for somebody else; you are doing it mostly for yourself. Either because you are terrified of the deity, you are scared of the almighty God, or you want to kind of bribe this higher spirit or whatever, show that you are good . . . so for me it was kind of unethical, and I firmly believed that we can do greater good without religion.

Tatiana similarly emphasized how religion discouraged people from assuming responsibility for their acts here and now:

> So, like these ten commandments . . . like don't kill! Don't lie! Don't steal! I don't need someone up here watching me to do them. And if I do something bad it is my own responsibility to say that I am sorry. I don't need to go to my god and say, please forgive me! Like, you know, the holy month of Ramadan, it is what? Like you sinned for the whole year, and then you do whatever you can in just one month, and then you can start over! And then, I saw once a Dubai commercial, and they were preparing for the holy month of Ramadan, how they helped each other and fed the poor and bla bla bla . . . like a responsible human being would be like that all the time.

What my atheist interlocutors saw as an increasing Islamization of society in the years since the breaking up of the Soviet Union involved the increasing dominance of a perception of time that, in their view, tended to divert people's attention from what mattered most.

"IT IS JUST DOING THE MOTION": DISENGAGEMENT AS TIME WORK

Amir, who was originally from the Uzbek part of the Ferghana Valley but had moved to Bishkek, described how, when visiting his family in his native town, he felt increasingly appalled by "traditions" there: the way women were treated and the way children were raised. However, he also felt that there was no way he could avoid "following tradition" and participating in the events that underpinned community life: "Just how can you not do this? It would be really strange if you did not do this . . . You would offend people, endangering your life and so on. The machine is so much bigger than you."

My atheist interlocutors, indeed, often referred to communal life as a "machine" or "machinery," conjuring up the image of something big and powerful—something made by human hands, but something so powerful that it seems to have a life of its own, and something one person acting alone cannot change or interfere with—a machine that provides meaning and direction to people's lives, lending a rhythm to social life that is difficult not to go along with to some degree at least.

What does atheist agency mean in this context? How do atheists resist the efforts of the "machinery" to impose itself on their experience of time (Flaherty 2011: 2)? Critical though they were toward Islam, and not least its eschatology, they also felt that there was no way they could completely escape participating in communal life, and especially the rituals central to it. It became a matter not of avoiding religious events or openly criticizing them, but of creating small spaces where one could breathe within the machinery. For Amir, for example, it was a matter of going along with the rhythm of social life, participating in the rituals, but in a disengaged way. As he put it, "I am going through these motions, because this is a part of culture. It is almost like standing up and making your bed, like going to somebody's funeral, or somebody's festive event and to say a prayer, or to follow somebody saying a prayer and doing the motion. It is just doing the motion."

"It is just doing the motion" is Amir's description of his effort to deny the movements or phrases involved in the rituals any meaning beyond themselves, a rejection of their eschatological dimensions. Similar experiences of going through ritual practices or saying prayers while depriving them of meaning were shared by several of my interlocutors. Aibek, for example, saw himself as a convinced atheist, but nonetheless prayed together with his religious friends whenever they asked him to. When I asked him how he felt about it, he said that he did not care. He did not think of anything in particular; he just did the movements.

Martin Demant Frederiksen (2017) has produced a fascinating exploration of the lives of a group of Georgian nihilists. They "live in a sphere of disengaged repetition where turning the future into something that 'doesn't matter anyway' becomes a way of handling boredom in the present in an *in*active manner" (Frederiksen 2017: 9). With this research, Frederiksen critically examines the tendency within the social sciences to view individual subjects as inherently intentional. Studies of marginality, he argues, have often focused on how individuals or groups are distanced from a hoped-for life as a result of structural, economic, or political circumstances, and how this may result in unwanted experiences of boredom. For the Georgian nihilists, however, the lack of direction and disillusion do not inhibit life but are seen as basic conditions *of* life (Frederiksen 2017: 10), conditions they embrace by deliberately disengaging and "doing nothing" in the sense of negating whatever happens.

There are many similarities between the Georgian nihilists as described by Frederiksen and my atheist interlocutors in Kyrgyzstan. Like the Georgian nihilists, they are marginal to the dominant telos in society, but they are not marginal in the sense of being distanced from a hoped-for future they share with the majority. Rather, they deliberately disengage from the generally hoped-for future—the afterlife as promised in Islam. They "do the motions" of the rituals that are central to communal life, but in a disengaged way that may be seen as a deliberate cultivation of boredom, seen as "that which happens when nothing happens" (Sjørslev quoted in Frederiksen 2017: 9); or, put differently, the denial that anything happens at all, apart from random bodily movements or the uttering of meaningless phrases—a kind of time work that works through the "affective toning of concrete bodies" (Dalsgaard 2014).

However, contrary to the Georgian nihilists, who embraced negativity in a state of "joyful pessimism," as Frederiksen terms it, for my atheist interlocutors in Kyrgyzstan, their disengaged engagement—doing the motion and cultivating inner states of boredom—was meaningful in terms of another telos: that of care for their families and intimate others. This concern with the wellbeing of others was perhaps not always so clearly articulated. It nevertheless always lurked behind their reflections on why they rarely openly criticized the religious telos they found so appalling.

Firuza, for example, contributed to her relative's tombstone so her family would not get into trouble because of her. Amir also emphasized that he did not want to put his family and friends at risk in the community. Whereas he had the freedom to leave the *mahalla* (local community) whenever he liked, his family, relatives, and friends were stuck there and would get into trouble if he expressed his atheist convictions and refused to participate in communal ritual events. Being of Tatar background, they were initially seen by many as "Russians" and had to make a special effort to be accepted as part of the community. Now they were well integrated in the *mahalla*, and Amir did not want to put their hard-won position there at risk (Louw 2019). Sometimes, then, communal life was experienced not so much as an anonymous "machinery," but rather through the efforts of intimate others to live up to society's expectations, revealing how much (time) work it also takes to maintain a (temporal) structure. The efforts of young atheists to hold on to the importance of the present was thus driven not merely by a concern with rationality, but also, and perhaps even more importantly, by ethical concerns.

"IT IS NECESSARY TO BRING PRAYER RUGS": JOKING AND PLAYFULNESS AS TEMPORAL ENGAGEMENT

Dastan had grown up in a "moderately" religious family, as he termed it. His mother would occasionally fast during Ramadan, but she, as well as the other members of his family, had largely accepted that he was an atheist. When it came to his wedding, though, the family insisted that it include the *nikah* (an Islamic wedding ritual performed by a *mullah*, a religious authority). Life-cycle rituals are at the core of religious and communal life in Kyrgyzstan, and many of the discussions that take place on online fora for atheists in the country touch on the question of how to handle the religious aspects of these rituals, aspects that have come to occupy a more prominent role in recent years (McBrien 2006). Dastan and Gulnara, for their part, assured their families that they had already performed the *nikah*, although they actually had not done so, and now their successful circumvention of the expectations of their families and communities had become an amusing story that was shared in their close circle of atheist friends, for fun as well as for inspiration.

Apart from cultivating a state of disengagement—"just doing the motion"— when having to participate in religious rituals and being confronted with religious phrases, my atheist interlocutors would also often emotionally detach from the dominant Islamic telos and regain a sense of agency through joking and playfulness. In his discussion of storytelling as a means for symbolically altering subject-object relations, Michael Jackson (2001: 182) has remarked that while "tragedy is an outcome of being arrested, stuck, immobilised or trapped in a situation *that one is powerless to do anything about*," the comic, by contrast, "is defined by the relief, release, and distance it provides from just such binds, which is why laughter may be compared with the freedom of being able to breathe, speak or move again after a moment of suspense."

Several of my atheist interlocutors had stories to tell where humor became a release from a feeling of being caught up in situations with a dominant religious telos. One of Firuza's relatives, she recounted, had recently died. He was found dead in his apartment where he had lived by himself. Another of her relatives told her that, when arranging for the man's funeral, he had started to feel the presence of the deceased, his body and his soul. Firuza emphasized that she was respectful of those who had ideas like these, and reasoned that they might become particularly important when a person is grieving, but she did not like to be involved with them. In this particular case, then, she had jokingly suggested to her relative that he contact *The Battle of the Extrasensory*, a popular Russian TV show in which psychics compete with each other. As this example shows, efforts to deal with religious ideas, acts, and attitudes could occur not only in the company of like-minded others, but also when atheists are with religious others. Aibek similarly emphasized that while he would pray with his religious friends when they asked him to, at other times, he would joke with these same friends about the "ridiculousness" of what was written in the Quran. As he reasoned, however, he was only able to do so because they knew each other well, and they knew that he was not a bad person after all.

It has frequently been remarked that humor—the appreciation of which often depends on implicit knowledge—can be a form of symbolic and tacit resistance or expression of dissent and solidarity among oppressed groups in contexts where outspoken resistance or the expression of dissent is risky or even impossible. One never knows how exactly to understand humor; it only hints at serious truths and only discloses serious truths to those who know them beforehand. In a sense, humor may also be seen as a kind of time work. If the Kyrgyzstani atheists confront a dominant narrative that tends to see the present as a passing, and not particularly important, moment in a larger temporal framework where the past is present through the interference of ancestor spirits, and where the afterlife is an ever-present concern, the jokes they make about it may be seen as anti-narrative. The jokes reveal that such narratives are not straightforward representations of reality, but in fact narratives that could have been told in a different way, directing attention toward the here and now as the point of departure for any temporal representation.

My atheist interlocutors would often feel freer to joke with religion in their shared social media spaces, including the Facebook group started by Dastan. In 2017, for example, when Ramadan was just about to start, Damira posted an invitation to an informal get-together with followers of the Facebook page for atheists and agnostics. She ended her text in this way: "Please note Ramadan: remember to bring prayer rugs with you!"

Joking is an inherently ambiguous discourse that may contain, or hint at, several (contradictory) truths at the same time. You never know what people *really* mean (in this case, whether Damira made fun of those around her who prayed and followed Ramadan, or whether she made fun of the way she and her fellow atheists sometimes resembled religious people in their devotion to the atheist cause, or perhaps both), and that is exactly the idea. Some of the more active members of the Facebook group had received threats—including death threats—and often had to tread a fine line so as not to create trouble for themselves and others, also on social media. Similarly, the playful commentaries on the rituals surrounding marriage enacted and posted on Facebook by Dastan, Gulnara, and Damira around the time of Dastan and Gulnara's wedding could be seen as critiques of these rituals and their religious dimensions, but they could also be seen as being done for the sake of mere fun.

THE LIMITS OF TIME—AND OF TIME WORK: FUNERALS

While my atheist interlocutors generally had resigned themselves to their inability to withdraw completely from the religious aspects of communal life or criticize it unambiguously, there was one subject that left many of them frustrated and eager to change things: the question of what to do about their own deaths and funerals.

In Islam, as mentioned previously, worldly life is seen as a mere prelude to, or preparation for, the afterlife, in which every person will be judged by God and given rewards or punishments according to his or her good and bad deeds. Though lurking in the background during the whole life of a Muslim, the eschatological dimensions of Islam become more foregrounded as one ages. In Kyrgyzstan, when people get older, they are expected to start thinking more about, and preparing for, their afterlife. They may start praying more regularly and—in the case of men—attending the mosque. When a person has passed away, performing funeral rituals in the proper manner is seen as particularly important—both for the afterlife of the deceased as well as for the family and community whose lives move on without him or her. Funeral rituals are often elaborate and expensive (Kuchumkulova 2007: 190).

Many of my atheist interlocutors had an intense wish to determine the manner in which their remains would be handled after death. Specifically, they wanted to be cremated and have their ashes spread. Damira had heard of a biodegradable urn designed to convert you into a tree after death and found the thought of transforming into a tree very appealing. More generally, and similar to atheists and humanists in other parts of the world (see, e.g., Engelke 2015 on humanist funerals in the UK), they wished for a funeral that would emphasize the fact that death meant one's self had come to a definite end. Thus, they viewed cremation as the best or most rational choice. Cremation, however, is considered *haram*, forbidden, in Islam, which requires that the deceased be cleaned, shrouded, prayed for, and buried with the head facing Mecca. Consequently, cremation was not yet a possibility in Kyrgyzstan. There were no crematoriums in the country, and even if there had been, it would have been difficult to persuade their families to perform a funeral rite that, in their view, would not only put the resurrection of their loved ones at risk, but would also very likely cause uproar in the community.

I was initially puzzled by this strong wish among some of my interlocutors to determine what happened to them after death—a wish that made some of them entertain the thought of migrating to a country where cremation was possible. Why does it matter what happens to you after death when you are in fact dead and this, according to atheist views, is the end of your existence? As Matthew Engelke (2015: 30) has remarked in a discussion of the attitudes of humanist celebrants in England to the presence of the coffin at the funerals they conduct, "The anthropology of death has, in essence, always been an anthropology of the body, of how the brute facts of mortality, of the body's putrescence and decomposition, get enfolded into social projects of triumph, of life's regeneration (if not resurrection)." The Quran, more particularly, teaches that the body slowly disintegrates, except for the tailbone. It is believed that, at the time of resurrection, Allah resurrects the body from the tailbone (which is why cremation is considered *haram*, as it would destroy the tailbone and prevent resurrection). For my atheist interlocutors, the idea that their very bodies would be left to slowly decompose in order to confirm beliefs they found irrational and unethical was appalling. Even more disturbing was the thought that there was nothing they could do about it. There was no way they could enjoy the satisfaction of performing the ritual in a disengaged way; it would be impossible for them to create a sense of agency through joking with the ritual. Thus, the frustrations felt when thinking about their own deaths and funerals served to highlight the importance of the time work they performed during other religious rituals for their personal integrity and sense of agency, although it may have seemed insignificant and hardly recognizable at first sight.

CONCLUSION

The younger generation of atheists in Kyrgyzstan tends to experience Islam as a "machinery" that is growing more powerful in society, structuring social life, imposing a rhythm on it, and making people experience the here and now as a prelude to their afterlives and as influenced by spirits from the past. Consequently, their efforts to live atheist lives, be true to their atheist convictions, and craft atheist selves and communities have an important temporal dimension that may be captured through the concept of "time work." What characterizes atheist time work, I have argued, is first and foremost the effort to hold on to the present, the here and now, with its ethical demands, when the attention of others seems to be focused on the past or the future. Yet these atheists often feel obliged to participate in ritual events and rarely feel that they are able to openly and unambiguously criticize the religious beliefs of others. Instead, they typically conform to the overt rhythm of social life while cultivating inner states of disengagement, or relate to it through a humorous attitude, which questions its telos, but does so in an ambiguous way. The time work they perform in order to maintain their atheist sensibilities in what is experienced as a predominantly religious context thus ranges from the more overt attempts to find or create alternatives to existing life-stage ceremonies—which places these atheist individuals in an alternative temporal structure than that proposed by Islam—to the more subtle, but no less important, affective work through which they disengage from its telos.

Maria Louw
Associate Professor, Department of Anthropology
Aarhus University, Denmark

NOTES

1. All names in this chapter are pseudonyms.
2. The chapter is based on ongoing fieldwork among atheists in Bishkek, as well as around nine months of fieldwork on everyday religion and secularism conducted in Kyrgyzstan in the period 2006–2012.
3. In this period, however, a smaller group of (mainly) scholars and intellectuals started promoting Tengrism, a pre-Islamic Kyrgyz, Turkic, or nomadic worldview centered around Tengri (Larouelle 2006, 2007; Toktogulova 2007). Converts to other religions, notably (charismatic) Christianity, also questioned the common assumption that Kyrgyz are Muslims by definition (Hilgers 2009; Pelkmans 2006, 2017).
4. Recently, there has been a growing interest in atheism and being atheist in many parts of the world—or perhaps it has just become more visible. Since the start of the new millennium, there has been an explosion in polemical literature arguing for or against atheism. For example, in the wake of biologist Richard Dawkins's (2006) book, *The God Delusion*, a fierce debate developed between what are now commonly called new atheists and anti-atheists. The debates touch on fundamental questions, such as whether or not a life may be meaningful without a religious or spiritual dimension, to what extent morality is linked with religion, whether science and religion are compatible, and to what extent and on what basis we may claim to know anything about the existence or nonexistence of deities and the transcendent. This new atheist resurgence is also apparent in the rise of atheist/"humanist" movements and organizations in different parts of the world: movements and organizations that seek to promote atheism, secure the right to live an atheist life, and, in some cases, to establish atheist rituals and ceremonies as alternatives to predominantly religious ones (see Geertz and Markússon 2010: 153).

REFERENCES

Cimino, Richard, and Christopher Smith. 2014. *Atheist Awakening: Secular Activism and Community in America*. Oxford: Oxford University Press.
Dalsgård, Anne Line. 2014. "Standing Apart: On Time, Affect, and Discernment in Nordeste, Brazil." In *Ethnographies of Youth and Temporality: Time Objectified*, edited by Anne Line Dalsgård, Martin Demant Frederiksen, Susanne Højlund and Lotte Meinert. Philadelphia: Temple University Press.

Dawkins, Richard. 2006. *The God Delusion*. New York: Houghton Mifflin.

Engelke, Matthew. 2015. "The Coffin Question: Death and Materiality in Humanist Funerals." In *Material Religion* 11 (1): 26–49.

———. 2017. "On Atheism and Non-Religion: An Afterword." In *Being Godless. Ethnographies of Atheism and Non-Religion*, edited by Ruy Llera Blanes and Galina Oustinova-Stjepanovic. Oxford: Berghahn Books.

Flaherty, Michael G. 2011. *The Textures of Time: Agency and Temporal Experience*. Philadelphia: Temple University Press.

Frederiksen, Martin Demant. 2017. "Joyful Pessimism: Marginality, Disengagement, and the Doing of Nothing." *Focaal: Journal of Global and Historical Anthropology* 78: 9–22.

Geertz, Armin W., and Gudmundur Ingi Markússon. 2010. "Religion Is Natural, Atheism Is Not: On Why Everybody Is Both Right and Wrong." *Religion* 40 (3): 152–65.

Hilgers, Irene. 2009. *Why Do Uzbeks Have to Be Muslims? Exploring Religiosity in the Ferghana Valley*. Berlin: Lit Verlag.

Isci, Baris. 2010. "'Proper' Muslim against 'Authentic' Kyrgyz: The Formation of Islamic Field and Secular Challenges in Bishkek, Kyrgyzstan." PhD diss., Washington University, St. Louis, MO.

Jackson, Michael. 2001. *The Politics of Storytelling: Violence, Transgression and Intersubjectivity*. Copenhagen: Museum Tusculanum Press.

Keller, Shoshana. 2001. *To Moscow, not Mecca: The Soviet Campaign against Islam in Central Asia 1917–1941*. Westport, CT: Praeger.

Khalid, Adeeb. 2007. *Islam after Communism: Religion and Politics in Central Asia*. Berkeley: University of California Press.

Kuchumkulova, Elmira. 2007. "Kyrgyz Nomadic Customs and the Impact of Re-Islamization after Independence." PhD diss., University of Washington, Seattle, WA.

Larouelle, Marlene. 2006. "Tengrism: In Search for Central Asia's Spiritual Roots." *Central Asia-Caucasus Analyst*, 22 March.

———. 2007. "Religious Revival, Nationalism and the 'Invention of Tradition': Political Tengrism in Central Asia and Tatarstan." *Central Asian Survey* 26 (2): 203–16.

Louw, Maria. 2011. "Being Muslim the Ironic Way: Secularism, Religion and Irony in Post-Soviet Kyrgyzstan." In *Varieties of Secularism in Asia. Anthropological Explorations of Religion, Politics, and the Spiritual*, edited by Nils Bubandt and Martijn van Beek, 143–62. London: Taylor & Francis.

———. 2017. "Haunting as Moral Engine: Ethical Striving and Moral Aporias among Sufis in Uzbekistan." In *Moral Engines. Exploring the Ethical Drives in Human Life*, edited by Cheryl Mattingly, Rasmus Dyring, Maria Louw and Thomas Schwartz Wentzer, 143–62. Oxford: Berghahn Books.

———. 2019. "Atheism 2.0: Finding Spaces for Atheism in Contemporary Kyrgyzstan." *Central Asian Affairs* 6 (2–3): 206–223.

McBrien, Julie. 2006. "Listening to the Wedding Speaker: Discussing Religion and Culture in Southern Kyrgyzstan." *Central Asian Survey* 25 (3): 341–58.

———. 2017. *From Belonging to Belief: Modern Secularisms and the Construction of Religion in Kyrgyzstan.* Pittsburgh: University of Pittsburgh Press.

Montgomery, David. 2016. *Practicing Islam: Knowledge, Experience, and Social Navigation in Kyrgyzstan.* Pittsburgh: University of Pittsburgh Press.

Nasridinov, Emil, and Nurgul Esenamanova. 2017. "The War of Billboards: Hijab, Secularism, and Public Space in Bishkek." *Central Asian Affairs* 4 (2): 217–42.

Northrop, Douglas. 2004. *Veiled Empire: Gender and Power in Stalinist Central Asia.* Ithaca, NY: Cornell University Press.

Pelkmans, Mathijs. 2006. "Asymmetries on the "Religious Market" in Kyrgyzstan." In *The Postsocialist Religious Question: Faith and Power in Central Asia and East-Central Europe*, edited by Chris Hann and the Civil Religion Group, 29–46. Berlin: Lit Verlag.

———. 2017. *Fragile Conviction: Changing Ideological Landscapes in Urban Kyrgyzstan.* Ithaca, NY: Cornell University Press.

Ro'I, Yaacov. 2000. *Islam in the Soviet Union.* London: Hurst and Co.

Toktogulova, Mukaran. 2007. "Syncretism of Religious Beliefs (*Kyrgyzchylyk* and *Musulmanchylyk*)." In *Mazar Worship in Kyrgyzstan: Rituals and Practitioners in Talas*, edited by Gulnara Aitpaeva. Bishkek: Aigine Cultural Research Center.

Part V

Reinventing the Past,
Present, and Future

Chapter 8

Inventing New Time

Time Work in the Grief Practices of Bereaved Parents

Dorthe Refslund Christensen and Kjetil Sandvik

◈

INTRODUCTION AND AGENDA

At a Danish cemetery, we find the grave of a baby boy who was born in 2007, lived for a few hours, and died. On his grave, his mother keeps a small laminated book for sharing photos, poems, and reflections on being the mother of a dead boy. At the time when the boy would have started in preschool at the age of six, she writes a celebration note to him with a photo of a Lego Ninjago backpack, fantasizing that this is the school bag he would have had if he had lived long enough to start school. A couple of years later, the family redecorates his grave for his birthday, making the grave more suitable for an older boy—in the same way as people redecorate their children's rooms as they grow older.

On a Danish online memorial page, a mother describes the glass ball with an engraved picture of her dead baby she has had made, explaining that she always hangs it on the tree at Christmastime because it *makes her feel as if her baby is celebrating Christmas with the family.* And a father explains that a tattoo in memory of his dead baby somehow keeps his baby and their relationship alive, helping the baby to share his life and experiences.

These are just a few short examples of how bereaved parents deal with their grief when they lose a baby—of how they continue to parent the dead baby and how they ritualize the continued presence of, and their relationship to, the baby. They are also examples of time work—of how bereaved parents, in many ritualized ways, produce and alter their temporal experiences following the death of their baby in order to keep the baby present in their lives. In this chapter, we analyze how this is done, based on Michael Flaherty's (2003, 2011) productive theories regarding time work, and we argue in favor of expanding Flaherty's theory by introducing a new, seventh category of time work, which we call *inventing time*.

DEATH AND TIME

Brief Introduction to Previous Research

Over the years, we have conducted extensive research on the grief practices of bereaved parents in Denmark after the death of their stillborn babies and infants. Here, we briefly introduce our basic findings following these studies (Christensen and Sandvik 2013, 2014, 2016). In a later section of this chapter, we present the time work analysis from 2013 in greater depth since it makes up the foundation of our analyses of temporal agency and of the conceptual addendum we suggest to Flaherty's theoretical work in this field.

In "Sharing Death: Conceptions of Time at a Danish Online Memorial Site" (Christensen and Sandvik 2013: 100), we argue that "with the death of very young children time itself is utterly distorted and the future of the parents disappears while the present is folded into the past, leaving the parents in some kind of non-time." Our empirical material was the mourning practices of bereaved parents at the Danish online memorial site Mindet.dk (*mindet* means "memory" in Danish), and we examined the way in which time work defines how bereaved parents ritualize grief and use various kinds of ritualization to negotiate, re-create, and reappropriate time (Christensen and Sandvik 2013: 105).

Our theoretical framework, besides Flaherty's (2011) concept of time work, consisted of Paul Ricoeur's (1980, 1984) extensive research on time and narrative, Mikhail Bakhtin's (1981) theory on the chronotope, and the ritual theories of Adam B. Seligman et al. (2008) and Catherine Bell (1997). We argue that the death of a baby locks the parents in the present time. They perceive the future with a sense of paralysis, and suddenly the narrated past seems irrelevant owing to the death of their baby. However, ritualization and time work enable these parents to gradually change the way they perceive and talk about time, making the future inhabitable again.

In 2008–2014, we carried out a qualitative study of a number of children's graves in order to analyze the parental practices connected to these graves. This work is presented in "Death Ends a Life, Not a Relationship:

Objects as Media on Children's Graves" (Christensen and Sandvik 2014). In our analysis, we demonstrated that the chronotopical qualities at stake at Mindet.dk are extended in various ways to the graves of the children concerned. The graves become "heterotopias" (Foucault 1984): spaces where the worlds of the baby and the parents merge. The graves also serve as ritual interfaces where the parents perform parenthood and communicate to and about their dead baby through various materialities that are turned into communicative objects and media. Our theoretical framework for this analysis was based on Meyrowitz's (1973) media metaphor theory, Bordewijk and Van Kaam's (1986) matrix of four communication flows, and Carey's ([1975] 1989) theory on communication as ritual. We argue that family life is not only represented on the graves but also mediated and re-mediated through the display of material artifacts such as seasonal ornaments and prototypical childhood objects including toys, poems, photos, sweets, inscriptions, and drawings—objects that gain media qualities and make possible two-way communication between the dead baby and its family as well as the social world. These studies did not include analyses of time work and temporal agency (see below for further details about this research).

Our article titled "Grief and Everyday Life. Bereaved Parents' Negotiations of Presence across Media" (Christensen and Sandvik 2016) is informed by our fieldwork regarding Mindet.dk and children's graves, as well as informal conversations and one in-depth interview on everyday life with the mother who placed the photo of a Ninjago schoolbag in the book on her son's grave, as presented above. We argue that bereaved parents are continually performing, negotiating, and (re)appropriating parenthood and inscribing their dead baby in everyday and family life through the use of existing media (photos, web applications, digital media); through physical objects working as what we term "occasional media," which are objects to which media qualities are occasionally ascribed; and even through the parent's own bodies (tattoos) (Christensen and Sandvik 2016: 105ff.). They use these media to resemble everyday parental activities, such as playing with their baby, reading bedtime stories, and celebrating birthdays.

Current theories on grief tend to suggest that the objective of grief is not to abandon relationships with deceased individuals but rather to "keep hold" of the dead as a prerequisite for "moving on": the "continuing bonds paradigm" (Klass, Silverman, and Nickman 1996; Stroebe et al. 2005; Walter 1996, 1999, 2017: xx). Our article contributes to the empirical understanding of questions such as these: How exactly do the bereaved move on? What does it imply to keep hold of the dead, and how is this keeping hold performed and experienced? We argue that by taking the dead with them into the realm of everyday life, the bereaved turn themselves into competent agents, an agency that includes their relations with the dead. By continuing their bonds to their dead baby in their everyday lives, parents can turn distance and absence into presence and the possibility of living with the dead despite their (physical) absence. Consequently, we suggest that grief and everyday life are two separate but mutually inclusive realms within the same space of agency, and that they coexist concurrently (Christensen and Sandvik 2016: 110).

Moving Beyond: Death, Presence, and Time Work

Death is a fundamental challenge to the ways humans experience time. On the one hand, death is finite because it draws an irreversible temporal line between *then* and *now*. The living move on, while the dead stop their journey when death occurs. The line marks a fundamental difference between being and nonbeing and produces a spatial difference between the realm of the dead (which may be either a secular or a religious realm) and the realm of the living. People who experience the death of a loved one might sense that the difference in realms seems insurmountable in ways that almost hurt physically, and that the distance between realms is impossible to comprehend, let alone accept.

However, when we think about the dead (and in particular when we talk about them), something interesting happens: in the first period after death occurs, we who are bereaved might experience difficulty or even reluctance in speaking of the dead in the past tense. Talking about the dead in the past tense not only feels weird and wrong, but also gives the impression that we have accepted their death. And the acceptance of death often takes time.

However, after some time (hours, days), we slowly start to switch between the present and past tense, although referring to a loved one in the past tense still seems too heartless to endure. We do not want to let go of them even though we are trying to come to terms with the fact of their death. Later on, we might get used to talking about the dead in the past tense, but at some point many of us feel that it is natural to switch between the two tenses because it gives us a feeling that talking in the present tense keeps the dead person with us and allocates a social space to them despite their absence.

This experience of being able to actually recapture some of the spirit of the dead or our experiences with them (or the fear of not being able to do this if we do nothing) motivates bereaved individuals to start producing rituals to commemorate the deceased. We suggest that these rituals, which involve negotiating the agency of the deceased in a new state of being and continuing to live with the deceased, can be understood as a *making present*. This is profoundly inspired by Heidegger's (1962: 469) statement that "saying now . . . is the discursive articulation of a *making-present*" (see also Christensen and Sandvik 2013, 2014, 2015, 2016). Bereaved individuals use rituals to "say now"—to drag the deceased back across the threshold of death and, for a moment, share a new life with them. This is the new, invented time that we elaborate on below. We will demonstrate that the idea of maintaining the *presence* of a baby (as opposed to its absence) is closely related to the temporal *present* (as opposed to the past), and that everyday ritualizing practices actually produce a "now" (a present time including the baby).

TIME WORK AND TEMPORAL AGENCY

In his article, "Time Work: Customizing Temporal Experience," Michael Flaherty (2003: 17) introduces his concept of "time work," covering "individual or interpersonal efforts to create or suppress particular kinds of temporal experience." In his original formulation, Flaherty (2003: 32) identified five dimensions of time work: "duration," "frequency," "sequence," "timing," and "allocation," which are various ways of manipulating or *doing* time (see below), and he concludes that "temporal agency is largely a product of existing arrangements and contributes to their reproduction." Later, in *The Textures of Time*, Flaherty (2011: 136ff.) develops his argument regarding the "spectrum of temporal agency" by introducing four degrees of temporal agency, three of which support the status quo ("consensual determinism," "cultural reproduction," and "reactionary agency"), while the fourth ("time play") is a more explorative and negotiating type of temporal agency. He also adds a new, sixth dimension of time work, which he refers to as "taking time." In our 2013 analysis, we argue that the grief practices of bereaved parents constitute various kinds of time work, and we apply Flaherty's dimensions to these parental practices.

Our theoretical and empirical argument for adding to Flaherty's productive conceptualization of time work is outlined below, adding a seventh variation—*inventing time*—to his six variations. We also explore the interrelations between inventing time and (some of) Flaherty's variations and types of temporal agency in order to argue that inventing time is indeed a seventh variation rather than a subcategory of Flaherty's six time work variations. Furthermore, we add the inventing time variation to Flaherty's four types of temporal agency and argue that inventing time is a subcategory of the fourth type, time play. In other words, we claim that inventing time enables bereaved parents to transgress the conservative and reproductive boundaries of Flaherty's first three types of agency and create the conditions needed to live on with the dead baby as an integrated family member with its own agency. With this aim, we revisit our material and elaborate on our previous theoretical and empirical work on grief, everyday life, and performing parenthood (Christensen and Sandvik 2013, 2014, 2016). We extend our analyses of this material to construct the foundation of our argument and suggest that bereaved parents, by inventing and performing new ritualized ways of keeping their baby present in everyday activities, profoundly negotiate basic temporal as well as social boundaries. The parents are, in fact, *not* merely reinstalling their temporal normality that existed prior to the death of their baby, nor reproducing many laypersons' taboo-laden view on how to mourn, let go, and move on. Instead, they are inventing delicate ways of keeping the dead baby present in their lives and ways of living on *with* rather than *without* their child.

The mourning practices of bereaved parents thus transgress the aim of returning to social normality (including the temporality of everyday life as it existed prior to the death of their baby), and can be seen as a way of creating a new time order in which their baby is made present through repeated ritualizations.

THE TIME WORK DONE BY BEREAVED PARENTS

We start by looking into temporal structures as they might be experienced by parents both before and after their baby is born and dies.

For most (Danish) couples, pregnancy is a period of expectation, waiting, and passing time. Three intertwined strategies seem to be essential. First, material construction, or being practical, which involves restructuring the home, collecting (buying and borrowing) clothes and other material items for the baby, painting walls and assembling furniture, decorating the nursery, etc. Second, the (re)construction of the families of the prospective parents[1] and social narratives in which the couple's history and family on both sides are revisited and renarrated to accommodate the forthcoming addition to the family: parents become grandparents; best friends are renamed as uncles and aunts; things that the mother and father used and loved as children (teddy bears, blankets) are brought out of the cupboard; family photos of the parents as children are found; and stories are told about preferences, habits, and so on. It could be argued that the past is renarrated and brought into contact with the present in this way in order to face the awaited future. Third, there is the plain "killing of time": during pregnancy, especially during the final phase, the present can be physically challenging

for the mother. But the most common feeling is often impatience and waiting, and the couple might try to "accelerate time" (see Flaherty 2011: 15ff.)
by doing things they do not usually do (going to the movies, driving out into
the countryside, cleaning the house over and over again, etc.). In this sense,
the future is the only thing that really matters. People wait impatiently for
the *new time*, with hopes for future events and family life instigated by the
coming of the baby. The new time is family time; the future is the family's
future; and it starts when the baby is born. However, as media scholar Maja
Sonne Damkjær (2016: 140) has suggested, the use of digital media such
as online pregnancy calendars, enrolment in due-date groups, and the an-
nouncement of the pregnancy on social media are all practices that have
contributed to a temporal expansion of parenthood and lead to people seeing themselves as parents of an unborn baby rather than seeing themselves
as parents-to-be.

The baby is given some kind of agency from very early on in pregnancy—
especially after the first scanning, which provides the parents-to-be with the
first physical documentation of the baby's existence in the form of scanning
photos (Damkjær 2016). As the mother begins to feel the fetus growing and
moving in her womb, she begins to read moods into the fetus's movements
and comment on and adjust to any sign of the fetus's daily rhythm and to
attribute agency (motivation, intentionality, temperament, moods) to certain kinds of movements inside her. In many cases, she will also regulate
her own habits and rhythms in accordance with her interpretation of the
baby's movements. For instance, if certain movements by the baby can be
interpreted as a reaction to her eating hot chili, she may well believe that the
baby is protesting and stop eating chili for the rest of the pregnancy. Or she
may believe that her baby is dancing with joy and continue to enjoy eating
chili. If certain music seems to calm the fetus, she might use this music to
make the fetus and herself relax together.[2] In other words, both parenthood
and the baby's life have already begun before the baby is born. And if the
baby dies, the future remains unresolved.

When a baby is stillborn or dies after a very short life, time collapses:
all preparatory efforts—and thus, the past—become immediately irrelevant,
and all the narratives and interpretations of the baby's character that have
been built on sensation and expectation become meaningless. The present
is unbearably painful and inconceivable, while the future (in terms of its
shape and expected content) is suddenly nonexistent—or, more precisely, it
cannot be achieved due to the baby's death. Ricoeur (1984) has argued that
it is a basic human condition to always be stretched between a past, present,
and future, with experiences and narratives moving across temporalities. In
this case, the parents seem trapped in a black void that erases all sense of

meaning since the past, present, and future are all meaningless or irrelevant in the form in which they were expected, narrated, and hoped for by the parents. The time which actually *is*, without the baby, is not bearable.

We argue that building an online memorial indicates that bereaved parents are actually establishing a chronotope—that is, an "intrinsic connectedness of temporal and spatial relationships" (Bakhtin 1981 in Christensen and Sandvik 2013). Here, time-space ritualizations (Seligmann et al. 2008) and time work are performed through which reality is gradually experienced and transformed through the subjunctive potential of ritualizing.[3] The chronotope of Mindet.dk helps establish small subjunctive temporal and narrative units or small fragments of parallel spaces and temporal structures where the parents can narrate and perform some of the experiences and events they would have shared with the baby had it lived. We call this "invented memories" (Christensen and Sandvik 2013). This aspect in particular is core to the development of parental practices and fundamental to the temporal argument we are developing in this chapter.

We argue in favor of three stages in this process.[4] The first stage of ritualizations and time work consists of the parents stretching time: they produce narratives of the baby's short life, imparting *duration* to it and giving it agency, as well as sorting out the *succession/sequencing* of events leading to the baby's death. The endpoint of this seems to be the parents actually appropriating the death of their baby by being the ones to say "this is our baby, and our baby is dead."

The second stage consists of the often very frequently repeated ritualizations of lighting a candle and writing small updates to and about the baby and family. These updates typically take place around bedtime, leading us to hypothesize that this is a ritualization replacing tucking the baby in for the night and a basic way of performing parenthood. One dominant trait of these ritualizations seems to involve establishing a bearable and persistent relationship with the dead baby, by placing it in a different social realm, and developing narratives of where the baby is thought to reside. This is done within the chronotope of Mindet.dk as a small social, temporal, and spatial sphere (a sociality or community of mourners), developing relations to the baby as well as other mourners and their children, commenting on each other's updates and photos, and sharing a language about the dead baby—they are often talked about as angels and located in heaven or sitting on clouds (Christensen and Sandvik 2013; see also Walter et al. 2011; Walter 2016, 2018). Moreover, the children seem to be given some kind of agency—for instance, possessing superhuman qualities (they protect the family or serve as confessors).

The third stage is, logically, a continuation of the second, although the updates become less frequent and are eventually limited to red-letter days

such as the baby's birthday, date of death, date of months or years passing since death (Christensen and Sandvik 2013: 116–17). We can see from
the updates that activities in other social spaces are also performed (on the
grave, in the countryside, and in the family home).

In accord with Flaherty's (2003) conclusion, the time work in these activities of the parents can largely be seen as a reproductive activity contribut-
ing to the status quo of the social world of the bereaved parents. This world
was profoundly destroyed by the death of their baby, but by engaging in
time work through their various performances of grief, they reinstall a temporal normality that makes sense of the past, present, and future and return
to their regular temporalities, activities, and agencies (their social world).
This narrative indicates that the baby is at a distance, yet given some agency.
The resulting narratives do not seem to break with regular expectations
concerning temporality and agency. However, in this chapter we argue that
the invented parts of memory mentioned above, which sometimes occur in
parental narratives, are the foundations for *inventing a new form of time*. They
allow the parents to say "now" (see Heidegger 1962) and include the baby
in their present, gradually forming new narratives about the agency of the
baby.

If we include the children's graves in our argument, at least two important temporal perspectives can be observed: First, the *duration* of the baby's
life is dealt with, although this is a form of engagement that is different
from online practices. This might be because the practices performed on the
graves go on for a longer period than those observed at Mindet.dk, where
the highest frequency of activity is often in the first months after the baby's
death. At Mindet.dk the duration of temporal experience that parents seek
to manipulate or stretch is the time prior to the baby's death and, to a lesser
degree, the baby's life after death. It is the baby as a living being during
pregnancy and until the point where it is stillborn or dies shortly after birth
that is in focus—this is the period that is processed in an attempt to understand what went wrong. The social and temporal experience sought through
these practices seems to be "normality"—the sense that the world and life of
the parents go on after the loss.

On the graves, this perspective seems to change over time. The duration
strategies clearly show that the baby's life actually goes on in the narratives
and lives of the bereaved. The objects displayed show that the baby has a life
that the family affirms and performs constantly by changing objects on the
grave. The duration strategies are combined with the strategy of sequencing
events in the lives of the children and their families, with a view to tying
the two together—for instance, by displaying seasonal objects connecting the
social world and the baby, thereby showing the baby what time of year it is

and including it in the celebration of Christmas and Easter. Siblings might also give presents to their dead brother or sister (for instance, drawings, handprints and footprints, little painted stones, postcards, or bead plates), or they might play at the grave with some of the items on display (see Christensen and Sandvik 2014).

Second, but closely related, through the continued performance of parenthood, it can be argued that the parents try to extend the lives of their children, with the baby's physical death no longer being perceived as coinciding with its social death. This indicates that the parents have moved beyond the sole affirmation of conservative temporal and social boundaries (Flaherty 2003, 2011). We argue that these practices increasingly fall into the fourth of Flaherty's (2011: 146) types of agency: "time play"—that is, a mode of being temporarily creative, experimental, and inventive, where one "customize[s] temporality for the sake of personal preferences. . . . There is temporal exploration. One plays with time to see how things turn out if matters are handled in a certain fashion." We propose that the time play done by parents is a way of inventing new time and that through their practices the parents not only allocate time from the time their baby died to fantasies about a prolonged life; they also create rituals that produce new time, a way of *saying now* (Heidegger 1962: 469)—a *present* where the presence of the baby is felt and developed into new family narratives and traditions (Nünning, Nünning, and Neuman 2010).[5] In some of these narratives and rituals the baby also grows older, like the baby boy mentioned at the beginning of this chapter. However, babies do not always grow older in the practices we observed.

Three important aspects of the practices of bereaved parents are central to the point we are trying to make. First, their time work seems to shift from being about taking their leave of the dead baby to continuing to have and live with a dead baby. Second, there is a shift in efforts and narratives from being parents-to-be to not being parents, and to actually being parents of a dead baby. Third, the parents start to develop strategies of how to parent this baby and keep it in the life of the family.

These ideas have been supported by conversations and interviews we have had with bereaved parents over the years, and we are still exploring what is implied by these practices and how to study them. Many of the aspects that seem crucial for a culturally contextualized understanding of the situation of bereaved parents are closely related to temporal issues. In other words, understanding the temporal conditions and time work of parents is one key to understanding this field.[6]

One way of revealing the differences between losing a grandmother aged ninety-two, a father in his sixties, and a baby in infancy is by using references to time. A ninety-two-year-old grandmother has presumably had a full life, and the time that is potentially left for her to live— that is, her space left for action—is not very long. A father dying in his sixties has had a substantial proportion of his life, although he might have enjoyed many more years in the company of his loved ones. The younger you die, the larger is the time left that you might have lived. A stillborn baby leaves nothing but potentiality—potential time, actions, relationships, agency, and so forth. This is difficult for parents to process because of the painful recognition of so much potential life lost. Furthermore, when parents lose a baby, they actually lose someone that they were responsible for, as opposed to losing an older relative. The feeling of responsibility, and maybe even guilt, makes it crucial for many bereaved parents to continually care for and show responsibility for their baby and, at the same time, they seem to have an ongoing need to parent. Philosopher Claude Romano (2009: 115, referred to in Christensen and Sandvik 2013: 110) has argued that "in bereavement, where the cataclysm of death is felt by a human being, it is not only because we have lost *the other* [and to Romano we are only humans insofar as we are ourselves to 'another']; rather, it is because when the other dies we are no longer needed by him or her and in this process we die not only to the deceased but to ourselves." So, the immediate feeling of losing one's role as a primary caretaker and parent, according to Romano, is part of being bereaved.

Moreover, bereaved parents have only very little memory of living *with* their baby, limited to the sensations and interpretations they had and produced during pregnancy as opposed to the memories and narratives of relations and events when an older person dies. With a stillborn child, crucial narratives must be established after the baby has died without ever having lived outside the womb. On the other hand, we suggest that the situation also contains meaning-making potential for the parents because it can be filled with experiences and relations in the ongoing life of the family through performative narratives. However, due to the attitude of Danish society toward bereavement in general and to losing a baby in particular, this requires both effort and a lot of courage.

Another important difference between losing a dear person who has lived a long life and losing a baby who dies in infancy is related to the afterlife. Looking at death as a social process, the dead must be narratively processed to another realm, whether this is a well-defined afterlife or a more diffuse religious or secular conceptualization of where the person resides after death. A dead adult has been a physical being in and of this world, but a baby who dies in infancy has been alive either for only a very short time or for no time at all. Such a baby almost already belongs to another realm—it is its continued relation to *this* world that must be established, performed, negotiated, and secured through repeated actions. One of the crucial ways of doing this is by inventing a new concept of time and new traditions, and by repeatedly including the baby in events and social practices, *inventing time*, "saying now."

Inventing Time: Arguing for a Seventh Variation of Time Work

Before moving on in our argument, let us briefly sum up: in our first major study of the grief practices of bereaved parents at Mindet.dk, we established that parental time work primarily involves *duration* (making the short life of the baby last longer by stretching time), *sequencing* (narrating the events leading to the birth and death of the baby and establishing a succession in these events), and *frequency/timing* (for instance, lighting candles at the online memorial site at the same hour every day—like tucking the baby in for the night). But *allocating time*, or maybe even *taking time* from the afterlife by giving the baby some kind of agency and time in this world, is also common. When it comes to temporal agency, we argue that the majority of parental practices belong to what Flaherty (2003: 32) terms "existing arrangements" in that they contribute to the reproduction of existing social and cultural norms. Moreover, we suggest that they belong to his second type of temporal agency, "cultural reproduction" (Flaherty 2011: 142 ff.), since they do exactly that: reproduce values and norms relating to expecting, giving birth to, and losing a baby. One exception is the *invented memories*, that is, small fragments of memory-like stories inscribing the baby in ongoing life, such as writing "we went on a holiday by the sea. I guess you would have loved to swim in the ocean." This might be said to break with the conservative logic of cultural reproduction, since such stories have the character of small joyful fantasies. We still argue that narratives like this *allocate* some kind of imagined time to the dead baby, but we simultaneously consider these narratives to be the foundations of the *inventing time* variation of time work we suggest in this chapter.

The time work practices apparent at children's graves are more ambiguous, and we have argued above that this might be due to the fact that these grave practices seem to go on for a longer period of time than the online memorials at Mindet.dk. The *duration* strategies we observe are different from the strategies employed at Mindet.dk, since they are no longer about stretching the baby's physical life after death. Instead, they focus on stretching the baby's social life and relations in this world. Neither are the efforts increasingly about *reallocating* time by replacing time in the afterlife with time in this world. Instead, they focus on producing heterotopic rituals (temporal, spatial, agentic) through which a new time of joint family life and ongoing relations can take place. This also moves the type of temporal agency from the reproducing kind to what seems to resemble *time playing* (see Flaherty 2011: 146ff.), with parents becoming more interested in exploring and negotiating in their ritualizations of temporal agency.

Our studies of the everyday life practices of parents suggest that there are clear distinctions between the types of temporal agency that reproduce existing cultural norms dominating the practices of bereavement. The continuous *making of presence and present* is not tied to certain situations but can, indeed, happen anywhere. Yet, at the same time, our findings clearly suggest that in each family (and also for each bereaved parent or sibling), certain rituals (temporal, spatial, and situational) are repeated and eventually turned into routines (see Bakardjieva 2011) that become focal points for continuing to live with the dead.

Based on the empirical findings presented here, we suggest that a seventh variation of time work, *inventing time*, should be introduced. When inventing time, the parents (and others) create a spontaneous or routinized moment or series of moments during which the family and the dead baby can retain close contact. The ritualizations constitute "saying now" and should be understood as a performative form of time making that transgresses the implication that something is taking place in the present tense as opposed to in the past. Instead, it establishes the time that it proclaims. For this reason, *inventing time* is a new variation of time work: it makes possible (and constitutes) the core of living with the dead, and is the basic premise on which the idea of the living inhabiting the same world as the dead depends. It exceeds the boundaries of the other time work variations that, in parental grief practices, are about coming to terms in various formats with the passing of the dead baby, "constituting a transport between states of being, not being and new configurations of being" (Bjerregaard et al. 2016: 1). This transport is delayed through duration time work by keeping the baby in this world or stretching the time it had here, by narrating stories of its courage and perceived strength as it fought for its life, by allocating more time to its life in this world and thereby taking time from the afterlife. The outcome of inventing time presupposes these kinds of time work: they are preparatory to everyday life with the dead baby.[7]

The *inventing time* variation clearly transgresses the conservative and reproductive categories of agency suggested by Flaherty (2003: 32). When inventing time, parents overcome the limitations of this world, of the afterlife, and of the predominant ideas about who can possess agency and invent temporal and social spaces, thereby opening up ideas of agencies and relations that are not commonly acknowledged in the twenty-first-century

Western world. They employ cultural formats that are more widespread in other parts of the world and have to do with ideas, cosmologies, rituals, and everyday life practices that are much more inclusive of the dead than practices in the current mainstream Western world.[8]

The frequent claim that death is still a taboo in the twenty-first-century Western world could be contested (Jacobsen 2016; Walter 2017; Christensen et al. 2017), but there is no doubt that many bereaved individuals feel that talking about their ongoing life with the dead *is* indeed taboo. Many bereaved parents feel a great reluctance among their friends, relatives, and colleagues to talk about their lost ones, and this might be due to the fact that losing a baby is the greatest fear of many parents. In addition, losing a baby is no longer a commonly shared experience since death in infancy has been greatly reduced during the past century. Many bereaved parents report that their families expect grief to have an endpoint and want the parents to move on. Such families may suggest that they have another baby, or content themselves with the children that they already have (if they have any).

Grief as time work suggests that part of the taboo has to do with negotiating whether or not it is socially acceptable to reallocate time among the living to the dead baby. Talking in the present tense about the baby's life and performing an inclusive "now" might be regarded as a very disturbing sign that the parents have not come to terms with their baby's death. But nothing could be further from the truth. The parents in our study are perfectly aware that their babies are dead, and referring to them in the present tense is not a sign of regression but a strategy in long-term "grief work"[9] that allows the space and time needed for a continued presence and relationship and continued parenting. *Inventing time* means reinventing parenthood and securing family life.

CONCLUSION AND PERSPECTIVES FOR FURTHER RESEARCH

Death is a fundamental challenge to the ways in which humans experience time. At the same time, as we have demonstrated throughout this chapter, death is an instigator of new human experiences of the way time works, or, perhaps more accurately, the way temporal experiences can be manipulated and changed through ritualized actions. We have suggested an addition to Flaherty's time work theory: a seventh variation which we call *inventing time*. With regard to the time work done by the bereaved parents that we studied, this invented time is a *new present*, in the sense that ritualizations actually make the parents capable of feeling that they can include the child in their ongoing everyday lives, thereby adding to the short or nonexistent time that the baby had outside the womb. These parents feel that their baby can take part in family life, can be addressed, and, sometimes, can answer back (for instance when a parent believes that a windmill whirring around on a grave is the voice of their child).

Some people might find this controversial: claiming that a dead baby is talking to its parents through a windmill on the grave. However, every human being who has suffered severe loss and bereavement due to the death of a loved one has had similar experiences: a widow asking her husband what to do in a certain situation and asking for a sign of approval for a certain decision; a son feeling his father's intense presence when doing something he used to do with his father. Situations like these are very common. If the dead do not approach the living themselves, ritualizations are produced as a means to make the dead present when needed: smelling her perfume every morning, kissing his picture every night at bedtime, cooking his favorite dish and talking about him while eating, walking by the sea in places we used to walk with our beloved—these are all examples of actions taken in order to bring the deceased back across the threshold of death so that their presence can be sensed once again. But such actions are only possible for bereaved individuals who have shared some of their lives with the deceased person. Things are more complicated for bereaved parents: they have only their own expectations, narratives in the making, family traditions, and a cultural reservoir of prototypical childhood objects that have not actually belonged to their baby—objects that their baby might have possessed if it had lived.

We suggest that the basic difference between the ritualizations produced in relation to a lost baby and a dead adult might just be the variations of time work that are employed to obtain the desired presence. The time work that goes on after the death of an adult could be described as the grief work involved in continuing to live with the dead person by ritually *reinventing* the time that has already passed: memories, situations, treasured moments that were once shared in life and are now reinvented in order to take the dead with us. The time work that goes on after the death of a baby, on the other hand, involves the *invention of time*: each unit of time is new, and each ritualized moment is indeed an invention.

Dorthe Refslund Christensen
Associate Professor, Department of Aesthetics and Communication
Aarhus University, Denmark

Kjetil Sandvik
Associate Professor, Department of Media, Cognition, and Communication
University of Copenhagen, Denmark

NOTES

1. This is, of course, clearest when it is the family's firstborn who dies—which was the case in most of the deaths in our material.
2. On knowing the fetus through the senses, see Tom Kjær 2003.
3. Seligman et al. (2008) argue that ritualizations basically create a subjunctive space—that is, an "as if" or "could be" universe where fundamental human experiences of the world can be negotiated. They also claim that this experimental mode is a quality that is not limited to religious ritualizations but tied to ritualization itself as an action mode. See also Christensen and Sandvik 2013: 106.
4. Our references to stages does not indicate concurrence with the stage-based models of grief suggested by, for instance, Elisabeth Kübler-Ross (1969). While the long narratives of pregnancy and the events that occurred around the birth/ death of a child certainly seem to be chronological at first, the various phases still overlap and are to some extent nonchronological even though there do seem to be different kinds of time work involved (Christensen and Sandvik 2013).
5. See Nünning, Nünning, and Neuman's (2010) understanding of narrative as a practice that produces worlds and matrices for life performance.
6. In Denmark, the mortality rates for both babies and infants are very low. Every year, around two thousand babies either die in the womb after the first twelve weeks of pregnancy or are stillborn. To put this into perspective, in 2017 in Denmark, 61,397 babies were born. This means that expectant parents in Denmark generally assume that their baby will be born alive and will stay alive during infancy. This is an important factor in understanding the response to a baby's death in Denmark.
7. One might object that *inventing time*, rather than being construed as a seventh variation of time work, might be construed as a variation or a metacategory to Flaherty's six variations. In this chapter, however, we have chosen the first take since our material does not suggest that inventing time is a precondition of all of the six variations. We aim at developing and refining this argument in future research.
8. Stefania Matei (2018: 84), in her illuminating work on agency and online commemorative environments, suggests breaking with classical approaches to agency as the performance of "intentional" actions and replacing it with an approach to agency as "relational" made possible by actor-network theory. The agency of the dead babies, we suggest, resembles Matei's (2018: 85) third category, "posthumous extended agency," that is, "when deceased persons receive a form of simulated presence in the world. . . . This extension is possible by developing resources that simulate posthumous presence" through media and materialities.
9. Lindemann (1944) suggested the term grief work.

REFERENCES

Bakardjieva, Maria. 2011. "The Internet in Everyday Life: Exploring the Tenets and Contributions of Diverse Approaches." In *The Handbook of Internet Studies*, edited by Mia Consalvo and Charles Ess, 59–80. Malden, MA: Wiley-Blackwell.

Bakhtin, Michail. 1981. "Form of Time and Chronotope in the Novel." In *The Dialogic Imagination: Four Essays*, edited by Michael Holquist, 84–258. Austin: University of Texas Press.

Bell, Cathrine. 1997. *Ritual Perspectives and Dimensions*. New York: Oxford University Press.

Bjerregaard, Peter, Anders E. Rasmussen, and Tim F. Soerensen, eds. 2016. *Materialities of Passing: Explorations in Transformation, Transition and Transience*. Studies in Death, Materiality and the Origins of Time series, vol. 3, edited by Rane Willerslev and Dorthe R. Christensen. Abingdon: Routledge.

Bordewijk, Jan. L., and Ben van Kaam. 1986. "Towards a New Classification of Tele-Information Services." *Intermedia* 34 (1): 6–21.

Carey, James. (1975) 1989. "A Cultural Approach to Communication." In *Communication as Culture*, 13–36. Boston: Unwin Hyman.

Christensen, Dorthe R., Ylva Haard af Segerstad, Dick Kasperowski, and Kjetil Sandvik. 2017. "Bereaved Parents' Online Grief Communities: De-Tabooing Practices or Relation-Building Grief-Ghettos?" *Journal of Broadcasting and Electronic Media* 61 (1): 58–72.

Christensen, Dorthe R., and Kjetil Sandvik. 2013. "Sharing Death: Conceptions of Time at a Danish Online Memorial Site." In *Taming Time, Timing Death: Social Technologies and Ritual*, edited by Dorthe R. Christensen and Rane Willerslev, Studies in Death, Materiality and the Origins of Time, vol. 1, 99–118. Farnham: Ashgate/Routledge.

———. 2014. "Death Ends a Life, Not a Relationship: Objects as Media on Children's Graves." In *Mediation and Remediating Death: Studies on Death, Materiality and the Origins of Time*, edited by Dorthe R. Christensen and Kjetil Sandvik, vol. 2, 251–71. Farnham: Ashgate/Routledge.

———. 2015. "Death Ends a Life Not a Relationship: Time Work and Ritualizations on Mindet.dk." *New Review of Hypermedia and Multimedia* 21 (1–2): 57–71.

———. 2016. "Grief and Everyday Life: Bereaved Parents Communicating Presence across Media." In *The Media and the Mundane: Communication across Media in Everyday Life*, edited by Kjetil Sandvik, Anne Mette Thorhauge, and Bjarni Valtysson, 105–18. Göteborg: Nordicom.

———. 2018. "Making Presence: Time Work and Narratives in Bereaved Parents' Online Grief Work." In *Mirrors of Passing: Unlocking the Mysteries of Death, Materiality, and Time*, edited by Rane Willerslev and Sophie H. Seebach, 187–201. New York: Berghahn Books.

Damkjær, Maja S. 2016. "Medialiseret forældreskab i overgangen til familielivet." In *Medialisering: Mediernes rolle i social og kulturel forandring*, edited by Stig Hjarvard, 125–56. København: Hans Reitzels Forlag.

Flaherty, Michael G. 2003. "Time Work: Customizing Temporal Experience." *Social Psychology Quarterly* 66 (1): 17–33.

———. 2011. *The Textures of Time: Agency and Temporal Experience*. Philadelphia: Temple University Press.

Foucault, Michel. 1984. "Of Other Spaces, Heterotopias." *Architecture, Mouvement, Continuité* 5: 46–49.

Heidegger, Martin. 1962. *Being and Time*. New York: Harper and Row.

Jacobsen, Michael H. 2016. "Spectacular Death": Proposing a New Fifth Phase to Philippe Ariès's Admirable History of Death. *Humanities* 5 (2): 1–20.

Kjær, Tom. 2003. "At være forældre til et dødt spædbarn." Danish online article: http://www.kirkenherlevsygehus.dk/upload/kjær_fra_korr.pdf.

Klass, Dennis, Phyllis R. Silverman, and Steven L. Nickman, eds. 1996. *Continuing Bonds: New Understandings of Grief*. Philadelphia: Taylor & Francis.

Kübler-Ross, Elisabeth. 1969. *On Death and Dying*. London: Routledge.

Lindemann, Erik. 1944. "Symptomatology and Management of Acute Grief." *American Journal of Psychiatry* 101: 141–48.

Matei, Stefania. 2018. "Responsibility beyond the Grave: Technological Mediation of Collective Moral Agency in Online Commemorative Environments." *Design Issues* 34 (1): 84–94.

Meyrowitz, Joshua. 1973. "Images of Media: Hidden Ferment—and Harmony—in the Field." *Journal of Communication* 43 (3): 55–66.

Nünning, Ansgar, Vera Nünning, and Birgit Neuman. 2010. *Cultural Ways of Worldmaking: Media and Narratives*. Berlin: De Gruyter.

Ricoeur, Paul. 1980. "Narrative Time." *Critical Inquiry* 71: 169–90.

———. 1984. *Time and Narrative*. Vol. 1. Translated by K. Blamey and D. Pellauer. Chicago: University of Chicago Press.

Romano, Claude. 2009. *Event and World*. New York: Fordham University Press.

Seligman, Adam B., Robert P. Weller, Michael J. Puett, and Bennett Simon. 2008. *Ritual and Its Consequences: An Essay on the Limits of Sincerity*. New York: Oxford University Press.

Stroebe, Wolfgang, Henk Shut, and Margaret S. Stroebe. 2005. "Grief Work, Disclosure and Counseling: Do They Help the Bereaved?" *Clinical Psychology Review* 25: 395–414.

Stroebe, Margaret, and Wolfgang Stroebe, eds. 1994. *Handbook of Bereavement: Theory, Research, and Intervention*. Cambridge: Cambridge University Press.

Walter, Tony. 1996. "A New Model of Grief: Bereavement and Biography." *Mortality* 1 (1): 7–25.

———. 1999. *On Bereavement: The Culture of Grief*. Maidenhead, PA: Open University Press.

———. 2016. "The Dead Who Become Angels: Bereavement and Vernacular Religion." *Omega: Journal of Death and Dying* 73 (1): 3–28.

———. 2017. *What Death Means Now*. Bristol: Policy Press Shorts Insights.

———. 2018 "Imag(in)ing the Dead as Angels." In *Malady and Mortality*, edited by Helen Thomas, 255–70. Newcastle-upon-Tyne: Cambridge Scholars Publishing.

Walter, Tony, Rachid Hourizi, Wendy Moncur, and Stacey Pitsillides. 2011. "Does the Internet Change How We Die and Mourn." *Omega: Journal of Death and Dying* 64 (4): 275–302.

Chapter 9

Now Is Not

Future Anteriority and
a Georgian in Russia

Martin Demant Frederiksen

⧉◇⧉

*En passant, the only origin there [is]. The now [here] a never, no here for the [now],
no now for the never. Thus some traces of the en route, an after, no[t] before.*
—Julia Hölzl, *Transience: A Poiesis, of Dis/Appearance* (brackets in original)

MOSCOW 2019

Sitting in the backseat of a limousine, I am interviewing Gosha—lead singer in one of Russia's most popular rock bands. They have a new album out, and it is climbing the charts. Spring has arrived and we are driving toward a concert venue. Or maybe it is a press conference. We discuss his incredible success, but we also touch on his early life, some ten years ago, when the band had only recently formed and they were all still living in Batumi, a coastal city in neighboring Georgia. Those were hard times, Gosha lets me know, but luckily they are now over. Although the band is busy with promoting their new album and preparing for their upcoming tour, Gosha and I meet quite often. I am currently writing pieces for *Rolling Stone* magazine, and with the number of stories and amount of background information I get about Gosha and his band these days, this is likely to go on the cover of the upcoming issue.

COPENHAGEN 2017

It was news of hoverboards that made me think about Gosha again. In 1989, the film *Back to the Future Part II* presented a vision of the future in which hoverboards, flying cars, self-drying jackets, and the premiere of *Jaws 19* were part of present-day life (Zemeckis 1989). Yet some twenty-five years after its premiere, as the future that had been envisioned finally came around, there was a widespread lack of self-drying jackets and *Jaws* sequels. Hoverboards, however, had begun to materialize, but it was one of the only once-envisioned aspects to do so. Unsurprisingly, the future had been difficult to predict in detail; it had merely been imagined.

Hoverboards made me think of Gosha because I realized that we were also approaching a future that Gosha had once predicted, one that we had talked about at great length, imagining ourselves to already be living in it. The *Rolling Stone* interview that I conducted with famed lead singer Gosha did not, of course, really take place in Moscow in 2019. It took place in Georgia in 2009, when Gosha was merely an unemployed young musician desperate to migrate to Russia, and I was merely an anthropologist. At the time, Gosha had been extremely reluctant to talk about his past and present from the perspective of the present. In a sense, the present was *too present*, too troublesome to talk about. Instead, he had insisted on the two of us setting up interview situations in an idealized future in which he had already migrated to Russia, where he was now remembering his past life in Georgia. He was, in this sense, narrating his life from a future-anterior perspective—that is, the perspective of that which will have been. This entailed that I was equally assigned a fictional role in this hoped-for and imagined future, and that we were both in Russia looking back at the present together. My research was thus temporally reconfigured from being an anthropology based only on coexperiencing the present to being one that equally entailed a coexperiencing of the future, taking what Charles Stewart (2017: 130) calls "digressive narrative leaps" forward and backward in time.

Writing about the seemingly objective aspects of time, such as clocks and the number of weekdays, Michael Flaherty (2018: 3) notes that "although it is not easy to revise temporal orientations, they are subject to change," though we most often must come to terms with these objective systems in order to socialize and coordinate actions with others. But whereas objective time is more or less invariant, subjective time is not. The latter is a question of "weaving our desires and circumstances together," a question of time work as the "effort directed toward provoking or preventing various forms of temporal experience" (Flaherty 2018: 21). Flaherty notes that time work can be classified into different dimensions: duration, frequency, sequence, timing, allocation, and taking time. Out of these, it is particularly the question of sequence that I am interested in here—that is, time work as attempts to customize an order of succession of activities and experiences. In most cases, this is done by looking forward, but in the case presented here it is a question of "time traveling" to the future in order to *look back* upon a sequence of events that have not yet happened. Sequencing here is thus not as such a question of setting up a linear timeline, but one of nonlinearity and time travel, and a form of time work that enables a dissolving or re-creation of the present (or the "now") through future-anteriority.

In the following, I trace Gosha's story as it unfolded from 2009 to the present, along with my own initial skepticism toward how Gosha could make future-anteriority as a principle of temporal agency *work*. In doing so, I relate future-anteriority as time work to the theoretical perspectives of Pierre Bourdieu and Michael Taussig (via Franz Kafka and Walter Benjamin). I aim to show that, in a Bourdieusian perspective, future-anteriority stands forth as a detachment from reality, whereas in a Taussigan perspective, it is a displacement of the self. Whereas the former represents an imagined future that—despite the implied impossibility of that endeavor—seeks to break with the present, the latter represents a generative moment where the relation between present and future becomes porous as the pre-creation of the future involves a re-creation of, rather than a break with, the present. But first I want to briefly outline the societal setting and carve out the context of Gosha's future-anteriority.

BATUMI 2009

I met Gosha while conducting fieldwork in Batumi about experiences of marginality, boredom, and time among local unemployed, underemployed, or semicriminal young men (Frederiksen 2013). At that time, unemployment rates in the Ajara region, where Batumi is located, were at around 25 percent. Once a haven for tourists from throughout the Soviet Union, Batumi and the Ajara region had faced harsh economic challenges as Georgia gained independence in 1991. Through the leadership of Aslan Abashidze, Ajara became sealed off from the rest of Georgia as a self-declared Autonomous Republic. On the one hand, this meant that the region steered clear of the civil wars that severely marked other parts of Georgia during the 1990s. On the other hand, the isolated status entailed a steep decline in tourists, along with a breakdown of formerly significant agricultural industries, such as tea and citrus plantations (Pelkmans 2006; Frederiksen 2013; Khalvashi 2015).

By 2009, Ajara had once again become part of Georgia proper, Aslan Abashidze having been ousted in 2004 following the Rose Revolution. But most locals were still struggling financially. As had many others within his age group, Gosha had been working odd jobs in the tourism sector during the short-lived summer seasons, and sometimes he had earned a little by washing cars off season. But most often he had to rely on petty cash from family members to get by. He was twenty-four at the time, divorced after a brief marriage, and now living with his two brothers and his young son, Nika. When the Russian-Georgian war broke out during the early weeks of my fieldwork, the situation for many locals went from bad to worse. Although the war was short-lived, it had dramatic effects. Fear of renewed invasion was widespread; tourists quickly disappeared; food and gas shortages set in; and work was nowhere to be found (Frederiksen 2013, 2014a). In some sense, paraphrasing Anne Allison (2013: 7), the war intensified a precarity already in existence, and migration was seen by Gosha and many others as the only feasible option—an option that had already been used by numerous Georgians since the country gained independence in 1991.

By 2013, around 770 thousand Georgian migrants were residing abroad—roughly 20 percent of the population—out of which 635 thousand were living in Russia (MPC 2013). In the following years, up to 100 thousand people annually emigrated (State Commission on Migration Studies 2017). Added to this are the number of Georgian citizens living in Russia as illegal immigrants; some estimates say up to 300 thousand people, although these numbers vary. Obtaining a visa to Russia was impossible after the 2008 war, and deportation of Georgians from Russia took place on several occasions, although the latter had happened regularly even before the war. Gosha was certainly up against the odds in dreaming about Russia. Yet despite these circumstances, whenever he and I were talking about the present from the future, we were always in Russia, driving around the streets of Moscow in a limousine.

AARHUS 2010

It was when I was originally writing up and trying to analyze Gosha's story that I first became acquainted with Michael Flaherty's (1999, see also Flaherty 2011) notion of time work, and his examinations of how people seek to alter or customize their individual experiences of time. I had also found inspiration in Susan Whyte's writings on the subjunctive mood. Whyte (2002: 175) defines subjunctivity as "the mood in which intentional subjects address possible outcomes." It is the mood of doubt, hope, will, and potential, and it was a notion that I believed fit well with theoretical conceptualizations of hope as being directed toward the future, carrying both negative and positive aspects, and one that seemed to fit well with the story of Gosha. During a presentation of a paper seeking to develop some of these thoughts, a fellow PhD student noted how there was a certain irony in the fact that, objectively seen, there was probably a bigger chance of me managing to go to Moscow as a journalist in 2019 than of Gosha managing to go there as a rock star—even though it was his dream and not mine. As with his friends and neighbors in Batumi, the people to whom I retold Gosha's story were skeptical about his ability to succeed.

TBILISI 2012

It was during a discussion with Nana, a local, Tbilisi-based NGO worker in 2012, at a point where I had in some sense put the story of Gosha behind me, that I first became acquainted with the notion of future-anteriority. Nana had been working with internally displaced people from the Georgian-Russian conflict and, for a series of years, attempted to maneuver within the multitude of reforms that the then-current government had been initiating within the sphere of psychosocial aid (and elsewhere). The government at stake was that of Mikheil Saakashvili, who had been a leading figure in the Rose Revolution and who had built up a reputation for being inclined to put form over content in his political practice, and for claiming reforms successful long before they were even implemented (Dunn 2014; Di Puppo 2015; Frederiksen and Gotfredsen 2017). Because of these political practices, Nana said, the present was not problematic because of what had happened in the past, but because of what would happen in the future. And as a consequence, the precarity of life consisted not only of post-traumatic stress (a problematic past repeating itself) but also of pretraumatic stress: a future that rendered problems in the present irrelevant despite their presence (Frederiksen 2014b). In short, the politics of the government was based on that which would have happened in the future.

One example of this was when the country's formerly liberal visa regulations were altered in order to make it more difficult for foreigners to enter the country. The government argued that this was done in compliance with the Association Agreement with the European Union, and a date was set for when the new rules would be in effect. Yet, already in the weeks prior to this date, officials in Tbilisi International Airport began complying with them, refusing foreign citizens entry to the country on the grounds that the rules would be changed in the time to come, although they had not yet changed.

In this sense, politics and reform processes came to operate as something that had already happened, although it was not yet reality—politics did not work *toward* the future but *back from* the future. Indeed, future-anteriority may be defined as a negation or a refusal of the present moment (e.g. Walsh 2001), an absenting of the present (Frederiksen 2014b) despite the continuous presence of the present.

COPENHAGEN 2017

Jarret Zigon (2009: 254) argues that hope should not merely be seen within an active/passive dichotomy, nor as solely an orientation toward a better future. Rather, hope should be viewed within the "shifting and slipping temporalities that partially constitute living in the social world." And it is, as noted by Stef Jansen (2016), surprising that while the way in which hope is tied to time and temporality is often seen as one of its primary characteristics, there is very little variety in conceptualizations of hope, despite the fact that there are numerous conceptualizations of time and temporal experience: Siegfried Kracauer's (1969) notion of "cataracts of time," Foucault's (1967) ideas about heterochrony, Russell West-Pavlov's (2013) "temporal strands," Sarah Sharma's (2014) notion of "power-chronography," Manpreet Janeja and Andreas Bandak's (2018) discussion on the politics and poetics of waiting, and Achille Mbembe's (2001) writing on the "interlocking" of times, to mention just a few.

The work of Pierre Bourdieu has been pivotal in many recent analyses of time, hope, and agency, not least through his description of the relation between subjective hope (*illusio*) and objective chances (*lusiones*). Although all individuals within this framework are agentive beings pushing toward the future through their investments, hopes, and interests, they are never free from the structures governing the particular field, or from the "meta-capital granting power of the state" (Bourdieu 1999: 57). What is seldom acknowledged, however, in the work of Bourdieu, is that he in fact does offer an opening to transformative rather than reproductive agency. As he writes, "It would be wrong to conclude that the circle of expectations and chances cannot be broken" (Bourdieu 2000: 234). This transformative agency most often occurs in situations where individuals feel that they are playthings of external constraints, and engage in activities that offer an escape from a life without possible investment; it entails a transgression of a social frontier that enacts the unthinkable. Bourdieu (2000: 226) refers to this transgression as being "detached from reality"—for instance, through following prophecies, magic, or millenarian movements and engaging in acts taking place in an imagined future that is not connected to the present. As noted by Bridget Fowler (2016: 76), such an open potentiality "is delineated as the rational pursuit of feasible Utopia . . . an image of alternative futures." That the determinism of structure otherwise predominant in Bourdieu's theory can be challenged by imagining alternatives, and through this imagining carve out the potential of flexibility or freedom, rests upon both habitus and field being marked by extreme uncertainty. This is why it remains marginal, and most often "unreal and foolhardy." It resembles what Tamta Khalvashi (2015: 102), also drawing on Bourdieu's (2000) *Pascalian Meditations*, refers to as "impossible optimism," which denotes the continuous attachment to something that you do not have.

This relation to time had seemed to fit well with Gosha's story in terms of revealing how a subjunctive mood gains prominence in situations marked by crisis and uncertainty. Yet as hoverboards made me remember Gosha, it also struck me that, when originally writing his story, I had potentially given his hope a wrong direction. His hopes were not merely directed toward the future, as a subjunctive mood would indicate, but rather directed back to the present from the future. And as a means to overcome the present he seemed to engage with the same kind of future-anteriority as the government. It should be noted that Gosha was not mimicking the future envisioned by the government. In fact, he had nothing but contempt for politicians' visions of the future, visions in which he could see no place for himself. Rather, he was copying the government's manner or structure of hopefulness, its practice of future-anteriority, by mimicking a hoped-for or imagined future, one that from his own perspective was neither unreal nor detached. Hence, while I had used the subjunctive "if it were to be," he had in fact used the future anterior "it will have been"; I was directing his hope toward the future, while he was directing himself back from the future, and in directing his hopes forward I had in some sense allowed them to stand forth as unreal and even foolhardy in the Bourdieusian sense.

Gosha had noted at one point, with reference to our talks-from-the-future, that "the time will come, where we will sit in Europe, somewhere away from this place, and we will drink tea or maybe coffee and we will say, 'Remember, Martin,' 'Remember, Gosha.' . . . We will remember this time as a joke" (Frederiksen 2013: 87). Note how the certainty of "will" is repeated: time *will* come, we *will* sit, we *will* drink, we *will* remember. The only uncertainty involved is whether we will be drinking tea or coffee.

KRASNADOR 2015

The Georgian population grew increasingly skeptical toward the future-anterior promises of politicians. A new government was elected in 2013, although this did not entail future-anteriority disappearing from politics. Similarly, people who knew Gosha grew increasingly skeptical about whether he would ever actually go to Russia and become a musician there. And I cannot completely exclude myself from that category, even though, at one point, I played a significant part in his future-anterior stories. As it would turn out, whatever skepticism I might have had was eventually put to shame.

I knew that Gosha had, in fact, managed to migrate to Russia some years ago. He had done so via marriage to a Russian girl he had dated online (see Frederiksen 2014c). But to be honest, I was a bit surprised when I learned in 2015 that Gosha had also actually become lead singer in a popular local band in Krasnador. And it struck me, as I read the promotional material of his new band, how his appearance in Russia was described in terms that were almost religious, as if his coming to Russia was a "coming" that had been predestined: "The band was formed in 2005. Lots of things changed since then. And the major change was when HE appeared. . . . he took a role as the vocalist and a spiritual leader of the band." But why would that strike me with surprise? It *had* been predestined. Gosha had said it many times, and I had noted it down, long ago. Yet while I had been writing about it as an experimentation with reality, and while many of his friends, family members, and neighbors had been talking about it as slightly delusional, Gosha had slowly turned it into reality. Or, said differently, he had lived it as reality until it became recognizable as reality for everyone else.

COPENHAGEN 2017

Can one actually participate in another person's hope? There has, within anthropology, been much discussion about questions related to the temporal aspects of field work and analysis (e. g., Dalsgaard and Frederiksen 2015; Dalsgaard and Nielsen 2015; Otto 2013), and problems related to the tense with which we later write (Birth 2008; Fabian 1983) or the use of temporality as an analytical category (Ringel 2016).

If Gosha's future-anterior mood mimicked that of the state, I was in a sense also mimicking Gosha. I accepted my role as a journalist from *Rolling Stone* magazine, and we played out the future together. The difference was that while Gosha insisted on negating the present, I went on to insist on the presence of the present. In my later writing, I continued to focus on the precariousness of Gosha's then-present daily life, while this was really what Gosha had attempted to avoid and overcome. In my perspective, the "now" was problematic; in Gosha's perspective the "now" was not, which was what made the "now" tolerable.

In *Frames of War*, Judith Butler (2010: 15) writes,

> We imagine that when the child is wanted, there is celebration at the beginning of life. But there can be no celebration without an implicit understanding that the life is grievable, that it would be grieved if it were lost, and that this future anterior is installed as the condition of its life. . . . "This will be a life that will have been lived" is the presupposition of a grievable life, which means that this will be a life that can be regarded as a life, and be sustained by that regard.

Let us dwell on the latter part of this statement for a moment: "a life that can be regarded as a life." There were many aspects of Gosha's 2008 life that were surrounded by grief. He had an extremely strained relationship with his ex-wife—the mother of his son, whom he feared mistreated the boy; he struggled with depression and increasing dependence on both pre-scription and nonprescription drugs; it had proven almost impossible to set up shows in Batumi or Tbilisi where he and the band could expose their music; and he had no idea as to how he would ever get to Russia and what would happen to his son if he did. In a sense, grief was not just a part of life, it *was* life; it was an all-consuming presence. And the future-anterior perspective seemed to be exactly what made it both grievable and thus manageable; rather than it being "a life that is not a life," it became a life that *will have been lived*, and it will have been one aspect of one point in life, but not all of life.

PANAMA, LAND OF THE CUNA, TWENTIETH CENTURY

Mimesis refers to a process of re-creation (Gebauer and Wulf 1996). The notion is probably most well known from the writings of Franz Kafka and Walter Benjamin in their explorations of the mimetic faculty—that is, the human property or ability to become or behave like something else, an approach Michael Taussig (1993) developed further in *Mimesis and Alterity*. I want to touch briefly on each of these authors.

In "A Report to an Academy," Kafka (2007) presents us with the story of an ape captured on the Gold Coast. Realizing in his cage that escape is impossible, the ape seeks an alternative "way out" by imitating the people around him—aping humanity and learning to spit, talk, smoke, and drink. "Nobody promised me," reports the ape, "that, if I became like them, the bars would be removed. Promises like that based on apparently impossible terms just aren't made. But if the terms are met, later on the promises turn up exactly where they were formerly sought in vain" (Kafka 2007: 85). After five years of mimicry, the ape has succeeded to a degree where he is invited to give a report to an academy about his former life as an ape. Yet, he states, although he is not yet fully human, he has forgotten most things about this former existence in freedom. As such, he has lost freedom in mimicking what it means to be human, and, as he never fully does become human, he remains caught between two modes of existence. There will always be a "tickling in his heels" reminding him of his apehood and his freedom, an experience he claims to share with every human being who pretends to having forgotten their apehood (81). Humans may not, as such, be apes, but we all continue aping. Agency here (if that is at all the right word to use) is not a question of rational choice. Kafka's aping ape himself calls his actions "lofty goals hazily entering his mind" (85). It is instead the ability or faculty to mimic something that is Other—a life that is Other or a structure that is Other—to a degree that allows for this imagined alterity to reveal itself as partly real in time.

Walter Benjamin often related to or wrote about the work of Kafka (Osborne 2000; Comay 2000). In "On the Mimetic Faculty," he shares Kafka's position of seeing mimicry as something humanity has always done. For Benjamin (2007: 333), mimicry is the compulsion "to become and behave like something else," and a foundational aspect of early mankind seen, for instance, in their mimicking of the surrounding world through dance. It is a form of playing with reality and may also be observed in the world of children, he notes: "Children's play is everywhere permeated by mimetic modes of behaviour, and its realm is by no means limited to what one person can imitate in another. The child plays at being not only a shopkeeper or teacher but also a windmill and a train" (Benjamin 2007: 333). It is thus a faculty that we all have, and although it may be that we in the modern world make less use of it as adults, we continue to have the ability to "read what was never written" (Benjamin 2007: 336), to mimic and behave as someone or something Other.

In *Mimesis and Alterity*, Michael Taussig (1993) departs from Kafka's ape aping humanity's aping and Benjamin's compulsion to become Other. His exploration of mimesis is based on old anthropological accounts of wood figurines among the Cuna Indians in Panama that have seemingly adopted images of Western pop culture while at the same time distancing themselves from the West. The magic of mimesis, he notes, consists in the fact that the copy (or the mimicry) affects "the original to such a degree that the representation shares in or acquires the properties of the represented" (Taussig 1993:

47), and it is through mimesis that people gain "the freedom to live reality as really made-up" (255). Through a re-creation of an Other, mimesis creates a generative possibility in the present through a radical displacement of the self. As such, it creates a suture, attaching the real and the really made-up to each other. And it is, Taussig (1993: xvii, 86) argues, in this place between the real and the really made-up that we all live our lives, theatricalizing, factualizing, and suturing through mimicry. In the aptly named preface, "A Report to the Academy" ("the," not "an"), he uses this standpoint to present a critical view on social constructivism. "With good reason," he writes, "postmodernism has relentlessly instructed us that reality is arti-fice yet, so it seems to me, not enough surprise has been expressed as to how we nevertheless go on with living, pretending—thanks to the mimetic faculty—that we live facts, not fictions" (Taussig 1993: xv). Engaging with Otherness, with magic, with the really made-up is not a detachment from reality, as Bourdieu would have put it, but actually an attachment, a suture. It may not objectively be seen as real, but it is lived as real, which is what makes it work.

MOSCOW 2019?

The attainment of adulthood, Deborah Durham (2017) has recently argued, seems increasingly to create anxiety for young people throughout the world, and even as they attain it, it may well remain elusive. In this vein, Gosha's story is not remarkable or unique but inserts itself as one case among many in which young people are forced to experiment with new ways of being or alternative ways of making both the present and the future more concrete (e.g., Cole 2010; Frederiksen and Dalsgaard 2014). Yet the future-anterior aspect of Gosha's time work does not entail making the present concrete as much as it entails dissolving it enough to make it livable. This does not imply breaking with the present (as in a Bourdieusian perspective), but rather re-creating it to what it will have been. Paraphrasing Allen Feldman (2015: 126), who also draws on Benjamin and the relation of mimesis to future-anteriority, this becomes a question of enacting "what has yet to be enacted" (see also Lertzman 2003: 12), of bringing together different times in order not just to rearticulate possibilities (see Del Pilar Blanco and Peeren 2013; Spivak 1995), but to view the present from a different perspective. Taussig (2018) himself later turned to the principle of the "magic hour" as an example of this form of fusing together different times—night and day, past and future—into a single moment that is experienced as a particular kind of generative now.

When finishing this chapter, I made one last attempt to track down Gosha. I logged into an old account on the Russian website odnoklassniki.ru—a place where Gosha and I had had much contact some ten years ago, but both of us more or less subsequently abandoned the site. To my surprise, I did find a message from him, simply stating "Helloooo Brother!" It had been written from Krasnador in 2015 as a response to a message that I had sent him in 2013. Another thing occurred while finishing the chapter: I was invited to visit Moscow, although various circumstances prevented me from doing so. It would have been quite serendipitous to actually sit in Moscow and finish this chapter, although most likely I would have been sitting there without Gosha. Then again, with so much else once-foreseen partly coming true, I would have restrained myself from being surprised had Gosha suddenly walked down the street. Futures rarely unfold exactly as they are planned or perceived, but sometimes, despite all odds, they come incredibly close.

I initially thought it a shame that I could not get hold of Gosha. Aside from writing him on odnoklassniki.ru, I tried contacting the manager of his new band in Russia, who did not reply, and I contacted some of our old mutual friends in Batumi, who did not have his direct contact details, either. But I had already played my part of what is now Gosha's present, as I had talked to him about it and written about it years ago, although, mistakenly, I had separated what I believed was either real or really made-up, while Gosha had been suturing the two. And I have increasingly come to realize that, when we were talking about (or from) the future, we had perhaps not been talking about the same thing at all. At the least, we had been engaged in different moods and directions while doing so. As noted earlier, I had been skeptical about whether Gosha's time work would work—whether he would ever reach the future he was envisioning. But that was not the work it was meant to do. Instead, Gosha was working on the present via the future just as much as he was working on the future in the present.

My aim here has not been to say that hope is always a question of future-anteriority instead of subjunctivity. On the contrary, it has been to bring attention to the role of what we might term the mood swings of hope and the practices of mimicry involved when people position themselves in time and are positioned in time by those who study them. And it has been to bring attention to time work as a digressive leap that allows one to live the present by re-creating it through enactments of hoped-for futures.

Martin Demant Frederiksen
Associate Professor, Department of Anthropology
Aarhus University, Denmark

NOTE

I owe my thanks to all who have commented and made suggestions for this chapter, and particularly to Robin May Schott, Noa Vaisman, and Clarissa Martins, and to the editors of this volume for their comments along the way.

REFERENCES

Allison, Anne 2013. *Precarious Japan*. Durham, NC: Duke University Press.
Benjamin, Walter 2007. "On the Mimetic Faculty." In *Reflections: Essays, Aphorisms, Autobiographical Writings*. New York: Schocken Books.
Birth, Kevin 2008. "The Creation of Coevalness and the Danger of Homochronism." *Journal of the Royal Anthropological Institute* 14 (1): 3–20.
Bourdieu, Pierre 1999. "Rethinking the State: Genesis and Structure of the Bureaucratic Field." In *State/Culture: State Formation after the Cultural Turn*, edited by George Steinmetz, 53–76. Ithaca: Cornell University Press.
———. 2000. *Pascalian Meditations*. London: Polity Press.
Butler, Judith 2010. *Frames of War: When is Life Grievable?* London: Verso.
Cole, Jennifer 2010. *Sex and Salvation: Imagining the Future in Madagascar*. Chicago: University of Chicago Press.
Comay, Rebecca. 2000. "Benjamin's Endgame." In *Walter Benjamin's Philosophy: Destruction and Experience*, edited by Andrew Benjamin and Peter Osborne, 252–92. Manchester: Clinamen Press.
Dalsgaard, Anne Line, and Martin Demant Frederiksen. 2015. "Out of Conclusion: On Recurrence and Open-Endedness in Life and Analysis." In *Time and the Field*, edited by Steffen Dalsgaard and Morten Nielsen, 50–64. London: Berghahn Books.
Dalsgaard, Steffen, and Morten Nielsen. 2015. "Introduction: Time and the Field." In *Time and the Field*, edited by Steffen Dalsgaard and Morten Nielsen, 1–19. London: Berghahn Books.
del Pilar Blanco, Marìa, and Esther Peeren. 2013. "Introduction: Conceptualizing Spectralities." In *The Spectralities Reader: Ghosts and Haunting in Contemporary Cultural Theory*, edited by Marìa del Pilar Blanco and Esther Peeren, 1–29. London: Bloomsbury.
Di Puppo, Lili. 2015. "Marketing Reforms: The Dimension of Narratives in Georgia's Fight against Corruption." In *State and Legal Practice in the Caucasus: Anthropological Perspectives on Law and Politics*, edited by Stephane Voell and Iwona Kaliszewska, 223–42. London: Routledge.
Dunn, Elizabeth. 2014. "Humanitarianism, Displacement and the Politics of Nothing in Postwar Georgia." *Slavic Review* 73 (2): 307–22.
Durham, Deborah. 2017. "Elusive Adulthoods: Introduction." In *Elusive Adulthoods: The Anthropology of New Maturities*, edited by Deborah Durham and Jacqueline Solway, 1–39. Bloomington: Indiana University Press.

Fabian, Johannes. 1983. *Time and the Other: How Anthropology Makes Its Object*. New York: Columbia University Press.

Feldman, Allen 2015. *Archives of the Insensible: Of War, Photopolitics, and Dead Memory*. Chicago: University of Chicago Press.

Flaherty, Michael G. 1999. *A Watched Pot: How We Experience Time*. New York: New York University Press.

———. 2011. *The Textures of Time: Agency and Temporal Experience*. Philadelphia: Temple University Press.

———. 2018. "An S-Shaped Pattern in the Perceived Passage of Time: How Social Interaction Governs Temporal Experience." *Language and Cognition* 10: 1–25.

Foucault, Michel. (1967) 2008. "Of Other Places." In *Heterotopia and the City: Public Space in Postcivil Society*, edited by Michiel Dehaene and Lieven de Cauter, 13–31. New York: Routledge.

Fowler, Bridget. 2016. "The State, the Enlightenment and the Scottish Literary Field." In *Bourdieusian Prospects*, edited by Lisa Adkins, Carey Brosnan and Steven Threadgold, 71–91. London: Routledge.

Frederiksen, Martin Demant. 2013. *Young Men, Time and Boredom in the Republic of Georgia*. Philadelphia: Temple University Press.

———. 2014a. "Heterochronic Atmospheres: Affect, Materiality, and Youth in Depression." In *Ethnographies of Youth and Temporality: Time Objectified*, edited by Anne Line Dalsgaard, Martin Frederiksen, Susanne Hojlund, and Lotte Meinert, 81–96. Philadelphia: Temple University Press.

———. 2014b. "The Would-Be State: Reforms, NGOs, and Absent Presents in Post-Revolutionary Georgia." *Slavic Review* 73 (2): 307–22.

———. 2014c. "To Russia with Love: Hope, Confinement and Virtuality among Youth on the Georgian Black Sea Coast." *Focaal* 70: 26–36.

Frederiksen, Martin Demant, and Anne Line Dalsgaard. 2014. "Introduction: Time Objectified." In *Ethnographies of Youth and Temporality: Time Objectified*, edited by Anne Line Dalsgaard, Martin Demant Frederiksen, Susanne Højlund, and Lotte Meinert, 1–21. Philadelphia: Temple University Press.

Frederiksen, Martin Demant, and Katrine Bendtsen Gotfredsen. 2017. *Georgian Portraits: Essays on the Afterlives of a Revolution*. Winchester, UK: Zero Books.

Gebauer, Gunter, and Christoph Wulf. 1996. *Mimesis: Culture–Art–Society*. University of California Press.

Hölzl, Julia. 2010. *Transience: A Poiesis, of Dis/Appearance*. New York: Atropos Press.

Janeja, Manpreet, and Andreas Bandak. 2018. *Ethnographies of Waiting: Doubt, Hope and Uncertainty*. London: Bloomsbury.

Jansen, Stef. 2016. "For a Relational, Historical Ethnography of Hope: Indeterminacy and Determination in the Bosnian and Herzegovinian Meantime." *History and Anthropology* 27 (4): 1–18.

Kafka, Franz. 2007. *Metamorphosis and Other Stories*. London: Penguin.

Khalvashi, Tamta. 2015. "Peripheral Affects: Shame, Publics, and Performance on the Margins of the Republic of Georgia." PhD dissertation, University of Copenhagen.

Kracauer, Siegfried. 1969. *History: The Last Things before the Last*. New York: Oxford University Press.

Lertzman, Renee. 2003. "The Future Produced, Perceived and Performed: Reading Green Futures." Working Paper. Accessed 24 November 2017 from http://www .cardiff.ac.uk/socsi/futures/futureproduced.pdf.

Mbembe, Achille. 2001. *On the Postcolony*. Berkeley: University of California Press.

Osborne, Peter. 2000. "Small-Scale Victories, Large-Scale Defeats: Walter Benjamin's Politics of Time." In *Walter Benjamin's Philosophy: Destruction and Experience*, edited by Andrew Benjamin and Peter Osborne, 59–110. Manchester: Clinamen Press.

Otto, Ton. 2013. "Times of the Other: The Temporalities of Ethnographic Fieldwork." *Social Analysis* 57: 64–79.

Pelkmans, Mathijs. 2006. *Defending the Border: Identity, Religion, and Modernity in the Republic of Georgia*. Ithaca: Cornell University Press.

Ringel, Felix. 2016. "Beyond Temporality: Notes on the Anthropology of Time from a Shrinking Fieldsite." *Anthropological Theory* 16 (4): 390–412.

Sharma, Sarah. 2014. *In the Meantime: Temporality and Cultural Politics*. Durham, NC: Duke University Press.

Spivak, Gayatri Chakravorty. 1995. "Ghostwriting." *Diacritics* 25 (2): 65–84.

State Commission on Migration Studies. 2017. *2017 Migration Profile of Georgia*. Tbilisi: Secretariat of the State Commission on Migration Studies.

Stewart, Charles. 2017. "Uncanny History: Temporal Topology in the Post-Ottoman World." *Social Analysis* 61 (1): 129– 42.

Taussig, Michael. 1993. *Mimesis and Alterity: A Particular History of the Senses*. New York: Routledge.

———. 2018. *Palma Africana*. Chicago: Chicago University Press.

Walsh, Lisa. 1002. "Between Maternity and Paternity: Figuring Ethical Subjectivity." *Differences: A Journal of Feminist Cultural Studies* 12 (1): 79– 111.

West-Pavlov, Russell. 2013. *Temporalities*. Oxon, UK: Routledge.

Whyte, Susan Reynolds. 2002. "Subjectivity and Subjunctivity: Hoping for Health in Eastern Uganda." In *Postcolonial Subjectivities in Africa*, edited by Richard Werbner, 171–91. London: Zed Books.

Zemeckis, Robert, dir. 1989. *Back to the Future Part II*. Universal Pictures.

Zigon, Jarret. 2009. "Hope Dies Last: Two Aspects of Hope in Contemporary Moscow." *Anthropological Theory* 9 (3): 253–71.

Part VI

Time and Deprivation

Chapter 10

The Work of Waiting

Boredom, Teatime, and Future-Making in Niger

Adeline Masquelier

❦

On a balmy night in Niamey, Niger's capital city, a dozen young men are sitting together by the side of the road running along the east bank of the Niger River. Four of them are playing cards while the rest appear to be listening to a radio broadcast. A few feet away, a young man by the name of Mourtaba is intently watching a tiny, bubbling kettle resting on a bed of hot coals. "Tea drinking, it started with unemployment," he tells me as he carefully picks up the kettle with a small piece of cardboard—the handle is very hot. He pours the contents into a metal cup before swiftly pouring it back into the kettle with the smoothness, confidence, and economy of motion of someone who routinely performs these gestures. Pouring tea from a height aerates the liquid and creates a foamy layer on the surface that is said to enhance the drinking experience. When prepared by a skilled tea maker, the heavily sweetened concoction is a perfect marriage of tea and froth. "Young men had nothing to do. They would sit and drink tea," Mourtaba further explains. "Tea brought people together. It gave them something to do. So it became the pastime of young men as they waited for things to improve."

Mourtaba is the designated *teaman* (tea maker) of the *fada*, the "tea circle" or conversation group that meets daily at the same spot.[1] He is the fada's youngest member and a sophomore in high school. Every evening, after he has completed his school assignments, he makes his way to the fada—the term refers to both the group of friends and the meeting place—bringing with him the small brazier filled with coals and the metal tray holding the kettle and the metal cup, as well as small glasses used to serve tea. As he lays the blue kettle back on the burning coals, I notice the red initials painted on one side: S. M. They stand for "Super Mecs" (French slang for "Super Guys"), the name the young men have given to their fada. Meanwhile, the card players are still absorbed in their game and the others are now debating the merits of a new initiative the Nigerien government recently implemented to tackle youth unemployment. Though none of them appear to be paying attention to what Mourtaba is doing, they are all waiting for the tea to brew.

In the context of global shifts that fall under the rubric of neoliberalism (Ferguson 2006; Harvey 2005), waiting has become something of an endemic condition for young male urbanites unable to secure stable salaried jobs in Niger. *Samari* (unmarried young men) have created spaces specifically for waiting—the fadas—and they repair to those spaces frequently to socialize with friends, play cards, listen to music, and engage in a variety of pastimes and projects. Fadas generally bring together samari who have grown up in the same neighborhood or attended the same school. In some cases, they join young men who share similar musical interests, political views, or religious commitments. Though they are not entirely free of the rivalry that often tinges relations between young men competing for scarce resources,[2] fadas are described as places where samari do not have to pretend to be anything but themselves. They constitute a refuge from formal social constraints—a kind of "heterotopia" (Foucault [1966] 1994) that exists beyond the grasp of dominant social institutions and functions with its own temporalities, ethical codes, and forms of commensality.

If idleness is often what brings young men to join a fada, tea, by their own admission, is what keeps them together. At the fada, idleness (and its attendant anxieties) is transformed into an enjoyable and ultimately rewarding experience thanks to the way that "teatime"—during which tea is prepared and consumed—punctuates the temporality of boredom and endows waiting with a pragmatic, purposeful dimension. Michael Flaherty (2003, 2011) has coined the concept of "time work" to capture how temporal experience is constructed through people's efforts to intervene in the unfolding of events. In this chapter, I explore the agentive dimension of waiting at the fada through the analytical lens of time work. Focusing on teatime, I discuss how the fadas of young Nigerien men constitute what might be called workspaces-in-waiting. In particular, I consider how the emergence of a new sociality—epitomized through the practice of sharing tea—shapes the temporality and texture of waiting, helping boredom vanish and giving samari a fleeting sense of control over the spread of time.

Following a brief description of the economic conditions that have given rise to a widespread sense, among the younger generation in particular, that a future, once possible, is now imperiled, I consider the effects of unemployment, precarity, and idleness on the experience of time and productivity, and I describe the strategies samari have devised to reinsert flow and momentum into their lives. I discuss how the small pleasures that the fada, as a space of care and conviviality, affords its members lead to a restructuring of temporality such that, rather than being a source of anxiety and ennui, time becomes a resource. Teatime, I argue, is a kind of production, a social practice that shapes—and is itself shaped—by notions of time, sociality, and futurity. In the way it resituates young men in the rhythm and tempo of daily life, teatime provides opportunities for hope to nest and for dreams of a good life to be nurtured. However, when teatime clashes with other temporalities, such as the regimented schedule of daily prayers Muslims are enjoined to follow, it becomes an expression of impiety. In the end, it also suggests that youth understand time and apprehend the future very differently from elders, while providing yet another demonstration of how, to paraphrase Flaherty (2003), time and agency work together. The settings for my ethnographic study are Dogondoutchi, a small provincial town of heterogeneous Hausa speakers, and Niamey, a multiethnic and multilingual metropolis.

COMPROMISED ADULTHOODS

In the early years of independence, Nigeriens who sought upward mobility through education were assured of being admitted to the civil service.[3] Formal education was widely advertised as the ticket to a better life. Today, however, having a high school or university degree does not automatically translate into prosperity and success. In the 1980s and 1990s, the World Bank, the International Monetary Fund (IMF), and other international lenders imposed severe limitations on state spending as part of a neoliberal program of reforms aimed at spurring economic growth. The Nigerien state shrunk social services and stopped acting as a job provider, relying instead on flexible, disposable labor to dispense minimal and largely inadequate education, healthcare, and security. Instead of leading to economic growth and encouraging foreign investments, the reforms undertaken in the name of fiscal responsibility plunged the country into economic decline and stagnation. The quality of education declined; employment opportunities dwindled; and the lucky few who found jobs often received salaries far too modest to sustain households. Consequently, social inequalities have widened, and most young people, regardless of their educational status, lead lives of considerable precarity.

While educational credentials have not led to the valued government jobs that would enable samari to marry (and care for dependents), they have spawned aspirations that make it shameful for them to engage in labor-intensive, low-paying work. Every year, large numbers of *jeunes diplômés* (educated youth) join existing cohorts of unemployed rather than take jobs they consider beneath them. Added to the fact that jobs are few and far between, there is a perception that the system is rigged against poor candidates who cannot benefit from the politics of patronage and nepotism that favor well-off job candidates with connections. Intensified exposure to global media has also created expectations of rapid mobility among the less educated who are navigating the informal economy, working as fruit vendors, motorcycle taxi drivers, shoe shiners, and so on. Yet the means of support they cobble up through a combination of hustling, hawking, and economic ingenuity are limited, and many of them are forced to defer their plans of marriage and family.

This state of affairs is hardly specific to Niger. Throughout the Global South (and increasingly in some parts of the Global North, as well), young people are marginalized by the workings of capital. Having come of age in an era of great uncertainty, many of them negotiate volatile economic contexts without ever being assured of securing stable livelihoods. Trapped in the imposed presentism of daily survival, they often feel robbed of the futurity that previous generations took for granted (Allison 2013; Mains 2013; Weiss 2004). Scholars have referred to the period of stagnation, helplessness, and vulnerability experienced by young unemployed college graduates in the Middle East, Africa, and elsewhere as "waithood" (Dhillon and Yousef 2009; Honwana 2012; Singerman 2007). The concept of waithood implies that young people are somehow stuck in a kind of "arrested liminality"—a preadulthood—because the social prerequisites for adulthood are too hard to reach (Durham and Solway 2017; Sommers 2012: 5; Utas 2005). As a unidirectional holding pattern, waithood only tells us one side of the story, however. Though life transitions are never so definitive as their models suggest, the concept of waithood operates on the assumption that the move to adulthood, no matter how delayed, is inevitable and irreversible (Johnson-Hanks 2006). Because it homogenizes the period of suspension young men find themselves in, waithood cannot account for the diverse twists and turns that the trajectories of youth take in Niger and elsewhere.

Nigerien society is divided into youth and elders, but since juniority and seniority are situational notions, this may be interpreted differently depending on the context, enabling people to claim particular age statuses. When they turn seven, boys reach the age of reason and are old enough to be sent away from home (to study with a Quranic teacher, for instance).

Gender norms governing social life take on their full meaning after puberty, when boys become samari. Samari are given separate sleeping quarters; their access to other men's houses is restricted. Since social adulthood is a matter of providing for a dependent, samari become fully adult upon marrying their first wife. According to this cultural logic, young women become adults when they give birth to their first child. Many of them marry early: female sexuality must be imperatively regulated by marriage. This means that women's experience of youth is shorter than men's and their transition to adulthood is not hampered to the same extent by austerity and joblessness, though they, too, may find their futures compromised, especially if education is their chosen path to economic stability.

In the face of limited prospects, samari have sought spaces of relevance in a landscape of unevenly distributed access to work and wealth. The fada is a haven where they can buffer themselves from the alienating effects of marginalization. It is a place where they can wait and hope. Waiting may be experienced as a suspension of time but it is hardly ever a suspension of activity (Jeffrey 2008; Kwon 2015; Miyazaki 2004). Nor does it inevitably translate into a passive, aimless mode of anticipating the future (Dungey and Meinert 2017). In this regard, the daily making and consumption of tea, or what I call teatime, cannot be reduced to a simple tactic for passing time. It is also energizing, stirring samari into setting up lines of activity that launch some kind of future. In this chapter, I explore the micropolitics of waiting that are not easily accounted for by the macrotemporalities of waithood.

THE FADA OF YOUTH

In Hausa, Niger's most widely spoken language, the word "fada" traditionally refers to the chief or emir's court. The fada is a masculine space par excellence, specifically suited to the work of conflict resolution and public deliberation. When Nigerien university students went on strike in Niamey in the early 1990s in an effort to push the state to transition to a multiparty democracy, they adopted the term to designate their own informal gatherings as they sat in the street and debated the future of their country. To pass time, they drank Tuareg tea, a heavily sugared infusion of green tea that is typically consumed in company. In a matter of years, the fadas had replaced the traditional youth associations created in the 1970s by the state to channel youthful energies toward public works and food crop production. At the fada, samari struggling to carve out their place in society found a refuge from harsh social realities and an outlet for the performance of masculinity. In the company of similarly penniless peers, many of them forgot the shame of having to depend on elders for survival. The fada was also where they learned to map out possible futures. One could say the fada was a place where yearning for "aspirational normativity" (Berlant 2011)–an expectation that, rather than having to merely survive, one actually belongs in the world–was encouraged.

As fadas emerged in other urban areas where male youth struggled with unemployment, boredom, and social exclusion, the culture of tea drinking spread among samari–"like a virus," a young man once put it. Tea soon became the centerpiece of fada life everywhere and a prime expression of male conviviality. For elders, for whom a man is often known by what he does for a living, the tea drinking of unemployed samari symptomatized laziness, hedonism, and irresponsibility. If not properly controlled, it could lead, along with tobacco, drug, and alcohol consumption, to moral decadence and even crime. With time, however, most elders reconciled themselves to the fact that fadas were here to stay. Since their emergence in the 1990s, fadas have led to a drastic reconfiguration of public space and of the modalities of male sociality.

There are many kinds of fadas, with some composed essentially of un-(der)employed samari and others made up of stably employed men who meet daily after work. A large number of them have a diverse membership composed of university students as well as petty traders, unemployed graduates, and temporarily employed teachers. Fadas often join young men with shared interests; yet not all fadas are united by the same vision of sociality and citizenship. Some are but informal conversation spots. Many of them are fairly structured organizations, headed by a governing body and animated by a spirit of civic-mindedness. Their configuration and mission notwithstanding, a spirit of egalitarianism suffuses the fadas. Whether they are relatively well-off or impoverished, salaried or working in the informal economy, educated or illiterate, all members enjoy the same rights and privileges. "Life is hard," samari say; "it is critical that we be supportive of one another." What this often means is that whoever has money will pay for sugar and tea. In some cases, stringent rules dictate that members pay their dues if they wish to remain in good standing. Though hierarchy occasionally regulates certain practices (such as the order in which tea is served), solidarity, respect, inclusion, and parity are the fada's foundation.

Modeled after the council of elders, an all-male governing structure, the fada is centered on male pastimes, concerns, and aspirations. It is also part of street culture. In an overwhelmingly Muslim society, where women's access to public spaces is constantly policed, the street is largely controlled by men. Young women seen in the street are usually going somewhere, not loitering. Any social gathering they attend mostly takes place inside someone's home. In contrast, samari assemble at the fada in plain view of passers-by, reminding us of how differently men and women occupy public space in gender-segregated societies. Since the fada is designed to fulfill men's desire for sociality and self-affirmation, the presence of women disrupts its social dynamics and its carefully cultivated intimacy. To be sure, there are exceptions to this rule: a very small percentage of fadas have a mixed membership (educated youths who are comfortable in gender-mixed settings). Generally, however, young women passing by a fada do not linger, fearful of the social opprobrium their presence at these male gatherings might generate. When they do visit, it is generally under the cover of darkness and wearing a hijab to escape parental control. At night, the fada thus becomes a discreet rendezvous space for lovers—an issue that has prompted religious Muslim elites to lash out against the fada system.

The names fadas bear—often borrowed from hip-hop music or alluding to distant destinations—betray their members' cosmopolitan aspirations and their infatuation with the tough expressions of heroic masculinity promoted by global popular culture.[4] They also reveal the kind of futures to which samari aspire. Like young Ugandan musicians who, in their attempts to court fame and success, take evocative names that they hope will bring them closer to their desired future (Meinert and Schneidermann 2014), samari often chose names that condense their visions of the life they want to live one day. By relying on the magic of words to bring hoped-for worlds into being, they are effectively "naming the future" (Meinert and Schneidermann 2014: 170). In the way it "predicts" a future that is closely aligned with the present, naming one's fada after a famous hip-hop star or a sought-after destination is a form of temporal agency—a refusal to accept that the future may be foreclosed. Some of them function as nongovernmental organizations or rotating credit associations, while others provide informal professional training. During elections, a number of fadas become campaign headquarters for political parties. Others are looking to generate social capital through their engagement in musical activities. Not all have a civic mission: a few of them serve as nodes of redistribution for drugs or stolen goods. Yet, insofar as they have largely reconfigured the forms that social and political engagements take among young men, fadas can be referred to as "street parliaments" (Banégas, Brisset-Foucault, and Cutolo 2012: 5).

To mark their presence in a neighborhood, samari etch the name of their fadas (together with other decorative motifs) on the walls against which they typically sit; the trend has given rise to a brand-new scriptural economy in urban Niger whose rules and regulations are controlled by samari (Masquelier 2019). Predictably, the iconic teapot figures prominently (along with hearts, dollar signs, stars, and skulls and bones) on the facades colonized by fadas. Although fadas continue to incite controversy, notably among Muslim religious leaders, who characterize them as dens of immorality and irreligiosity (samari often "forget" to pray), they have become part of the urban fabric. This is something growing numbers of parents recognize and, in some cases, approve of. For some members of the older generation, however, the sight of young men sipping tea in the street remains synonymous with indulgence and frivolity.

THE BURDEN OF TIME

Samari have their own take on what makes tea such a central ingredient of fada sociality. Among other things, they point out that tea is beneficial to their health. They like to enunciate the healing properties of green tea (it cleans the arteries) and stress its soothing effects. If many of them are increasingly aware that an excessive consumption of sugary tea may be linked to rising rates of diabetes, they nevertheless insist that tea must be appreciated for its restorative qualities. Above all, they note, tea is an effective remedy against boredom. Boredom is the inability to fill time through the kind of meaningful engagement with the world that makes one forget time. By giving samari not only something to do but also something to look forward to and something to remember with fondness, teatime—which includes the experience of waiting for the tea to brew—resituates them in time, making them feel part of the world. Samari who are unemployed or intermittently employed do not experience the regular alternance of work and rest that ideally gives one a sense of stability as well as forward momentum. They feel disconnected from a world regulated by the rhythm and pace of industrious life. By puncturing what previously felt like a dead stretch of time, teatime reintroduces a sense of pattern, as well as a rhythmic quality, in the lives of idle samari. It structures and segments time meaningfully. As such, it provides a useful lens through which to consider how temporal experience is "customized" (Flaherty 2003) at the fada, helping socially adrift samari regain a sense of control over how time is passed and life is lived.

When people are engaged in activities they find productive, enriching, or simply fun, they feel part of the world and in the flow of things. They gain a sense of control over their situation and lose the self-consciousness (that often translates as restlessness or anxiety) that may have initially distanced them from their activities. Moreover, their experience of time is altered. How fast time appears to flow (or, as English speakers say, "fly") thus provides a measure of the intensity of their engagement (Csikszentmihályi 1990). Those who feel bored, on the other hand, often describe time as an excessive, alienating presence that overwhelms their attempts to carve out spaces of belonging and fully experience life. Some jobless *samari* thus describe time as an elongated stretch of experience or as an emptiness that they try to "fill" or "kill" through various means. They speak of being stuck (*"ils nous coincent"*), unable to move forward. In urban Ethiopia, unemployed young men speak of having an "overabundant and potentially dangerous quantity" of time (Mains 2012: 10). In Accra, Ghana, the *kobolo* (street lounger) looking for employment similarly seeks to escape the burden of time (Quayson 2014). Feeling excluded from the future that policy makers and politicians are crafting for the citizenry, underprivileged young men in post-Soviet Georgia exist in a state of "temporal marginality" (Frederiksen 2013: 11). For the disenfranchised, fighting boredom translates worldwide into efforts to control the passing of time so that the perceived duration of a temporal stretch is altered (Flaherty 2003). The goal is to make time pass more quickly by imbuing the moment with the "qualities" it previously lacked (Goodstein 2005). This is precisely what teatime is about.

THE PLEASURES OF TEATIME

At the fada, preparing *shai* (tea) takes time. Not only should the process not be rushed but each step is the object of a careful, deliberate, and quasi-ritualized procedure that an experienced teaman performs with polish and precision: once the water and, later, the tea are boiling, and the sugar (often purchased with funds that members contribute weekly to the fada) has been added, the contents of the kettle have to boil for a long while before the tea is considered ready. "There are twenty-three rules for making and serving tea," a tall, wiry young man with round glasses once volunteered. When I asked what these were, he laughed before admitting he had forgotten most of them. With time I learned many of these so-called rules (though I also found out they differ from fada to fada). Some rules apply to the way tea is poured and the order in which assembled fada members are served. Others have to do with the way one drinks one's share of tea: for instance, the foam (created when the hot liquid is poured from a height) covering the tea can be tasted with a lick of the tongue but not swallowed entirely, for there are others waiting for their turn.

Each step of the tea-making process enables participants to savor by anticipation the delights that await them when they are handed a tiny glass of the dark amber liquid. Not only is the air permeated with the sweet smell of tea escaping from the bubbling kettle but also the performance of the tea maker is visible to all participants so they can measure his progress and

from time to time evaluate how close they are to enjoying a sip of tea. The
crunching sound of hot coals being stoked, the hissing made by drops of
liquid falling on the embers, and the gurgling of the tea being poured from
a height by the tea maker are all part of the sensual experience of teatime.
Time here is appreciated multisensorially.

Each tea session is made of three rounds. This means that each clump
of tea leaves is used three times: the first round of tea is the strongest (and
bitterest), while the last one is the weakest (and only fit for women, as far
as some samari are concerned). As noted earlier, teatime is as much about
waiting for the tea to brew as it is about drinking it.[5] It is a collective form of
waiting that creates opportunities to catch up with friends, strengthen social
connections, brainstorm about a new project, or simply sit contentedly in
the company of one's peers. Samari often say that a fada without tea is not
a fada. In so doing, they stress not only that teatime is a critical element of
fada temporality but also that the very act of sharing tea forges the social
connections that constitute the fada's fabric.

Jobless young men who experience the sting of poverty and the sense of
worthlessness arising out of their economic disenfranchisement speak of the
considerable anxiety they feel at the thought of their imperiled future. "Our
future is bleak. We do odd jobs so we don't die of hunger. But there are so
many *chômeurs* [unemployed people], and we become more numerous every
year. We wait for jobs that do not come, and time passes," explained a wor-
ried young man with a degree in history who spent much of his time at his
fada. Another member of the fada described how out of sorts he felt when,
after unsuccessfully trying to secure employment for several years, he went
back to school: "I graduated from middle school seven years ago. Last year,
there was a qualifying exam for *l'école normale* [the teachers' training school]
in my hometown. I was there with my brother who's seven years younger
than me. I was the smallest in size but the oldest in age. It was hard."

The wait for jobs is stressful because it is open-ended. In the current
economic slump, the tremendous uncertainty young men face means they
are living with an unclear time horizon. Some are hopeful that things will
improve if only they can be patient (patience is a particularly valued quality
that all *mutumin kirki*—good, honorable people—possess), but many live with a
gnawing sense that the future they so desperately yearn for may never come
to pass. Either way, they feel dispossessed, "deprived of property, work, and
entitlements" (Humphrey 2002: 21) as well as futurity.

For those who must put their lives on hold, the fada provides a set of
mechanisms for coping with excess time and alleviating the stress of not
knowing what will happen (or when something will happen). "*On fait le thé
pour se calmer. Le thé, c'est bon*" (We make tea to calm ourselves. Tea is good)

is how an eighteen-year-old high school student put it. He was alluding not to the chemical properties of shai but to the way that teatime, as a mode of customizing temporality, momentarily reinserts young men who are "lost in time" in the texture of lived experience.[6] Waiting for tea is not about stilling time; rather, it gives one a sense of forward direction. The "not-yet" (Bloch 1986) quality of the time one experiences has a comforting predictability. One's awareness of the "now" is meaningfully anchored in a wider temporality that includes not just what is ahead but what recently happened. In other words, teatime is a multilayered experience, making space for anticipation—and the certainty of yet-to-come moments centered on the fraternal sharing of tea—as well as recollection—including memories of previous teatimes.

Tea-drinking sessions can fill the large part of an afternoon. They make time bearable, even enjoyable. Aside from being time "fillers," they engage young men in the kind of anticipation that—in contrast to the seemingly endless search for jobs—yields foreseeable pleasures. Samari describe the whole experience (not just the moment when they swallow a sip of tea) as being at once stimulating and comforting—in short, productive. Whereas boredom dulls experience, teatime replenishes it. Elsewhere, I have probed the role of pleasure in structuring the temporality of teatime (Masquelier 2013). Here, I simply want to note how the anticipation of sweet delights that constitutes teatime comes close to what philosophers have referred to as "jouissance." In the way it absorbs samari in the "now" of experience, teatime transforms pleasure into a duration that is seemingly endless. One hopes the tea will be ready soon and, at the same time, one wishes for the experience not to end. Waiting for tea, even when it is mediated by light conversation or a game of backgammon, is a purposeful form of engagement that counters the oppressive weight of boredom by grounding those who wait in the pleasure of here and now and giving them a sense of "inner time or *durée* within which [their] actual experiences are connected with the past . . . and the future" (Schutz in Flaherty 2003: 18).

THE CUSTOMIZING OF TEMPORALITY

Recent scholarship has shed light on the temporality of precarity, pointing to the ways in which the experience of time is mediated by impoverishment and economic dislocation. Bruce O'Neill (2017) writes how in Bucharest, life for homeless people loses its pulsing quality, ultimately slowing down to a crawl. Anne Allison (2013: 91) describes the presentist concerns of the "precariously employed, forever youthful [Japanese] youth" for whom there is no longer a distinction between life and work because so much of life is spent working odd jobs or looking for jobs. Others have also noted how a characteristic of precarious time is precisely the fusion of work and non-work times to the extent that the quest for viable livelihoods absorbs every moment. In the process, time loses its texture, its rhythms, and its "eventfulness." Significantly, boredom amounts to a similar feeling that life has no flow or momentum. Among those for whom life is synonymous with "plenty of nothing," as Michael Raposa (1999: 42) puts it, time lacks definition. Because they are deprived of the rhythmic contrast between productive work and enjoyable rest (or idleness), their experience of the world is "without qualities" (Goldstein 2005). Young, unemployed Ethiopian men told anthropologist Daniel Mains (2007) that the only change they experienced in their lives was watching the shadows slide from one side of the road to the other with the quotidian movement of the sun in the sky.

In such contexts, the customizing of temporality focuses on the manipulation of frequency and sequence (Flaherty 2003). This may mean increasing the frequency of certain activities or dividing what seem like overly long, homogeneous intervals of time into shorter segments so as to produce a punctuated temporality. To (re)create marked distinctions between "work" and "leisure," homeless youth in Kinshasa model their lives after the temporalities of stably employed homeowners (Geenen 2009). They thus schedule Sunday visits to kin in an attempt to reinsert themselves in a rhythmic temporality regulated by routines which *they* control. By planning their own activities rather than letting circumstances dictate what they can do and when, they gain a measure of agency over their lives.

Though it may be less formally scheduled than weekly visits to one's family, teatime at the fada also involves some form of planning. The teaman does not start making tea on the spur of the moment (something one does, I have been told, with a bag of Lipton tea, which involves minimal preparations and can be consumed on an individual basis). Teatime is above all social time. It signals an effort to implicate as many people as possible in the experience despite the fact that the quantity of tea prepared remains the same. At one level, teatime is often part of the routine, the set of motions one engages in day after day, whose regular recurrence provides a sense of familiarity and comfort—a sense of control over one's time. At another level, teatime requires of the teaman and other participants that they be attuned to others, their needs, their constraints, and their aspirations.

In the language of the fada, tea is synonymous with conviviality. Though samari often joke that the sight of a bubbling kettle attracts everyone (including occasional passers-by and anthropologists) to the fada, a good teaman nevertheless waits for others to arrive before he sets things in motion. The timing and frequency of tea sessions are predicated on the comings and goings of fada members, how long they stay, how often they come, and how busy they are. Insofar as teatime (its planning, its realization, and the kind of attunement it requires of participants) can be said to be a form of time work, it is also affective work—a collective attempt to create a sociality with its own time and space.

Paradoxically, fada activities occasionally interfere with prayer time. Muslims are expected to pray five times a day at scheduled times. When they hear the *adhan* summoning the faithful for mandatory worship, men are expected to interrupt their activities and walk to the nearest mosque (women pray in the confines of their homes). Some samari waiting for tea reportedly ignore the muezzin sounding the call to prayer. Occasionally they admit to being so absorbed in a game of cards or checkers that they do not hear the call to prayer. Their purported inattention to the Muslim prayer schedule, widely described as a troubling symptom of impiety, has been virulently criticized by pious Muslims. Examined through the analytical lens of time work, it exemplifies samari's efforts to "realize [their] temporal desires" (Flaherty, this volume: 16). Whether or not members of a particular community choose to conform to a socially approved schedule of activities tells us something about the workings of temporal agency. Here, samari's response (or rather their lack of response) to the call to prayer signals an effort on the part of the younger generation to intervene in the trajectory of events.

By postponing the performance of prayer (or avoiding it altogether) to make time for idle pleasures, samari resist the imposition of normative temporalities that impinge on what they construct as leisure time. For a number of Muslim youth in Niger, being Muslim does not necessarily translate into religious observance at this particular stage in their lives. At one level, this means that age has something to do with the level of piety one demonstrates, with youth expected to be less pious than elders (LeBlanc 2000; Debevec 2012). At another level, it is a reminder that the public performance of religious acts is often a way of asserting maturity and performing adulthood. The relative importance young people attribute to their Muslim identities can shift significantly as they move along the life course and learn to juggle multiple, often conflicting, commitments. As an enactment of temporal agency, missing prayer is predicated on the possibility of short-term as well as distant futures, to which samari are attuned. Most young men operate under the assumption that there will be time later to catch up with the performance of missed religious obligations—whether "later" means a day or a decade. Put differently, folded within their seemingly trivial acts of resistance to the rigid prayer schedule is a potential future that includes the punctual performance of worship as a means of claiming adulthood. As a space of and for youth, the fada, I have tried to suggest, operates on its own time.[7] If the transition to adulthood hinges on securing a job and enjoying financial security, it is nevertheless critical for samari that they start demonstrating temporal conformity by praying on time.

THE WORK OF WAITING

When waiting is triggered by factors beyond individual control, such as imprisonment, unemployment, or forced relocation, it is experienced as a form of subjugation because it challenges a person or a collectivity's capacity to plan their own future. In this regard, the concept of waithood, coined by scholars to capture the experience of disablement produced by structural violence, hints at the way that waiting is about stuckness. Much of the waiting people do on an ordinary basis does not fit neatly into that category, however. For one thing, waiting is not simply a "gap" but also a critical path to the unfolding of possible futures. Rather than conceptualizing waiting as an interruption between events anticipated in a structure of events, I take it to be part of "duration," the experiential aspect that involves a range of emotive orientations and a sense of being-in-the-world (Cole and Durham 2008; Dalsgård et al. 2014). Moreover, while waiting has conventionally been understood strictly as inactivity or apathy—a mode of doing nothing—close attention to the ways in which people wait reveals they often engage in deliberate interventions into the structuring of time to produce particular outcomes—minor as they may be. In the way it "integrates agency with temporality" (Flaherty 2003: 19), the concept of time work allows us to trace the less visible forms that temporal agency takes in quotidian practice and examine how people position themselves in relation to the future.

At the fada—itself a critical part of the infrastructure designed by samari to "wait out the crisis" (Hage 2009)—waiting has become something of an art, with its own rules and regulations. In this chapter, I have tried to sketch out how the practice of preparing and drinking tea at the fada brings about a certain temporal experience, designed to enhance the participants' sense of self-determination, given the connection between time and agency. "We are bored; the fada gives us a sense of purpose," a young man told me. It was at the fada that Mourtaba learned to use a laptop, thanks to the support of an older fada member, who recommended he work on his English if he wished to maximize his brushes with opportunity. Mourtaba told me he planned to visit the American Cultural Center to read US magazines and practice his conversational English. He yearned to travel and see the world. After talking with friends, he decided to apply for a scholarship to study abroad. He credited the fada for developing his "capacity to aspire" (Appadurai 2013).

Aspiring entails a mode of anticipating the good life that must be constantly nurtured by signs that the conditions of flourishing exist and that one's personal circumstances can (and will) improve. Among un(der)employed samari, it is often undercut by disillusionment, disempowerment, and a sense of failure; in other words, an inability to hold on to the sense that the good life is part of one's future. Emptied of its forwardness, life becomes dull, depleted. In the warm embrace of the fada, young men re-experience the flow and momentum of life. As they partake in the restorative pleasures of tea drinking, they invent new rhythms for living while holding off despair and despondency. Part routine, part ritual, teatime enmeshes participants in the anticipation of sensual delights and shatters the numbness of boredom. At the same time, it creates ideal conditions for actualizing aspirations, cobbling together new practices of self-making, and transforming time into capital. "Tea encourages discussion. It is while we drink tea that we get ideas. And we can talk while our friends encourage us. We can plan the future," is how one young man put it. By resituating participants within the flow of time while simultaneously bracketing the practice of tea consumption as leisure, teatime is a prime instance of time work.

Adeline Masquelier
Professor, Department of Anthropology
Tulane University, USA

NOTES

1. Conversations with young Nigeriens were conducted in French, Niger's administrative language and the language children learn in school, and in Hausa, Niger's lingua franca. Young urbanites often insert English words in their vocabulary or cobble up terms to demonstrate their cosmopolitanism. "*Teaman*" and "*shaiman*" (a combination of "*shai*," the Hausa word for tea, and the English word "man") are typical examples of such linguistic bricolage.
2. Initially, fadas operated more like gangs, with members of rival fadas engaging in violent altercations against one another. I am told the days of fighting are over.
3. A former French colony, Niger earned its independence in 1960.
4. The names of fadas are drawn from a wide variety of registers: geography (Amerika); ethics (Adaltchi [justice]); hip-hop (Kash Money); aspiration (Territoire des Milliardaires [territory of billionaires]); proverbs (L'Union Fait la Force [unity makes strength]) and so on.

5. It may take as long as forty-five minutes for the tea to brew, whereas it often takes samari less than five seconds to swallow the shot of tea they are handed.
6. Tea is usually described by samari as a stimulant that imparts energy and focus. Students say their tea consumption spikes dramatically during examination periods.
7. Since they have no jobs to get up for, unemployed youth stay up late and sleep during part of the day. They claim to keep guard on their neighborhoods while others are sleeping, which is why they need tea to stay awake (Masquelier 2019).

REFERENCES

Allison, Anne. 2013. *Precarious Japan*. Durham, NC: Duke University Press.
Appadurai, Arjun. 2013. *The Future as Cultural Fact: Essays on the Global Condition*. New York: Verso.
Banégas, Richard, Florence Brisset-Foucault, and Armando Cutolo. 2012. "Parlements de la rue: Espaces publics de la parole et citoyenneté en Afrique." *Politique Africaine* 127 (3): 5–20.
Berlant, Lauren. 2011. *Cruel Optimism*. Durham, NC: Duke University Press.
Bloch, Ernst. 1986. *The Principle of Hope*. Vol. 1. Cambridge, MA: MIT Press.
Cole, Jennifer, and Deborah Durham. 2008. *Figuring the Future: Globalization and the Temporalities of Children and Youth*. Santa Fe, NM: School for Advanced Research Press.
Csikszentmihályi, Mihali. 1990. *Flow: The Psychology of Optimal Experience*. New York: Harper & Row.
Dalsgård, Anne Line, Martin Demant Frederiksen, Susanne Højlund, and Lotte Meinert, eds. 2014. *Ethnographies of Youth and Temporality: Time Objectified*. Philadelphia: Temple University Press.
Debevec, Liza. 2012. "Postponing Piety in Urban Burkina Faso: Discussing Ideas on When to Start Acting as a Pious Muslim." In *Ordinary Lives and Grand Schemes: An Anthropology of Everyday Religion*, edited by Samuli Schielke and Liza Debevec, 33–47. New York: Berghahn Books.
Dhillon, Navtej, and Tarik Yousef. 2009. *Waiting: The Unfulfilled Promise of Young People in the Middle East*. Washington, DC: Brookings Institution Press.
Dungey, Claire Elizabeth, and Lotte Meinert. 2017. "Learning to Wait: Schooling and the Instability of Adulthood for Young Men in Uganda." In *Elusive Adulthoods: The Anthropology of New Maturities*, edited by Deborah Durham and Jacqueline Solway, 83–104. Bloomington: Indiana University Press.
Durham, Deborah, and Jacqueline Solway. 2017. *Elusive Adulthoods: The Anthropology of New Maturities*. Bloomington: Indiana University Press.
Ferguson, James. 2006. *Global Shadows: Africa in the Neoliberal World Order*. Durham, NC: Duke University Press.
Flaherty, Michael G. 2003. "Time Work: Customizing Temporal Experience." *Social Psychology Quarterly* 66 (1): 17–33.

———. 2011. *The Textures of Time: Agency and Temporal Experience.* Philadelphia: Temple University Press.

Frederiksen, Martin Demant. 2013. *Young Men, Time, and Boredom in the Republic of Georgia.* Philadelphia: Temple University Press.

Foucault, Michel. (1966) 1994. *The Order of Things: An Archaeology of the Human Sciences.* New York: Vintage Books.

Geenen, Kristien. 2009. "'Sleep Occupies No Space': The Use of Public Space by Street Gangs in Kinshasa." *Africa* 79 (3): 347–68.

Goodstein, Elizabeth. 2005. *Experience without Qualities: Boredom and Modernity.* Palo Alto, CA: Stanford University Press.

Hage, Ghassan. 2009. "Waiting Out the Crisis: On Stuckness and Governmentality." In *Waiting,* edited by Ghassan Hage, 97–106. Carlton: University of Melbourne Press.

Harvey, David. 2005. *A Brief History of Neoliberalism.* New York: Oxford University Press.

Honwana, Alcinda. 2012. *The Time of Youth: Work, Social Change, and Politics in Africa.* Sterling, VA: Kumarian Press.

Humphrey, Caroline. 2002. *The Unmaking of Soviet Life: Everyday Economies after Socialism.* Ithaca, NY: Cornell University Press.

Johnson-Hanks, Jennifer. 2006. *Uncertain Honor: Modern Motherhood in an African Crisis.* Chicago: University of Chicago Press.

Kwon, June H. 2015. "The Work of Waiting: Love and Money in Korean Chinese Transnational Migration." *Cultural Anthropology* 30 (3): 477–500.

LeBlanc, Marie-Nathalie. 2000. "Fashion and the Politics of Identity: Versioning Womanhood and Muslimhood in the Face of Tradition and Modernity." *Africa* 70 (3): 443–81.

Mains, Daniel. 2013. *Hope Is Cut: Youth, Unemployment and the Future in Urban Ethiopia.* Philadelphia: Temple University Press.

Masquelier, Adeline. 2005. "The Scorpion's Sting: Youth, Marriage, and the Struggle for Social Maturity in Niger." *Journal of the Royal Anthropological Institute* 11: 59–83.

———. 2013. "Teatime: Boredom and the Temporalities of Young Men in Niger." *Africa* 83 (3): 470–91.

———. 2019. *Fada: Boredom and Belonging in Niger.* Chicago: University of Chicago Press.

Meinert, Lotte, and Nanna Schneidermann. 2014. "Making a Name: Young Musicians in Uganda Working on the Future." In *Ethnographies of Youth and Temporality: Time Objectified,* edited by Anne Line Dalsgård, Martin Demant Frederiksen, Susanne Højlund, and Lotte Meinert, 153–74. Philadelphia: Temple University Press.

Miyazaki, Hirokazu. 2004. *The Method of Hope: Anthropology, Philosophy and Fijian Knowledge.* Palo Alto, CA: Stanford University Press.

O'Neill, Bruce. 2017. *The Space of Boredom: Homelessness in the Slowing Global Order.* Durham, NC: Duke University Press.

Quayson, Atto. 2014. *Oxford Street, Accra: City Life and the Itineraries of Transnationalism.* Durham, NC: Duke University Press.

Raposa, Michael. 1999. *Boredom and the Religious Imagination.* Charlottesville: University of Virginia Press.

Sommers, Marc. 2012. *Stuck: Rwandan Youth and the Struggle for Adulthood.* Athens: University of Georgia Press.

Singerman, Diane. 2007. "The Economic Imperatives of Marriage: Emerging Practices and Identities among Youth in the Middle East." Working Paper 6, Wolfensohn Center for Development, Washington, DC.

Utas, Mats. 2005. "Building a Future? The Reintegration and Remarginalization of Youth in Liberia." In *No Peace No War: An Anthropology of Contemporary Armed Conflicts*, edited by Paul Richards, 137–54. Athens: Ohio University Press.

Weiss, Brad, ed. 2004. *Producing African Futures: Ritual and Reproduction in a Neoliberal Age.* Leiden: Brill.

Chapter 11

Balancing Blood Sugar

Fasting, Feeling, and Time Work during the Egyptian Ramadan

Mille Kjærgaard Thorsen and Anne Line Dalsgård

The holy month of Ramadan commemorates the first revelation of the Quran to the Prophet Muhammad. During Ramadan, Muslims worldwide are particularly observant of their prayers and other pious activities. Anthropologist Samuli Schielke (2009: S28) writes that "Ramadan as a time of exceptional morality demonstrates and enforces the supremacy of God's commands by constituting a time in which morality is not situational but strict and in which religious obligations *must* be fulfilled." Fasting during Ramadan, from sunrise to sunset, constitutes one of the five pillars of Islam and is obligatory for all Muslims (Kreinath 2012). However, the month of Ramadan not only engages individual bodies and minds through activities such as the fast and prayers; it also engages the collective body of Muslim communities across families, localities, and nationalities (Frankl 1996; Schielke 2009). On the collective level, Ramadan temporarily restructures public time and its content; on the level of individuality, it works through an exercising of the body, evoking certain emotions and concomitant micro-temporalities throughout the day and month. However, as we shall see in the present ethnographic case from Ramadan in Cairo, Egypt, people are not just subject to temporal orchestration through commemorative practices; they are also active subjects who try to shape their emotional and temporal experiences around the fast in creative ways.

Throughout the chapter, we will focus less on the pious and moral aspects of the particular act of fasting and more on what we will call the everyday temporal experiences of fasting. Spiritual aspects are, no doubt, an integral part of Ramadan. Based on her work in Cairo among female piety movements, Saba Mahmood (2012: 123) writes, "The attitude with which these acts [of Ramadan] are performed is as important as their prescribed form: sincerity, humility, and feelings of virtuous fear and awe are all emotions by which excellence and virtuosity in piety are measured and marked." But as Schielke (2009: S26) has argued, anthropological studies of Islam have a tendency to favor "the complete, the consistent, and the perfect in a way that does not do justice to the complex and often contradictory nature of everyday experience." For most people in Cairo, excellence and virtuosity in piety must be striven for while they also handle the ordinary demands of social relations, their financial situation, the state, and their own bodies. Ethnographic accounts of everyday life can appear elusive and diffuse in their attempt to describe the background conditions against which particular events stand out (Lewis 2000: 539). Nevertheless, this chapter is an attempt to catch some of the more ordinary experiences of fasting during the Ramadan. The fieldwork includes Thorsen's participant observation among families with members diagnosed with diabetes, as well as observations at various health care facilities in Cairo.[1] Drawing on Michael Flaherty's (2003, 2011) concept of time work, we will unfold how Thorsen's interlocutors act on their present situation during Ramadan in order to create or modify particular emotional and temporal experiences revolving around the fast. The kind of time work we focus on shows that biology and culture are not to be seen as separate domains (Lyon 1995). Fasting is an embodied action that interacts with physiochemical processes of the body, and in our exploration of the attempts that people make to deal with its effects, it is not completely evident who or what is the active part. We work with the notion that emotion is embodied (Lyon 1995) and explore emotion and temporality as intertwined phenomena (Lois 2010) that are mediated by the body. We specifically argue that the biochemistry of the body may provoke certain emotional and temporal experiences and drive the individual in a desire for a changed subjective state. However, the biochemistry of the body may also constrain the individual's attempts to make these changes come about. In other words, the agency of the individual and the effects of chemical substances beyond his or her immediate control may have a mutual impact on each other. This dynamic easily lends itself to an exploration inspired by actor-network theory (Latour 2005). However, the concept of time work laid out by Flaherty specifically emphasizes the (human) attempt to modify experience, and we shall stay close to this definition in the following.

In the present ethnographic case from Ramadan in Cairo, we will show how certain perceptions of time are evoked and how attempts are made to alter them by the people in Thorsen's study during the obligatory fast from dawn to dusk. In particular, we will show how time work is carried out by way of watching TV, sleeping, and preparing the body for the coming fast by eating and drinking in certain ways. Time work, we propose, is an embodied agency that relates back to specific bodies, each of which has its own specific capacities, constraints, and potential. We begin this chapter with one of Thorsen's ethnographic notes on fasting during Ramadan in Cairo in July 2015. At this time, temperatures reached a high of 55 degrees Celsius (131 degrees Fahrenheit) in the sun. Thorsen and a nine-year-old boy called Karim were experiencing the fast for the first time.[2]

DON'T YOU DRINK!

I am really thirsty. Almost hypnotized, I stare into the pot while stirring the pasta and ghee. It is Ramadan in July in Cairo. It's hot, it's dusty, and it's trying. We are preparing for *iftar*, the first meal of the day, shared at sunset and marking the end of a day of fasting. Karim is yelling from the living room: "*Mama* . . . I am thirsty. I am scared." Karim is nine years old and attempting to fast for the first time. Karim's mother is rinsing fruits in the sink next to me. She yells back at Karim: "Calm down, *habibi*, my love." Karim angrily shouts, "I am going to drink something!" Karim's mother leaves the fruit and goes into the living room to calm Karim down. I can hear him complaining. Karim's mother comes back to the kitchen. I can hear Karim crying in the living room. He screams at his mother, "I AM SCARED!" I keep stirring the pot. Karim's aunt, Maha, one of my good friends and the hostess of tonight's iftar, pours some buffalo soup over the pasta and ghee. Suddenly Karim runs to the bathroom next to the kitchen and slams the door shut. His mother drops the fruit and runs to the door: "DON'T YOU DRINK!" she yells while trying to open the door. "Open the door, Karim," she demands. I turn away, smiling in secret and in sympathy. Karim opens the door. His mother tries to calm him down and encourage him. He will get five pounds if he makes it all the way to iftar without eating or drinking.

More women and children are gathering at the house. Karim is sulking by the entrance to the kitchen and glancing at his mother. Maha serves a glass of ice-cold water to one of the younger children. Karim grabs the glass and desperately licks the condensation off the outside of the glass. His mother tells him to stop and to go into the living room. After a while I leave the pots in the kitchen and follow Karim. Karim is lying on the living room floor. One cheek resting on the cool ceramic tiles. He is staring at something (or maybe at nothing) under the couch. I talk to Maha for a while. Karim keeps moving farther and farther under the couch, until, finally, he is completely hidden away under it. Karim's cousin Yasmin is also on the floor, sleeping. She is eight and also fasting. One of the younger kids pulls her by the leg across the floor. Yasmin is still sound asleep. Maha asks if I would like to sleep, as well. I tell her yes. Please.

I go into the children's room and fall asleep immediately. At one point I dream about eating a banana. I wake up for a few seconds, biting my tongue. I finally wake up after two hours. My body feels far from rested—instead, I feel heavy and exhausted, thirsty and hungry. It is six o'clock. I am relieved that iftar is only an hour away. It feels almost impossible to move my body. I stare at the ceiling. The fan is spinning. Spinning and spinning. And spinning. I am able to move my eyes. But only my eyes. After a while I turn my head and look at the clock again. Still an hour to iftar. A whole . . . long . . . hour. My knees feel swollen. Eventually I move from my back to my side and slowly try to sit up. I am very dizzy. My head aches. I switch on the lights in the room. It is getting darker. A good sign of iftar getting closer. I get up and walk through the apartment.

Everyone is rushing to get the food ready on time. More and more people are gathering at the house, including the men: husbands, uncles, fathers-in-law, grandfathers. The TV is on and Karim and the other children are watching cartoons. Buffalo liver is frying in the kitchen. Maha's husband is helping the women set the table. Instructions are thrown his way by Maha and his sisters. Everyone is asking about the time. What time is it? *Now*, what time is it? How many minutes left? Suddenly, finally, one of the men shouts: "Allahu Akbar!" I hear the prayers from the mosques outside flowing through the house and then from the TV and cell phones, as well. It is finally time to break the fast. We all gather quickly in the living room. Glasses of water and milk with soaked dates are handed out. Most of us finish it at once. Karim's mother is lining up prayer blankets in the living room. The men get ready for prayer. Women and children gather around. Karim grabs a small chair and sits down next to his grandfather. Karim is close enough to touch his grandfather as he moves up and down in prayer. Karim studies him closely. For a short while the prayer brings a sense of community and solemnness to the room. A very present sense of belonging to each other. But then some of the women hurry back into the kitchen to put some final touches to the iftar meal. Karim's mother hands out pieces of sausages to the women and children, while the men finish their prayer. After the prayer we all gather around the table, the children on the floor in a circle around a big tray. Food is everywhere. Soups. Salads. Sausages. Bread. Meat. Stewed meat. Grilled meat. Fried meat. Water and juices and sodas are passed around. I eat slowly, feeling the textures of the foods and considering the tastes of each bite carefully. I feel thankful and almost in a trance as I eat my way through whatever is put in front of me. The food soothes my body. I am almost able to feel it disintegrate, transform, and reach every small cell of my body.

But no one sits at the table for long. I, too, quickly feel full and bloated and leave the table, as well. I sit in one of the armchairs in the living room, resting. The TV is on. Ramadan series are airing. Liquids are passed around: water, Pepsi, hibiscus juice. Someone says that she has been preparing the hibiscus juice for days: "You have to keep feeding it with sugar. It needs so much sugar!" The children are running around, laughing and high on energy. My head is aching again and I am overwhelmed with exhaustion. Someone hands me a glass of Pepsi. It feels like such a relief—cold and sugary. Karim's grandmother is lying on one of the couches. She is sleeping already, legs resting on the armrest, a spinning fan cooling her face. She has diabetes but is fasting anyway. Karim is happy and running around. He runs up to his father and proudly announces: "*Baba*, I fasted today!" Karim's grandmother, suddenly not so much asleep, opens one eye as she glares at Karim: "I think you drank something earlier," she observes. Karim looks shyly at his feet and repeats quietly to his father: "I fasted today." Karim's father kisses him on the forehead and smiles at him gently. Someone hands me a bowl of watermelon. I eat the whole thing in a couple of minutes. I look around and then wonder whether I should have shared the bowl with others.

The rest of the evening and night, I am served constantly with different foods and drinks. Mango juice with pieces of fruit and dates. Sandwiches with fried liver and sesame dressing. Hot tea with sugar. Sticky baklava someone has been given at work. I eat even though I feel full. Early in the evening the men leave to go to the mosque. They are given a big can of mango juice to take with them. Little by little, the women leave with their children, and eventually only Maha and I are left. Maha is sitting on the floor, legs stretched out in front of her. She is pregnant but has been fasting all day anyway. Her feet are swollen. She shows me her feet but quickly covers them up again with her skirt. She complains about the pain. She tells me her doctor tells her to drink a lot of water to get rid of the swelling, but this is impossible during Ramadan. The TV is on. Shows are airing on all channels, frequently interrupted by commercial breaks: charity projects, crisps, soaps, sodas, hospitals. We are gradually getting closer to the time of *sahuur*, the last meal before the sun rises. I feel full, tired, content, and happy. Maha reminisces about Ramadan when she was younger. A man would walk around the neighborhood knocking on doors and windows making sure people got up to have their last meal before the sunrise. "This was before cell phones and alarm clocks," Maha laughs. We talk, reminisce, eat, and drink, until it is time to sit down at the table for a proper sahuur. Maha's husband joins us at 2:30 a.m., and the three of us sit down. We have watermelon, yoghurt, cheese, and beans. Maha tells us to hurry. "Quickly," she says, as we finish our plates in a rush. Yoghurt fills my mouth as prayers from the mosques around the neighborhood make it through the walls of the house, marking a new day of fasting, cooking, and waiting, of endurance, spirituality, and community.

RAMADAN AS A RESTRUCTURING OF TIME

Standard clock time is the dominant time in the contemporary world, including Egypt. During the modern era, lunar and solar time have been replaced by mechanical clock time (Moran 2015). However, religious times like Ramadan (and the Christian Easter) follow the moon, and Ramadan also follows the sun for the daily start and end of fasting, thereby intersecting significantly with standard clock time. In the reversal of this relationship, the otherwise dominant position of the clock is partly suspended. Amitav Ghosh (1992: 75) writes about this in his ethnographical novel *In an Antique Land*, which takes place in Egypt: "From the very first day of the lunar month the normal routines of the village had undergone a complete change: it was as though a segment of time had been picked from the calendar and turned inside out."

The temporal synchronization for the sake of religious commemoration during Ramadan means that mealtimes are not "approximate" because everyone fasts and breaks their fast at exactly the same time.[3] When to eat and not eat spills over into all other aspects of everyday life, with the times to work, sleep, cook, shop, go to the doctor, and socialize being adjusted to suit the fixed eating times. This temporary—but recurring—structuring of time evokes a strong sense of community, which is characterized not only by the ascetic character of fasting, but also by a festive atmosphere (Schielke 2009). The restructuring of time is apparent in the shifting materialities, movements, and emotions during Ramadan. This was evident in Cairo while Thorsen was there: streets were decorated with colored garlands and pennants, flashing chains of lights and lanterns; long tables filled the streets, and food was offered for free to those in need or anyone passing by at the time of iftar; the streets were completely empty at certain times and crowded at others; children gathered on balconies to throw fireworks into the empty streets at the time of iftar; groups of men took exactly the same route toward their local mosques at night; the same men gathered inside and outside the mosques, moving in prayer as if they were one; children's laughter was heard throughout the night, mixing with the sounds of night-long prayers at a time when the streets would otherwise be empty and silent; and emotions ran high due to the trying hours of the fast but also due to a strong sense of belonging to a certain community, be it religious, regional, national, local, or familiar, or all of these at the same time. In Thorsen's experience, the collective efforts to control the timing of events (Flaherty 2011: 79–97) also included changes in working hours for most people, especially those working in the public sector. The working day was often cut short by a couple of hours. Everyone seemed to acknowledge that others would work at a slower pace during Ramadan, and most Cairenes participating in Thorsen's study would rush to get errands and appointments out of the way in the weeks leading up to this holy month. During Ramadan, most shops were open only for a couple of hours during the day and then again at night, when restaurants and coffee shops would also open. Generally, it seemed legitimate for many people to take more time off when needed—for example, during the first days of Ramadan when they were still trying to adjust to the fast. In hospitals and pharmacies, young employees would often work the more trying shifts, typically during the day, allowing more senior staff to come in at night. Generally, Thorsen's interlocutors aimed to spend more time at home than usual during the day, and planned any activities outside the home for the time after iftar, when their bodies were refueled with energy and the climate was less demanding. Going to the doctor, for example, would usually take place at night instead of during the day.

In other words, Ramadan restructures time on the collective level because the times at which people go to work, eat, sleep, socialize, and so on change in unison during this month. As Thorsen observed in Cairo, iftar (the end of the fast) and sahuur (the last meal before the sun rises) are strictly coordinated and shared. Indeed, social orchestrations of time, particularly through synchronized changes in the allocation of time (Flaherty 2011: 98), are not only characteristic of Ramadan. The organization of temporality (past, present, and future, but also experiences like duration, passage, and inevitability) into specific times, be it ritual time or clock time, has always tied societies together and coordinated social life (Moran 2015). Socially orchestrated and culturally meaningful times, be they everyday times or (like Ramadan) exceptions from the norm, necessarily affect individual bodies acting within these frames of time (we need only to think of the neophyte engaged in an initiation rite, who has to incorporate the psychological composure of manhood, or the industrial worker who wakes up in the dead of night to get to work for a morning shift). "Practice is not in time but makes time," writes Bourdieu (2000: 206), and, like any other practice, temporal practices engage the very flesh of the persons involved. Let us now return to the fasting bodies in Cairo.

THE FASTING BODY

Schielke argues that the primary motivating factor among Egyptians for fasting during the month of Ramadan is the prospect of Paradise (Schielke 2009: S26). This understanding was shared by Thorsen's interlocutors, but other reasons were also presented. First, fasting is one of the five pillars of Islam, so most Egyptians in Thorsen's study argued that you simply cannot be a Muslim unless you fast during the month of Ramadan. Some groups are religiously exempt from fasting—for example, the ill and the pregnant. However, this did not stop most of the people in Thorsen's study from fasting even though they had diabetes or were pregnant. Among the people in Thorsen's study there were constant discussions of when you were too ill or weak to fast, supported by articles in local newspapers (for example, on how to approach fasting when you were diagnosed with diabetes). Most of Thorsen's interlocutors also argued that fasting in public as well as in private was an expression of their true faith in God—an acknowledgment that God is all-knowing. A young man in Thorsen's study framed it this way: "No one will know if I go home and eat, but God will know, and I will know." Others argued that fasting was both healthy and purifying, as it liberated them from worldly affairs and addictions. Finally, almost all of Thorsen's interlocutors argued that fasting was a reminder that access to food is not a given, and that food should be shared with the hungry. Overall, everyone agreed that fasting during Ramadan allowed them to study, focus, and reflect on the teachings of Islam.

Biomedical literature on fasting has focused on mapping the biochemical effects on the human body (see, e.g., Cahill et al. 1966; Young and Scrimshaw 1971). Some of this literature draws a distinction between fasting and starvation, depending on the specific biochemical reactions in the body, comparing the human body to that of various animals, discussing how some animals may fast for long durations of time and still fuel their cells with energy, whereas the human body depends on foods and liquids on a much more regular basis (see, e.g., Castellini and Rea 1992). Some biomedical literature has picked up on the fasting aspect of Ramadan specifically, attempting to map the physiological effects of fasting from dawn to dusk throughout the period of the holy month (see, e.g., Benaji et al. 2006).

Physiologically, the human body depends on sugars (such as glucose) and other elements to survive. When fasting, most organs draw on a variety of different nutrients stored in the body to keep functioning, but the brain depends specifically on glucose to work properly. Among other things, a lack of glucose results in the decreased ability to concentrate. If the glucose level (blood sugar) drops too low, the brain will perceive this as a life-threatening situation. It then signals the body to counter-regulate the blood sugar level by releasing hormones that increase the amount of glucose in the blood-stream. Some of these hormones are stress hormones, and when released they promote responses such as aggression. In addition, a specific brain chemical is released when the blood sugar drops, acting on a variety of re-ceptors in the brain, including a receptor that specifically regulates anger and aggression. All of the above mechanisms thus explain physiologically why experiences of hunger often coincide with experiences of cognitive im-pairment, impatience, and aggression (see, e.g., De Almeida et al. 2015; Karl et al. 2004; Rosenthal et al. 2001; Salis 2015).

In Thorsen's experience, and from observing people fasting around her, depriving the body of foods and liquids from dawn to dusk caused phys-ical reactions not only of hunger and thirst, but also of dizziness, nausea, stomach pain, headaches, dryness in the mouth, fatigue, and lack of con-centration. Many of Thorsen's interlocutors complained about these physi-cal reactions to the fast—not only children, but also adults. The experience of thirst was far more serious than the experience of hunger. When asked about the fast during the weeks leading up to Ramadan, most of Thorsen's interlocutors agreed in general with Maha, Karim's pregnant aunt: "Not eat-ing is not a problem. Not drinking in this heat—this is a problem!" The great impact of thirst became evident during Ramadan when some of Thorsen's interlocutors discussed (and googled) whether or not producing excess sa-liva, and swallowing this saliva, was regarded as breaking the fast. It was also evident in Karim's desperate attempt to lick off the condensation of a glass of cold water served to the younger children or in his shout: "I am going to drink something!"

Thorsen's notes also reveal that hunger and thirst resulted in various emotional reactions. For instance, Karim expressed his hunger and thirst through anger, fright, and apathy. He had yet to learn to control these emo-tions and cognitively convince himself that this temporary abstinence from food and liquid was in fact not dangerous and that his anger was not a mor-ally correct response. As revealed by other studies of children's emotional education (a classic is Briggs 1970), "feeling rules" (Hochschild 1979) are incorporated over time by participating in a given social environment.

However, Karim was not alone in his emotional outbursts. In Thorsen's observations, emotions generally ran high in Cairo during the month of Ra-madan, especially in the hours leading up to iftar. At this time, the temper of the fasting body was unusually short, and fights would often break out among strangers (for similar accounts, see Schielke 2009: S27). This was especially evident during rush hour, when crowded trains and busses were trying to get people home in time for iftar. Here, people had heated arguments over space, seats, and mutual respect as the duration of their journeys (Flaherty 2011: 14) became difficult to manage. In order to end the argument, someone would usually shout something along the lines of "We are all tired! We are all in the same situation! We are all fasting!" The arguments would then dissolve quietly and in a second, as if people were all of the same understanding: our fasting bodies are arguing and fighting, not "you" and "me." Dealing with anger and frustration during the month of Ramadan by shouting "I am fasting! I am fasting!" follows the tradition of the Prophet, who reportedly said, "The person observing fasting . . . should not behave foolishly and impudently, and if somebody fights with him or abuses him, he should tell him twice, 'I am fasting'" (as narrated by Abu Hurairah, see al-Bukhari 1894). The month of Ramadan, in other words, was a period of great endurance, frustration, and anger—but was also characterized by a remarkable willingness to forgive such emotional outbreaks. This illustrates how the fasting body during Ramadan is greatly affected not only by the biochemistry of the body, but also by individual and collective efforts to control and modify the biochemical responses brought on by the fast. We will explore these efforts further in the following sections.

EMBODIED TIME WORK

As shown by Thorsen's observations, the passing of time was of great concern to everyone during Ramadan. At certain moments time passed slowly, while at other times it passed too quickly—usually as food was filling everyone not only with calories, but also with comfort and satisfaction. Experiences of time would change in an instant: one hour before iftar might be perceived as a short time one minute, only to transform and seem like a very long time the next. Thorsen's interlocutors all made different attempts to influence these temporal experiences, trying in particular to make time pass more quickly.

Most of the men and women in Thorsen's study turned to the TV as a way to make time pass more quickly during Ramadan. Massive and countless productions of Ramadan series air during that month, making both a great topic for conversation as well as a way to pass time by keeping up with the daily episodes. Most Ramadan series depict stories and plots irrelevant to the holy month, ranging from historical dramas to great love stories, comedies, and reality shows. Even though the series rarely deal with issues relating directly to Ramadan, a favorite topic of conversation during Thorsen's fieldwork was which shows should be considered most *Haram*, usually because they depicted women smoking or wearing too few clothes, or actors and actresses kissing too passionately on screen. Others would debate whether or not it was in fact *Haram* to even pass time during Ramadan by entertaining oneself with the TV in the first place. One of Thorsen's interlocutors joked, "Yeah, everyone discusses this in the commercial breaks, but no one gets up to actually switch off the TV." Watching TV was a great way to pass time, but at some point the rumbling sound of someone's empty stomach would interfere with this attempt at time work: the fasting bodies simply seemed to remind everyone that the usual time to eat or drink had passed. This was when almost everyone turned to a more intrapersonal way of trying to intervene with the experience of time: sleeping. Some people found that it helped to go to sleep instead of being awake, thereby attempting to make time pass unnoticed. Usually they would draw on this strategy in the hours leading up to iftar, when the body was particularly difficult to ignore and when they were exhausted. But even in sleep the physical reactions of the body to fasting would interfere—as experienced by Thorsen: food entered her dreams, causing her to wake up and bite her tongue.

Different fasting bodies had very different physical and emotional reactions to fasting. For instance, the diabetic grandmother in this material was especially tired during Ramadan, as well as being particularly irritable (although this is not evident in the above example). And the pregnant aunt had particular difficulty owing to the excess water in her body caused by both the pregnancy and the fast (she had swollen legs and hands), making moving around very painful. Differences in emotional reactions were evident when comparing the struggles of the inexperienced child (Karim) and the foreign researcher (Thorsen) with those of the people around them.

These differences in emotional reactions point to another aspect of the relationship between physiology and emotion: human emotions are not simply biologically given idioms of expression (caused, for example, by a low glucose level and reactions in the brain), but are also cultural artifacts (Hochschild 1979). As Clifford Geertz (1973: 46, 81) argues, without culture we would not know what we were feeling. Knowing what we are feeling and how to react is a culturally acquired faculty, informed by ideas about proper behavior, religion, health, hygiene, and many other aspects of life. As Michelle Rosaldo (1984: 143) put it, "Feelings are not substances to be discovered in our blood but social practices organized by stories that we both enact and tell." However, our point here is that enacting and telling are embodied actions that also interact with substances in the blood and other physiochemical processes in the body. Thus, when Rosaldo (1984: 143) also describes emotions as being "'felt' in flushes, pulses, 'movements' of our lives, minds, hearts, stomachs, skin," she brings us closer to our point: namely, that emotions both manifest on the level of biology and are known and worked upon through culture (see also Leavitt 1996).

The people in Thorsen's study also acknowledged that human agency is in fact embodied, and that the biochemistry of the body necessarily interferes with experience and reaction—not in a theoretical way, but as part of daily practices. This was revealed by the fact that everyone understood the importance of engaging their bodies actively in their time work (our conceptualization, of course, not theirs). This was done primarily by preparing one's body properly for the fast by eating and drinking in certain ways in the hours leading up to the fast in order to make fasting less difficult and essentially to pass the time more quickly. It was also revealed in the many instances of advice that Thorsen received from her Egyptian acquaintances about the importance of sahuur, the last meal eaten before the daily fast started: "Sahuur should contain yoghurt and of course other things but no salt"; "You should drink plenty of water at the time of sahuur because this is really all the body needs. Food is much less important"; "You should really not drink a lot of water. If you drink a lot of water, your body will get rid of it faster"; "You should definitely take vitamins throughout Ramadan"; "If you do all of this, fasting is not that bad. Time will pass by quickly." The internet speaks to the same tendency to prepare oneself properly for the fast, as "What is a healthy sahuur in Ramadan" was the number five trending question googled in Egypt during Ramadan in 2016 (Cairo Scene 2016).

Thorsen's interlocutors also advised her about how to break the fast, and how to make those hours comfortable and less harsh on the body: "You should really only have some dates and then some soup. And then wait for a couple of hours before eating anything else." Or "The body is like a machine. It has been off all day so be kind to it. It takes time for it to start working again. Slowly slowly." Another way to engage the body in a form of time work was to constrain the movements of the body—for example, by staying home during the time of day when the body was most exhausted and the sun and heat outside at its peak. Conserving energy in the body was thus another important way to make the time of the fast feel less difficult. Schielke similarly explains how football is used as a way for young men to pass time during Ramadan, especially in the hours just before breaking the fast. He argues that football is "a way to kill time that is not deemed immoral or un-Islamic" (Schielke 2009: S25). In line with our argument here, we could argue that playing football is not merely a way to "kill time" but also a way to engage the body in a certain time work, keeping the body, and not just the mind, occupied, as well as allowing the players to feed off the endorphins released in their fasting bodies during the football match.

A TIME OF SUBMISSION AND POISE

Anthropologist Saba Mahmood (2012) recounts two expressions invoked by her interlocutors in Cairo during Ramadan. These two expressions capture the idea that Ramadan is a month not only of spirituality, but also of everyday life experiences. The first expression goes as follows: "The first third of Ramadan is kindness of God, the second third is His forgiveness, and the last third is refuge from hell's fire" (Mahmood 2012: 49). The second expression counters the first: "The first third of Ramadan is cookies, the second third is expenses, and the last third is relatives" (Mahmood 2012: 49). We hope we have succeeded in acknowledging the religious aspects of Ramadan in this chapter, but we have also chosen to focus more on the simultaneous abstinence from and abundance of "cookies."

Jane Bennett (2010: 39) writes that food can be seen as an "actant inside and alongside intention-forming, morality-(dis)obeying, language-using, reflexivity-wielding, and culture-making human beings, and as an inducer-producer of salient, public effects."[4] In the case presented here, it is not food alone, but also its denial and administration by human agency that works upon bodies and produces public effects. Some of these effects are, as we have shown, temporal, but they are not *only* temporal. Our argument has been that commemoration, here during Ramadan, can be seen as collective time work that affects individual bodies by way of different allocations of time, demands on people's ability to endure duration (of, for instance, fasting), and synchronization (of prayers and eating times). However, the individuals taking part are not only subject to such time work and its bodily effects; they are also active subjects who try to shape their emotional and temporal experiences of commemoration in creative ways.

Drawing on Michael Flaherty's concept of time work, we have shown how people try to create or modify particular emotional and temporal experiences revolving around the fast. Fasting, we have argued, is an embodied action that interacts with physiochemical processes of the body and may create sensations of fatigue, impatience, or boredom, for instance. Initially these sensations tend to evoke negative emotions, such as frustration and anger. But most people have learned from years of repeating the fast how to deal with such emotions. This was done through spiritual work, which we have not addressed in this chapter, but also in more pragmatic ways, like shouting "We are all fasting," sleeping, or watching TV, and preparing the body physically before starting the fast. They worked upon their bodily sensations and emotions by working upon the experience of time and vice versa.

To conclude, "emotion work" (Hochschild 1979) or "temporal emotion work" (Lois 2010) may be terms which are just as relevant for the focus of our research as "time work." However, we have found it particularly interesting to explore how temporal orchestrations can engage physical bodies down to the microlevel of, for instance, blood sugar, and how time and emotion are balanced at this microlevel. Submission and poise may be achieved intentionally, but as Bennett (2010: 39) points out, food is "inside and alongside intention-forming," and experienced Cairenes know that.

Mille Kjærgaard Thorsen
PhD, Department of Anthropology
Aarhus University, Denmark

Anne Line Dalsgård
Associate Professor, Department of Anthropology
Aarhus University, Denmark

NOTES

1. The fieldwork was conducted over the course of six months in 2015 and three months in 2017.
2. All quotations are translated by Thorsen from Arabic into English.
3. This is not entirely accurate, as the breaking and ending of the fast depends on the call for prayer, which may vary by up to a couple of minutes across Egypt.
4. In her book, *Vibrant Matter*, Bennett uses the term "actant" to dissolve the split between subject and object, showing how matter (such as sugar, for instance) has capacity to make differences in the world by affecting the interrelationships of which it is a part. Likewise, the term is used in actor-network theory (Latour 2005), where everything social and material is seen as interchanging position in constantly shifting networks of relationship. As stated in the beginning of this chapter, we could have gone in that direction; however, we focused on human agency.

REFERENCES

Al-Bukhari, Sahih. 1894. "The Superiority of as-Saum (the Fasting)." In *Book of Fasting* Book 30, Hadith 4, chap. 2, as narrated by Abu Huraira.

Benaji, B., N. Mounib, R. Roky, N. Aadil, I. E. Houti, S. Moussamih, S. Maliki, B. Gressier, and H. El Ghomari. 2006. "Diabetes and Ramadan: Review of the Literature." *Diabetes Research and Clinical Practice* 73 (2): 117–25.

Bennett, Jane. 2010. *Vibrant Matter: A Political Ecology of Things.* Durham, NC: Duke University Press.

Bourdieu, Pierre. 2000. *Pascalian Meditations.* Cambridge: Polity Press.

Briggs, Jean. 1970. *Never in Anger.* Cambridge, MA: Harvard University Press.

Cahill, G., M. Herrera, A. Morgan, J. Soeldner, J. Steinke, P. Levy, G. Reichard, and D. Kipnis. 1966. "Hormone-Fuel Interrelationships during Fasting." *Journal of Clinical Investigation* 45 (11): 1751–69.

Castellini, M., and L. Rea. 1992. "The Biochemistry of Natural Fasting at Its Limits." *Experientia* 48 (6): 575–82.

De Almeida, R., J. Cabral, and R. Narvaes. 2015. "Behavioural, Hormonal and Neurobiological Mechanisms of Aggressive Behaviour in Human and Nonhuman Primates." *Physiology & Behavior* 143: 121–35.

Flaherty, Michael G. 2003. "Time Work: Customizing Temporal Experience." *Social Psychology Quarterly* 66 (1): 17–33.

———. 2011. *The Textures of Time: Agency and Temporal Experience.* Philadelphia: Temple University Press.

Frankl, P. J. L. 1996. "The Observance of Ramaḍān in Swahili-Land (with Special Reference to Mombasa)." *Journal of Religion in Africa* 26 (4): 416–34.

Ghosh, Amitav. 1992. *In an Antique Land: History in the Guise of a Traveler's Tale.* New York: Vintage.

Geertz, Clifford. 1973. *The Interpretation of Cultures.* New York: Basic Books.

Hochschild, Arlie Russel. 1979. "Emotion Work, Feeling Rules, and Social Structure." *American Journal of Sociology* 85 (3): 551–75.

Karl, T., S. Lin, C. Schwarzer, A. Sainsbury, M. Couzens, W. Wittmann, D. Boey, S. von Hörsten, and H. Herzog. 2004. "Y1 Receptors Regulate Aggressive Behavior by Modulating Serotonin Pathways." *Proceedings of the National Academy of Sciences* 101 (34): 12742–747.

Kreinath, Jens. 2012. *The Anthropology of Islam Reader.* New York: Routledge.

Latour, Bruno. 2005. *Reassembling the Social: An Introduction to Actor-Network-Theory.* Oxford: Oxford University Press.

Leavitt, John. 1996. "Meaning and Feeling in the Anthropology of Emotions." *American Ethnologist* 23 (3): 514–39.

Lewis, J. Lowel. 2000. "Sex and Violence in Brazil: Carnival, Carpoeira; and the Problem of Everyday Life." *American Ethnologist* 26 (3): 539–57.

Lois, Jennifer. 2010. "The Temporal Emotion Work of Motherhood: Homeschoolers' Strategies for Managing Time Shortage." *Gender & Society* 24 (4): 421–446.

Lyon, Margot L. 1995. "Missing Emotion: The Limitations of Cultural Construc-
tionism in the Study of Emotion." *Cultural Anthropology* 10 (2): 244–63.

Mahmood, Saba. 2012. *Politics of Piety: The Islamic Revival and the Feminist Subject.*
Princeton: Princeton University Press.

Moran, Chuk. 2015. "Time as a Social Practice." *Time & Society* 24 (3): 283–303.

Rosaldo, Michelle Z. 1984. "Toward an Anthropology of Self and Feeling." In *Culture Theory: Essays on Mind, Self and Emotion*, edited by R. A. Shweder and R. A.
Levine, 137–57. Cambridge: Cambridge University Press.

Rosenthal, J. M., S. A. Amiel, L. Yágüez, E. Bullmore, D. Hopkins, M. Evans, A.
Pernet, H. Reid, V. Giampietro, C. Andrew, J. Suckling, A. Simmons, and S.
Williams. 2001. "The Effect of Acute Hypoglycemia on Brain Function and
Activation: A Functional Magnetic Resonance Imaging Study." *Diabetes* 50 (7):
1618–26.

Salis, Amanda. 2015. "Health Check: The Science of 'Hangry,' or Why Some People
Get Grumpy When They're Hungry." *The Conversation*, 20 July 2015. Accessed
8 January 2020. http://theconversation.com/health-check-the-science-of-hangry-
or-why-some-people-get-grumpy-when-theyre-hungry-37229.

Schielke, Samuli. 2009. "Being Good in Ramadan: Ambivalence, Fragmentation,
and the Moral Self in the Lives of Young Egyptians." *Journal of the Royal Anthropological Institute* 15: S24–S40.

Young, Vernon R., and Nevin S. Scrimshaw. 1971. "The Physiology of Starvation."
Scientific American 225 (4): 14–21.

Afterword

A "Temporal Novel" Inspired by the Concept of Time Work

Carmen Leccardi

AN UNORDINARY BOOK

This book is special in many respects. It is, all in one, a book of social theory, a rich collection of ethnographic essays, and a compelling account of experiences revolving around the relationship with time and its many forms. These experiences are often quite different from one another, set in geographically and culturally distant areas of the planet. What they have in common is a capacity to reveal the many forms of agency related to time work—the theme of the book. And revealing they are in quite a literal sense in that they "unveil," shining a light in the darkness, making the invisible visible. Thanks to this unveiling process, and with the help of the narrative power of ethnographic analysis, we come in contact with different aspects of our experience throughout the chapters: life and death, illness, spirituality, existential aspirations and projects, power and politics.

Our daily experience is mirrored in the "stories" to which we are allowed access by the analyses related to time work, which are documented in the ten research chapters. This quality, certainly all but usual in scientific writings, gives the book the flavor of a "temporal novel." As in novels, the vivid narration we find in the ethnographic reports allows us to identify with the daily lives of the examined groups and individuals. Whether it is the Inuit and their struggle with the temporal order of the global North, which imposes the synchronization of activities with the sterilized time of clocks, or the Argentinian "living disappeared," who were children during the tragic years of the dictatorship and are now forced to confront the change of identity in a traumatic way, or the religious community of a slum in northern Uganda, who use prayer to come to terms with the spirits tied to memory of the war, or Danish adults contending with ADHD, the attention deficit hyperactivity disorder that forces them to deal every day with a mismatch between their accelerated inner time and the rules and rhythms of social institutions. In all these cases, as in the others, equally intriguing, related by the book, we witness a daily exercise in redefinition of the temporal coordinates.

The goal of this "time work" is to bargain with the grids of social temporality, bending them to one's needs whenever possible, making room for the exercise of self-determination and autonomy, the quintessential modern ideals. In short, time work aims to make these grids flexible, to "domesticate" them without erasing them. It creates islands of quality time within these grids that are tuned into inner time and its pace, subverting the social and temporal order without announcements or ideological stands. Control over time is achieved through minute negotiations, often through practices iterated in the daily dimension and sometimes ritualistic in nature. De Certeau (1984) would have defined them as micro daily tactics through which we give meaning to our being in the world and manage to "feel at home." Time work and the quest for autonomy and self-determination within a given existential and social context ultimately overlap and promote each other.

Time work—the different practices through which we aim to give a personal imprint to social time—is the instrument through which we seek control. Altering the representation of time in daily life (or biographical time) can be considered the goal of this practice—a practice in which agency is expressed, subjectivities become visible, and creativity unfolds.

The details of the practices that we are made privy to throughout the book are in many ways moving—which is why I used the term "temporal novel" to describe this edited collection. We find ourselves eagerly anticipating the next chapter instead of wondering whether we are devoting too much time to this read. We are "taken," caught by the negotiations with time about which we are gradually informed. As a professional reader, I have come to the conclusion that this particular pleasure is tied to the profound personal, affective, and ethical implications that each of the temporal tales contained in the book carries with it. The subjects with which we become acquainted throughout the diverse chapters introduce us to different aspects of our own experience of existential changes. Hence the emotions, and therefore the particular forms of knowledge they convey (Nussbaum 2003).

However, this is not the only kind of pleasure the book provides. Aside from the allure of first-person storytelling that characterizes ethnographic practice, which is especially able to captivate the reader/listener, another analytical dimension is directly implied: the connection between theory and research, a core issue of disciplines such as anthropology and sociology (especially in its qualitative methods). The collection of essays in this volume demonstrates the potential for mutual enhancement and growth of these two sides of the same coin.

The virtuous outcome of this positive interaction, in the realm of social sciences and humanities, is the production of scientific reflexivity—a perspective of strategic importance for the understanding of processes of social and cultural transformation. As Giddens (1979) pinpointed some decades ago, the sociological investigation of time reveals the dialectical relationship between structure and action. In a sociological framework, time is the expression of two different dynamics that are deeply intertwined and can only be distinguished by analysis: the structuring of social life and the construction of agency.

The concept of time work elaborated by Michael Flaherty (2002, 2003, 2011)—the conceptual compass that orients and evens out the different essays in this book—has the capacity to show at once the normative power of time and its institutions and the strength of human creativity in taming its coercive force. The fascinating quality of history lies in the fact that men and women, together with their communities—around which the book's narrations are centered—use their personal relationships with time to get on top of these forms of temporal hetero-structuring without which social life could not be built (Durkheim [1912] 2008; Zerubavel 1981) and biographies could not take form. Hence the always ambivalent nature of time work, which is faced with temporal rules that both constrain and enable the development of personal strategies of time domestication.

Therefore, this book is not only the demonstration that time work can be considered an inalienable trait of human action and interaction, the expression of human subjectivity and capacity for self-determination. As detailed in the research conducted by the interdisciplinary team of scholars at Aarhus University, and as properly mentioned in the introduction, for the first time since its formulation this concept is being explored outside of the United States. Even when applied to the different local contexts across the continents—that is, in the multiplicity of its cultural expressions—this concept still provides the possibility of understanding the game of time played by the subjects in their daily lives. This means that the intertwinement between forms of agency, time, and daily life holds a great cognitive (and transformative) power. When we focus our attention on this intersection, it becomes clear that one's personal sense of time can influence the social temporal rhythms, softening or canceling, when possible, the aspects that are most detrimental to individual and community welfare. In other words, there are forms of temporal resistance and resilience around us that need to be identified and studied. It is a full-blown political task to which time work is related, especially in a context such as that of the new century, where the fragmentation of the forms of social and political participation tends to obscure the strength of agentic practices. The book, in my view, entrusts us with the responsibility, as social scientists, to undertake this exploration.

In order to meet this goal, we first of all need to "see" these dynamics in a conceptual sense, and then focus our attention on the forms of action and interaction through which they are materialized in the social environment. The existing social theories concerning time (see Adam 1990) are the basis on which the intertwinement between the concept of time work and its various cultural expressions must be built.

In the introduction of a recent volume dedicated to the relation between concepts and theories on the one hand, and temporal, spatial, and learning contexts on the other, Birgit Neumann and Ansgar Nünning (2012) emphasize the constant re-elaboration of meanings as a specific trait of the former. A transformation able to produce ever new differences and elaborations. According to the authors, cultural analysis can gain important insight from this awareness. As we know, Karl Mannheim's (1952) sociology of knowledge, as well as Norbert Elias's (especially 1993) historical-social research, which—despite their differences—share similar interests, have derived much fruitful impetus from this vision. As the ways of knowledge transform over time, the transformation of concepts necessarily follows. Concepts are dynamic constructs, whose interdependence with other social phenomena must be underlined. In a context such as the contemporary one, which is characterized by ever faster transformation processes, this dynamic is especially meaningful. Having conceptual frameworks that suit the historical present also means having the right tools to capture political dynamics that are essential to democratic life. Moreover, the hybridization of concepts with multiple cultural and social realities—which is exactly the direction of this book—significantly expands their analytical power along with their argumentative force.

AN ILLUSTRIOUS KINSHIP: TIME WORK AND SOCIOLOGICAL IMAGINATION

Before we take into more direct consideration an aspect of time work I especially care about—its relationship with time control—I want to call attention to a noble kinship that characterizes the concept of temporal agency in its interrelation with the concept of time work. I am talking about the relation between the concept of sociological imagination proposed by Charles Wright Mills ([1959] 1971) in the fifties and that of time work created by Michael Flaherty (2002, 2003, 2011) in the new century. Both of these concepts, in my view, successfully connect biographies and history, daily life and society, social structures and agency.

When Mills proposed the sociological imagination as the guiding principle of his research, his goal was to give visibility to a specific sociological project. Sociology, in his eyes, should not be merely an instrument to "navigate" the social world by explicating what gets taken for granted upon first inspection. "The Promise" (of sociology), the title of the first chapter of Mills's ([1959] 1971) *The Sociological Imagination*, is based on a critical approach that is made possible by the very nature of this discipline. Mills viewed sociology as necessarily engaged in solving issues tied to the public and political sphere in the broader sense, not only because of the tight bond shared, in principle, by social structure, history, and biographies, but also because, as it strives to explicate these connections, sociology empowers individuals to become aware of their potential and therefore to become directly involved in the history-making process (Mills [1959] 1971: 10). In this knowledge process, subjects are not only confronted with "the troubles they endure in terms of historical change and institutional contradictions," and with the causes of these troubles, but also with the "well-being they enjoy," as they are able to recognize their links to their inner time (Mills [1959] 1971: 9). It is therefore imperative that sociology avoids being identified with an ensemble of "bureaucratic techniques" and that space is given to issues of public relevance and the exploration of their possible solutions.

Ultimately, sociology is called to engage in social analysis with an eye to critical exploration of present and future, especially focusing on the close interrelation not only between present and future actions, but also between our everyday ability to imagine a different future and the possibility to redefine present issues. Appadurai (2014) explores this crucial theme, emphasizing the relation between the construction of a future map based on the priorities and choices of the present and the capacity to aspire to a different future while staying open to possibilities. All of this relates present and future to action and participation. The sociological imagination can thus become a precious ally as we seek to discover links between the individual realm and the collective realm, enabling us to produce analyses that can identify the many, at times contradictory, facets of the relation between contemporary processes of individualization and the dynamics of social bonding (Leccardi and Volonté 2017).

Much like the sociological imagination, the concept of time work relates the micro and macro dimensions, the dynamics of the self to institutional processes, cultures and societies, and the power of subjects to the dominant powers. Thanks to the perspective opened by Flaherty, we are able to connect biographies, history, and social structures starting from the subjects' capability to shape their existential realms. However, it is important to remember—as Flaherty explicitly invites us to do (this volume: 16)—that individuals and social groups are not the only ones to engage in time work to confirm or manifest their desire for self-determination; so do "religions, corporations, schools, hospitals, prisons, governments, and other organizations." All these social institutions engage in time work with power finalities. "In one way or another, they attempt to control or manipulate the temporal experience of their own people or that of client populations" (Flaherty, this volume: 16). People, in turn, work every day to escape these forms of domination, which are considered unacceptable in a time of growing centrality of individuals and their choices. To this purpose, they devise representations and practices—also collective ones—aimed at not losing control over their personal time, keeping the helm firmly in their own hands.

We see this, for instance, in a group of Nigerian young men engaged in a daily struggle against the socially imposed condition of "waithood"—a condition that bars them from adult roles and responsibilities against their clearly opposite aspirations. The possibility of responding in a lively way to the long and empty time imposed by unemployment—a motionless time, devoid of agency—depends on the creation of a "rich" collective time: interactive, ritualized, and shared, reassuring in its everyday quality. It is the time of common and public tea drinking, which constitutes an alternate temporality that is able to block the sense of existential uselessness and promote the "capacity to aspire" (Appadurai 2013). Institutional time work results here in the destruction of young people's temporal experience. Their time work, built around the *fada* (a public rite of gathering to drink tea, carried out on a daily basis) and the relationships it fosters, consolidates their ability to generate time, rather than endure it.

I referenced this example, among the many made available by this collection of essays, because the political nature of the contraposition between destruction and re-creation of time is particularly evident here. The young Nigerians at the center of the study not only give meaning to their present through the ceremony of tea drinking; they also use this time as a lever to restate their will to not lose the future challenge: public institutions are denying their right to the future, and they are committed to reconquering it. Their temporal agency is built *against* institutional time work. It takes form through this opposition. This experience of temporal agency unveils the often political nature—in the sense of everyday politics—of time work.

Going back to the relationship between sociological imagination and time work, I am convinced that the latter can be primarily related to the "style of work" that grounds the vision of sociology promoted by Mills—beyond the contraposition between (abstract) theory and (empty) empiricism. I am also convinced that the relation between biographical and historical times can profit greatly from the analyses centered around time work. In the case of this book, as much as for the project behind *The Sociological Imagination* (see Mjøset 2013), the will to spread knowledge to a wide audience can be considered a top priority. In this respect, the three editors of the volume, Flaherty, Meinert, and Dalsgård, can be considered, to all intents and purposes, public intellectuals who are able to update Mills's political and scientific program to our historical time, promoting, in this way, the crucial theme of dialogue between cultures and valorization of differences and interdependence in a framework of civic culture.

ON TEMPORAL AGENCY: TEMPORAL CONTROL IN THE CONTEMPORARY SOCIAL CONTEXT

The theme of self-determination and agency, as the readers of this book have come to understand, is the heart of what could be called the scientific conversation on time promoted by Michael Flaherty as collected and inspired by the empirical research of scholars at Aarhus University. I would like to end these notes by calling the readers' attention to the ways in which the transformations in the modes of conception of time control represent, in our age, a vital matter also in relation to the present and future of time work. As Flaherty writes in this book's first chapter (14), dedicated to an in-depth analysis of the concept,

> Time work is rooted in human desire. One desires a certain form of temporal experience, but it will not occur without one's intervention. The individual must take steps to bring this temporal experience into being. Typically, this process entails deliberation and planning, perhaps even a local or personal theory that guides one's effort. The resulting temporal experience is a product of human endeavor. One chooses to experience time in a particular way.

Today, this crucial agentive process is forced to confront specific social and cultural dynamics I would like to briefly address.

In the new century, temporal experience in daily life is affected by the decreased capacity of institutions to offer temporal structures that can effectively shape biographical careers. The relation to the different social institutions, especially education and work, no longer provides a clear articulation of the status transitions that traditionally marked biographical stages (for instance, the transition to adult life). In this context, the subjective vision of individuals, the reflective gaze they direct at their own biographies, ends up being as important—if not, on closer inspection, even more important—as their objective "careers" (Hughes [1971] 1984). Concretely, this means that the numerous temporal structures we face every day cannot be hierarchically sorted as they were for the majority of the twentieth century in industrial societies: first the time of work, then family time, then leisure time, and so on, based on a temporal order that was able to signal institutional priorities in a simple and direct way as useful principles for time control as much as biographical structuring. In other words, in order to express temporal self-determination today, we need to define increasingly individualized forms of time management. The dynamic is clear: if institutional structures become less effective as reference points for the projection of oneself into the future (and therefore of biographical control), the responsibility to define those reference points rests entirely on the shoulders of the individual.

Personal autonomy, which is traditionally identified as individuals' capacity to outline their own priorities as part of a project of self, is therefore tied with a double thread to the possibility of exerting control over temporal experience in daily life. In this sense, control over time comes down to the capacity to have, and defend, "a world of one's own" (De Singly 2015), guarding it from outside pressures. This possibility is negatively influenced by the social acceleration of our lives (Rosa 2013) and by the concomitant loss of capability, on the part of social institutions, to propose guidelines that can give meaning to the daily exchange between personal time and social identity. The constant change that mars institutional life no less than the very idea of identity (who we are and what we want is increasingly dependent upon contexts and contingencies) tends to short-circuit this exchange mechanism. The occupational crisis, especially widespread precarity, emphasizes its inconsistencies on a level of meaning no less than on a level of practices.

The order and predictability attained through rigid control of daily rhythms tend to give way to a certain "independence from rules" and to forms of autonomous definition of times that are disengaged from institutional rhythmicity. In general terms, it is the aspect of temporality Simmel ([1907] 1978) defined as *Lebenstempo*—that is, the rhythm of life considered in relation to the social dynamics of change and their existential effects. While the intensification of *Lebenstempo* was already apparent at the beginning of the last century, nowadays the processes of economic globalization, along with the dynamics of virtualization of communication forms and their impact on the construction of normative ideals of simultaneity, tend to produce new dynamics of temporal acceleration and compression.

Based on these premises, the modalities through which time control is exerted are transforming. The absence of stable points, and the necessity of constantly revising prospective actions for time control in light of the possibilities or impossibilities that arise, is the framework in which a reflection on the forms of temporal autonomy available today can be set.

Commenting on Simmel's stances regarding the two opposing lifestyles that are at the basis of the time management practice of individuals and groups—a symmetrical-rhythmical lifestyle oriented toward temporal rigidity and a spontaneous, individualistic style oriented toward flexibility—Alessandro Cavalli (2011: 263) writes, "Time management modalities, like lifestyles, are nothing other than ways to approach the world." Cavalli's observation allows us to get to the core of another question I wish to explore. We are dealing with a constitutive ambivalence of our contemporary relationship with time. On the one hand, we have a powerful desire for control of the times of daily life as an expression of the need for personal autonomy; on the other hand, the conviction of being practically unable to exert forms of control—if this control is meant in a rigid sense—is just as strong.

A number of authors have addressed this ambivalence—from Gergen (2000) to Rosa (2012, 2013) to De Singly (2015), to only name a few. These different analyses—some of them more centered around identity transformations, others more interested in seeing these processes as indicators of changes in the very concept of the "good life"—draw attention to a common theme: that is, the need to see one's autonomy grow through the possibility of making choices with the least possible amount of constraints in light of the constantly fluctuating environment. These choices must be such that they do not preclude future choices. Being able to navigate highly unstable territories becomes, in this framework, a fundamental prerequisite for a positive exercise of agency. Being able to exploit the unexpected, to not adhere completely to routine, and/or to accept the contradictions and ambiguities of this context as opportunities become forms of rational agency when social discontinuities are intense. Ultimately, the speed of these changes calls for a similar speed in one's decision-making process, which requires that one avoid abiding by pre-established rules. In this scenario, which is characterized by the ideal of pluralization of choices and simultaneously by uncertainty, the meaning of autonomy tends to modify, along with that of time control.

According to Gergen (2000), for instance, the choice to abdicate the idea of control over one's surroundings (and interiority) can at certain times be a sensible decision to preserve one's autonomy. If the external/internal context is characterized by rapid and uncontrollable transformation processes, "choosing not to choose" can turn into an appropriate strategy to attain power over personal time. Giving up the need for control and authenticity—meant as the desire to set, once and for all, what one truly wants and where one's potential lies—can thus become the gateway to the "good life," a life tuned into the frequencies of our contemporary era, allowing for volatility and flexibility of value judgments according to the different contexts. We can live for the pleasure of being autonomous within the ever-changing circumstances rather than seeking to reach a specific goal associated with gratification. The refusal to identify autonomy with control and the choice to remain open to contingency creates new social scenarios and not yet fully explored ideas of time control that leave behind, at least in part, the ideals of modernity.

Elaborating on this perspective, de Singly (2015) has underlined how autonomy, meant as the capacity to have a personal world open to constant change, can gain more lights than shadows from this vision. The contemporary individual appears to be able to "learn itself" better through these swerving trajectories than through codified biographical paths. The traits that identify this version of agency are the attunement to self-exploration and relationships, the refusal of pre-shaped identities, and the attention to the everyday dimension with its forms of sociability. Vastly distant from a rigid conception of time control, this culture signals the possibility of an eclectic identity as an antidote to uncertainty and identifies autonomy as the capacity for indeterminate openness to the social sphere. Control over lifetimes would be achieved primarily by tuning into the creativity of agency (Cahill and Leccardi 2020). Empirical research will bear the responsibility to "test" these analytical leads and determine whether they can contribute to the understanding of time work dynamics specific to our age.

FINAL THOUGHTS AND ACKNOWLEDGMENTS

In the privileged position of one who concludes a path of analysis extraordinarily rich in stimuli—and therefore able to favor the formulation of further research questions—I would like to draw attention to one particular aspect.

When a concept proves capable of helping us not only specify lines of inquiry but also identify problems that can effectively orient present and future research, when it enables us to connect with diverse strands of social investigation, as is the case for the concepts of time work and temporal agency, we need to extend our sincere gratitude to those who conceived it, as well as those who fortified it with their own scientific journey. To Michael Flaherty, and to the whole Aarhus group, the international scientific community extends its heartfelt thanks.

Carmen Leccardi
Professor of Cultural Sociology
University of Milan-Bicocca

REFERENCES

Appadurai, Arjun. 2013. *The Future as Cultural Fact: Essays on the Global Condition.* London: Verso.

Cahill, Helen, and Carmen Leccardi. 2020. "Reframing Resilience." In *Youth and the New Adulthood: Generations of Change*, edited by Johanna Wyn, Helen Cahill, Dan Woodman, Carmen Leccardi, Hernan Cuervo, and Jenny Chesters, 73–87. Singapore: Springer.

Cavalli, Alessandro. 2011. "La categoria del tempo in Simmel" [Simmel's time category]. In *Momenti di storia del pensiero sociologico* [Contributions to the history of sociological thought], edited by A. Cavalli, 253–65. Milano: Ledizioni.

De Certeau, Michel. 1984. *The Practice of Everyday Life.* Berkeley: University of California Press.

De Singly, François. 2015. *L'individualisme est un humanisme.* La Tour d'Aigues: Éditions de l'Aube.

Durkheim, Émile. (1912) 2008. *The Elementary Forms of Religious Life.* Oxford: Oxford University Press.

Elias, Norbert. 1993. *Time: An Essay.* Oxford: Blackwell.

Flaherty, Michael G. 2002. "Making Time: Agency and the Construction of Temporal Experience." *Symbolic Interaction* 25: 379–88.

———. 2003. "Time Work: Customizing Temporal Experience." *Social Psychology Quarterly* 66: 17–33.

———. 2011. *The Textures of Time: Agency and Temporal Experience.* Philadelphia: Temple University Press.

Gergen, Kenneth J. 2000. *The Saturated Self: Dilemmas of Identity in Contemporary Life.* New York: Basic Books.

Giddens, Anthony. 1979. *Central Problems in Social Theory: Action, Structure and Contradiction in Social Analysis.* London: Macmillan.

Hughes, Everett. (1971) 1984. *The Sociological Eye: Selected Papers.* New Jersey: Transaction Publishers.

Leccardi, Carmen, and Paolo Volonté, eds. 2017. *Un nuovo individualismo? Individualizzazione, soggettività e legame sociale* [A new individualism? Individualization, subjectivity and social bonds]. Milan: Egea.

Mills, Charles Wright. (1959) 1971. *The Sociological Imagination.* Harmondsworth: Penguin.

Mjøset, Lars. 2013. "The Fate of the Sociological Imagination: Mills, Social Science and Contemporary Sociology." In *C. Wright Mills and the Sociological Imagination: Contemporary Perspectives*, edited by J. Scott and A. Nilsen, 57–87. Cheltenham, UK: Edward Elgar.

Neumann, Birgit, and Ansgar Nünning. 2012. "Travelling Concepts as a Model for the Study of Culture." In *Travelling Concepts for the Study of Culture*, edited by B. Neumann and A. Nünning, 1–22. Berlin: De Gruyter.

Nussbaum, Martha C. 2003. *Upheavals of Thought: The Intelligence of Emotions*. Cambridge: Cambridge University Press.

Rosa, Hartmut. 2012. "On the Concept of the 'Good Life' in Contemporary Sociology." Paper, New School for Social Research, New York, and Schiller-University, Jena.

———. 2013. *Social Acceleration: A New Theory of Modernity*. New York: Columbia University Press.

Simmel, Georg. (1907) 1978. *The Philosophy of Money*. Edited by D. Frisby. London: Routledge.

Zerubavel, Eviatar 1981. *Hidden Rhythms: Schedules and Calendars in Social Life*. Chicago: University of Chicago Press.

Index

www.ingramcontent.com/pod-product-compliance
Lightning Source LLC
Chambersburg PA
CBHW070923030426
42336CB00014BA/2512